Experimenting with Unconditional Basic Income

Experimenting with Unconditional Basic Income

Lessons from the Finnish BI Experiment 2017-2018

Edited by

Olli Kangas

Director, Equal Society Strategic Research Programme, Academy of Finland and Professor of Practice, Department of Social Research, University of Turku, Finland

Signe Jauhiainen

Senior Researcher, Research Unit, Social Insurance Institution of Finland, Finland

Miska Simanainen

Researcher, Research Unit, Social Insurance Institution of Finland, Finland

Minna Ylikännö

Specialist, Ministry of Economic Affairs and Employment and Adjunct Professor, Department of Social Research, University of Turku, Finland

Cheltenham, UK • Northampton, MA, USA

© Olli Kangas, Signe Jauhiainen, Miska Simanainen and Minna Ylikännö 2021

This is an open access work distributed under the Creative Commons Attribution-NonCommercial-NoDerivatives 3.0 Unported (https://creativecommons.org/licenses/by-nc-nd/3.0/). Users can redistribute the work for non-commercial purposes, as long as it is passed along unchanged and in whole, as detailed in the License. Edward Elgar Publishing Ltd must be clearly credited as the rights holder for publication of the original work. Any translation or adaptation of the original content requires the written authorization of Edward Elgar Publishing Ltd.

Published by
Edward Elgar Publishing Limited
The Lypiatts
15 Lansdown Road
Cheltenham
Glos GL50 2JA
UK

Edward Elgar Publishing, Inc.
William Pratt House
9 Dewey Court
Northampton
Massachusetts 01060
USA

A catalogue record for this book
is available from the British Library

Library of Congress Control Number: 2021938831

This book is available electronically in the Elgaronline
Sociology, Social Policy and Education subject collection
http://dx.doi.org/10.4337/9781839104855

Printed on elemental chlorine free (ECF)
recycled paper containing 30% Post-Consumer Waste

ISBN 978 1 83910 484 8 (cased)
ISBN 978 1 83910 485 5 (eBook)

Printed and bound in the USA

Contents

List of figures	vii
List of tables	viii
About the editors	x
List of contributors	xii
Acknowledgements	xiii

1   Introduction to the journey of the Finnish basic income
experiment   1
Olli Kangas, Signe Jauhiainen, Miska Simanainen and Minna Ylikännö

2   The Finnish social security system: Background to the
Finnish basic income experiment   6
Olli Kangas and Miska Simanainen

3   Making of the Finnish basic income experiment   18
Olli Kangas

4   Constitutional preconditions for the Finnish basic income
experiment   37
Anna-Kaisa Tuovinen

5   Evaluation of the experiment   44
Signe Jauhiainen, Olli Kangas, Miska Simanainen and Minna Ylikännö

6   Basic income and employment   55
Minna Ylikännö and Olli Kangas

7   Subjective health, well-being and cognitive capabilities   71
Miska Simanainen and Annamari Tuulio-Henriksson

8   Financial well-being in basic income experiment   89
Maarit Lassander and Signe Jauhiainen

9   The bureaucracy of claiming benefits   106
Miska Simanainen

10	Trust, capabilities, confidence and basic income *Olli Kangas, Minna Ylikännö and Mikko Niemelä*	117
11	What explains the popular support for basic income? *Miska Simanainen and Olli Kangas*	134
12	Life on basic income – Interview accounts by basic income experiment participants on the effects of the experiment *Helena Blomberg, Christian Kroll and Laura Tarkiainen*	150
13	Media coverage of the Finnish basic income experiment *Katja Mäkkylä*	169
14	The feasibility of universal basic income *Olli Kangas*	187
Index		197

Figures

2.1	The division of labour between residence-based and employment-based income transfer schemes in Finland	8
2.2	The structure of the Finnish unemployment benefit system	11
2.3	Composition of income formation of an unemployed person living alone and an unemployed single parent	14
3.1	The level and financing of benefits and the degree of the EU involvement in legislation	26
6.1	Estimated marginal means for employment at the end of the experiment, treatment and ability to work	65
6.2	Estimated marginal means for confidence in finding employment, treatment and ability to work	67
10.1	Heuristic model of associations between trust and receiving basic income and the background variables	127
10.2	Heuristic model on associations between capability and receiving basic income and the background variables	128
11.1	Summary of the relationships between demographic properties and labour market positions, political affiliations, views about deservingness, item-specific opinions concerning basic income, and support for basic income	146

Tables

3.1 Participation tax rates of an unemployed individual living alone in relation to the current model and basic income of €1000 and €1500 per month   23

3.2 Participation tax rates of a single wage earner living alone and a single parent with two children in relation to the current model and basic income of €550 and €750 per month   24

5.1 Register data sources and their contents   47

5.2 Demographic characteristics of the target group, survey respondents and in the re-weighted survey data   49

6.1 Results of logistic regression for probability to be employed in the end of the experiment   63

6.2 Confidence in finding work corresponding to one's qualifications and experience within 12 months. Logistic regression results   66

7.1 Response distributions of survey questions on (A) self-evaluated state of health; (B) existence and level of impediment of a disease, disability or mental disorder; and (C) usage of health services during the previous two years   77

7.2 Response distributions of survey questions on (A) mental distress (individual MHI-5 items and clinically significant mental distress); (B) experiences of depression and inability to enjoy or be interested in things during the previous year; and (C) experiences of loneliness   79

7.3 Response distributions of survey questions on memory functioning, ability to learn new things, and ability to concentrate   83

7.4 Regression results on clinically significant mental distress   84

Tables   ix

8.1	Proportions of self-reported feeling about household's income nowadays	95
8.2	Response proportions of subjective financial well-being (SFWB) in the treatment and control groups	96
8.3	Regression analysis results on subjective financial well-being (SFWB)	99
9.1	Demographic analysis of respondents (treatment and control group)	110
9.2	Experiences of bureaucracy by selected background factors	111
9.3	Regression analysis (binary logistic) on the association of participation in the experiment and experiences of bureaucracy	113
9A.1	Survey questions and response categories for the study and background variables	116
9A.2	Distribution of response on the experiences of bureaucracy	116
10.1	Institutional and generalised trust in the EU, in Finland and in the treatment and control groups (means)	124
10.2	Levels of confidence and perceptions of own capabilities in the treatment and control groups	125
11.1	Regression analysis results on the determinants of support for basic income in Finland 2020: income inadequacy and insecure employment	140
11.2	Perceived causes for unemployment and poverty among the Finns in 2020	141
11.3	Regression analysis results on the determinants of support for basic income in Finland 2020: deservingness and opinions on the characteristics of basic income, coefficients and p-values	143
11A.1	Means for item-specific question on the characteristics of basic income (0=fully disagree, 10=fully agree)	149
12.1	Interviewees' background information (number of persons)	154
13A.1	The number and percentages of persons interviewed in the media regarding the basic income experiment, according to a phone survey	186

About the editors

Olli Kangas (PhD) is Director of the Equal Society Research Programme funded by the Strategic Research Council at the Academy of Finland and Professor of Practice in the Department of Social Research, University of Turku. Previously, he was the Director of Governmental Relations and Head of the Research Department at the Social Insurance Institution of Finland (Kela). He has worked as an Olof Palme Professor at the Department of Political Science at Uppsala University; H.C. Andersen Professor at the University of Southern Denmark (Department of Political Science), Professor at the Danish National Institute for Social Research, and Professor in Social Policy, University of Turku. His research interests revolve around comparative analysis of social policy systems, their causes and consequences in terms of the macro-economy, income distribution, health and well-being of the population, and legitimacy of social institutions. His latest publications include: Simanainen, M. and Kangas, O (2020), 'Speaking to those who know it best. Does participation in an experiment explain citizens' attitudes toward basic income?' *Journal of International and Comparative Social Policy*, August 2020; Olafsson, S., Daly, M., Kangas, O. and Palme, J. (eds.) (2019), *Welfare and the Great Depression: A Comparative Study*. Oxford: Oxford University Press; and Varjonen, S., Kangas, O. and Niemelä, M. (2019), 'Partisanship, continuity and change: politics in Finnish unemployment benefit reforms 1985–2016,' *Social Policy & Administration,* 9 July 2019.

Signe Jauhiainen (DSc, Econ) is a senior researcher at the Social Insurance Institution of Finland (Kela). Previously she has worked at Pellervo Economic Research PTT, Finnish Centre for Pension and University of Jyväskylä. Her research interests are in policy-relevant empirical research on social policy, labour markets, public finance and immigration. This research contributes to topical questions on how economic policy and social security can tackle the challenges of a changing labour market. Jauhiainen has been a member of the evaluation team of the Finnish basic income experiment and she participates actively in public debate on economic policy in Finland.

Miska Simanainen (MSocSc) is a researcher at the Social Insurance Institution of Finland (Kela). His current research interests revolve around poverty and welfare dependency, with a special focus on tax-benefit policies: their origins (politics), performance (from a comparative perspective), and their potential impact on the poverty, well-being, and behaviour of the citizens. Previously, he was employed by Statistics Finland and the Helsinki Institute for Information Technology. His professional background ranges from research and policy evaluation projects to the production of official statistics and the development of policy evaluation methods.

Minna Ylikännö (PhD) is a specialist at the Ministry of Economic Affairs and Employment, and an Adjunct Professor at the Department of Social Research, University of Turku. Previously, she worked as a researcher in the Department of Social Research, University of Turku. She also worked as a researcher and the head of the research team in the Research Department at the Social Insurance Institution of Finland (Kela), and as a Professor of TOPSOS-postgraduate training programme in the Department of Social Research, University of Turku. Regarding her research, the main interest has been questions concerning labour markets, unemployment, social assistance, well-being, social experiments, and time use. Her latest publications include Saikkonen, P. and Ylikännö, M. (2020), 'Is there room for targeting within universalism? Finnish social assistance recipient as a social citizen,' *Social Inclusion* 8(1), and Salin, M., Ylikännö, M. and Hakovirta, M. (2018), 'How to divide paid work and unpaid care between parents? Comparison of attitudes in 22 Western countries,' *Social Sciences* 7(10).

Contributors

Helena Blomberg, Professor of social policy, particularly social work at the Swedish School of Social Science, University of Helsinki, Finland.

Signe Jauhiainen, Senior Researcher at the Research Unit of the Social Insurance institution of Finland.

Olli Kangas, Director of the Equal Society Strategic Research programme at the Academy of Finland and Professor of Practice at the Department of Social Research, University of Turku, Finland.

Christian Kroll, Senior lecturer of social work and social policy at the Swedish School of Social Science, University of Helsinki, Finland and Reader of Social Work at Lund University Sweden.

Maarit Lassander, Researcher at Folkhälsan Research Center, Public Health Research Programme, Helsinki, Finland.

Katja Mäkkylä, PhD candidate at the University of Helsinki, Finland.

Mikko Niemelä, Professor of Sociology at the University of Turku, Finland.

Miska Simanainen, Researcher at the Research Unit of the Social Insurance Institution of Finland.

Laura Tarkiainen, DSocSc, is a researcher at the Swedish School of Social Sciences, University of Helsinki and a university teacher in the Faculty of Social Sciences at Tampere University, Finland.

Anna-Kaisa Tuovinen, Researcher at the Research Unit of the Social Insurance Institution of Finland.

Annamari Tuulio-Henriksson, Lecturer at the University of Helsinki, Finland.

Minna Ylikännö, Specialist at the Ministry of Economic Affairs and Employment, and Adjunct Professor at the Department of Social Research, University of Turku, Finland.

Acknowledgements

Research is never the product of only the individuals whose names are written on the cover page of a book, research report or journal article. Irrespective of whether a paper has one or more authors or editors, one should always remember that research is a collective process. In the process of research, we communicate with our colleagues; base our investigations on existing theories, earlier studies and the findings of such studies; and discuss our results with our peers. This is particularly true of the current volume.

The Finnish basic income experiment began in 2015 in accordance with the decision of the then Finnish Government. The Social Insurance Institution of Finland (Kela) was responsible for planning, implementing, and evaluating the experiment and facilitating constant interactions among researchers, politicians, administrative experts, and competent and helpful experts within Kela itself.

Although Kela was extremely busy with the creation of major legislative reforms at the time, it ensured that the experiment's planning group received sufficient resources to plan the experiment's practical set-up, formulate the relevant legislation, and finally conduct the experiment. In this context, we thank Mikael Forss, Liisa Hyssälä, Esko Karjala, Pirjo Laitinen, Anna Mäki-Jokela, Tomi Ståhl, Marjukka Turunen, and others in Kela who made the experiment possible. In particular, the help and support rendered by Outi Antila and Liisa Siika-aho in the Ministry of Social Affairs played a decisive role in finalising the legislation required for the experiment's implementation. Finally, we extend special thanks to the entire steering group for providing constructive comments and raising thought-provoking questions in our meetings at different phases of experiment planning.

Once planning and implementation were over, the experiment required evaluation. The Ministry of Social Affairs and Health provided the necessary funds for data collection and evaluation. This support is gratefully acknowledged. Further, we thank Essi Rentola and Jere Päivinen from the Ministry of Social Affairs and Health for good cooperation. In addition, we acknowledge the efforts of the expert steering group during the evaluation phase.

We presented our research results in scientific academic gatherings and discussed our findings with prominent scholars having expertise in social experiments in general and basic income experiments in particular. All these discussions and debates were highly interesting and very useful in the xiv *Experimenting with unconditional basic income*

evaluation process. The formal completion of this process has been indicated in the reports that were officially delivered to the Ministry of Social Affairs and Health. However, more detailed analyses on specific topics related to the experiment will be conducted in future.

Communication plays an important role in ensuring the success of such large-scale social experiments. Hence, we express our gratitude to Kela Communications and Milla Ikonen, in particular, for successfully coordinating communications among various teams involved in experiment implementation and enabling the evaluation team to communicate effectively with the public, politicians, and the media.

We thank all experts, as well as their organisations, who significantly contributed to the evaluation process and dissemination of results. The researchers who wrote articles in this volume are affiliated with various scientific organisations and research projects. Olli Kangas and Mikko Niemelä thank the Academy of Finland Flagship Programme[1] and the Strategic Research Council of the Academy of Finland[2] for offering grants. Olli Kangas thanks the EU Horizon 2020 research and innovation programme for offering a grant for the project titled Beyond 4.0.[3] Olli Kangas and Signe Jauhiainen thank the Strategic Research Council of the Academy of Finland for offering a grant for the project Work, Inequality and Public Policy project.[4]

Finally, we sincerely thank the participants of the experiment. In particular, we thank those who contributed to the data collection by either answering the phone survey or participating in the face-to-face interview. Thank you very much for your time and hospitality and for sharing your experiences with us. Your contribution was truly invaluable.

Editors
Helsinki and Lieto
15 January 2021

---

[1] Grant Number: 320162
[2] Grant Number: 293103
[3] Project Grant Agreement: 822296
[4] Grant Number: 293120

1. Introduction to the journey of the Finnish basic income experiment

Olli Kangas, Signe Jauhiainen, Miska Simanainen and Minna Ylikännö

This book provides a broad picture of the Finnish basic income experiment – from the planning, through the implementation, and ending with an evaluation of the experiment – in a versatile collection of studies. The editors, together with the rest of the research group, have had the most interesting couple of years evaluating the Finnish basic income experiment. In fact, some of us have spent even more time with the experiment, by being involved in the planning phase. This has been quite a journey.

It is not every day that a researcher gets a chance to dive into such an adventurous journey, peep into the hidden chambers of political decision-making with its tensions, intrigues and compromises, and see how ideas are transferred into legislation and how legislation is implemented. The journey has provided the opportunity not only to work in a talented and dedicated research group but also to have the most fruitful discussions with fellow academics, passionate reformers of welfare states, and journalists from every corner of the world.

Interest in the Finnish experiment has been huge since the beginning of the experiment and it continues. Throughout the experiment and its evaluation, national and international media have reported the twists and turns of the journey, and followed the lives of some of the participants of the experiment, who eventually became famous, especially outside Finland. You can read more about the role of the media during and after the experiment in Chapter 13, by Katja Mäkkylä.

Some may ask, why all this fuss in a country that has already established comprehensive social security for all its residents? Is Finland not representative of a Social Democratic welfare state with universal transfer benefits guaranteeing decent income for all and free and good quality services from the cradle to the grave? Is Finland not a country that takes the top spots when it comes to poverty reduction, well-being, trust, happiness and life satisfaction, quality of life, democratic political freedoms, or economic competitiveness?

Well, it is not only happiness and prosperity for us in Finland. We also have people queuing for food aid, people without shelter, and people living in prolonged poverty. Moreover, we have a jungle or a labyrinth of benefits and services when people try to find someone to help them with their problems. Already exhausted from often multiple social and health problems, those desperately in need for help may not have the capabilities to find their way forward in this jungle, or out of it. There are both economic and bureaucratic disincentives and, due to them being built in the social security system, people may give up and continue to live on social security instead of seeking ways out of the social security net.

One main reason for experimenting with basic income was to determine whether it could diminish the bureaucracy and dissolve the monetary disincentives involved in today's social security system. The task of the experiment was to evaluate whether basic income would be a device for simplifying the system and making it more transparent. The main question was whether basic income could reduce various work disincentives and consequently increase the employment rate. Even a well-developed welfare state may have problems providing help to its clients, and it may submerge them in myriad social policy programmes that are not always interacting in a rational way.

Chapter 2 presents the current social security system and its rather complex structure, and introduces the reader to the reasons why the centre-right government of Prime Minister Juha Sipilä (nominated in 2015 and resigned in 2019) decided to write the creative words, 'We shall have a basic income experiment', into its governmental programme. For many in Finland, this came as a surprise. The Sipilä government consisted of three parties: the Centre Party, the National Coalition Party, and the Finns Party. While the first had shown some lukewarm support for basic income, the two other parties had been openly critical of basic income. The two parties that most eagerly advocated basic income in Finland, the Green League and the Left Alliance, were in opposition at that time.

Surprisingly, basic income was visibly and firmly on the political agenda, and the next question was who should be responsible for planning such a novel experiment. The Prime Minister's Office announced a competition for this, which was won by the research group led by the Research Department in the Social Insurance Institution of Finland (Kela). This was the start of a long and challenging journey for the research group. Numerous microsimulations were run, and models evaluated, and endless legal, practical, and political problems were more or less successfully solved during the planning of the experiment. The planning phase was full of inspiration, perspiration, and frustration. Chapter 3 by Olli Kangas contains a narrative about the making of the experiment, and Chapter 4 by Anna-Kaisa Tuovinen sheds light on what kind of constitutional and other legal aspects had to be considered when planning such a social experiment as the Finnish one.

Introduction to the journey of the Finnish basic income experiment 3

Against all odds, the basic income experiment began as planned on 1 January 2017, and the inspired planners of the experiment could take a moment to breathe. But not for long. The evaluation of the experiment had already started, a new crew was gathered around this evaluation, and a new phase of the journey begun.

The scientific evaluation of the experiment includes four sub-studies and involves several researchers from different universities and research institutes in Finland. The research is multidisciplinary, utilising both quantitative and qualitative data. In the evaluation, the interest has been mainly in the employment effects of the experiment, but also in other aspects of well-being and in the experiences and opinions of those selected for the experiment to receive unconditional basic income for two years. In Chapter 5, the editors describe how the evaluation of the experiment was conducted. The extraordinary Finnish registers and their various combinations give endless possibilities for further, more extensive, more detailed, and better studies.

Register-based results regarding the employment effects of the experiment have been reported in earlier publications.[1] In this book, we utilise the survey data gathered at the end of the experiment from the receivers of basic income and their control group (see Chapter 5). In Chapter 6, Minna Ylikännö and Olli Kangas focus on employment questions with a special interest in the survey respondents' subjective assessment of work ability and self-rated confidence in finding new employment. The findings in this chapter support the previously reported results from the register analysis, but they also open new perspectives to the debate on the link between basic income, employment, and ability to work.

When discussing basic income in general, and in the context of modern societies with developed social security systems, in particular, questions about the trade-off between comprehensive social security and labour supply always pop up. In these discussions, one should keep in mind that participation in paid labour always requires the ability to work. One must have the skills needed, be healthy enough, both physically and mentally, to search and find a job. The target group of the Finnish experiment consisted of unemployed job seekers, of whom the majority had been unemployed for a long period. Almost 80 percent of them had been unemployed for more than one year. It is not that rare for a person without work to have multiple barriers to employment, including health problems. That is why interest in the evaluation was also in multifaceted connections between basic income, health, and well-being, and not only on employment effects.

In Chapter 7, Miska Simanainen and Annamari Tuulio-Henriksson analyse associations between basic income, subjective health, and cognitive abilities; that is, those essential prerequisites for participating in paid labour. Stress, induced by poverty and scarce financial resources, is in turn of interest in

Chapter 8 by Maarit Lassander and Signe Jauhiainen. Prolonged stress can trigger various physical and mental health problems, and from this perspective, the possible effects of basic income to mitigate financial stress are also of great interest. For two years, the experiment guaranteed a participant a net income of €560 per month, which was unconditionally paid on the second banking day of each month to the participant's bank account.

As mentioned above, one aim of the experiment was to diminish the bureaucracy involved in the transitions from social security to work. In these transitions, there may be many hurdles. It may be that the work does not pay enough (as discussed in Chapter 2) or there may be bureaucratic hindrances, making the unemployed cautious of accepting possible job offers. Bureaucracy is the focus of Miska Simanainen's analyses in Chapter 9. He asks whether basic income made it easier for social benefit recipients to cope with the complicated social security system. The recipients of basic income did not have to regularly report themselves to the public employment services, and they were not subject to any sanctions as stipulated by the current unemployment benefit system. They could trust they would receive the basic income every month, and no paperwork or screening of any kind was needed to prove the right for the benefit.

In a way, basic income is 'money of trust'. In the basic income system, the residents are trusted and expected to make rational decisions for themselves and, in the end, decisions that benefit societies at large. The proponents of basic income argue that universal and unconditional income transfer as basic income would eventually free people from bad quality jobs and enable them to do voluntary work or in other ways contribute to the well-being of others. Hence, by enhancing social capital bridging in society, they would also build a more trusting environment. When being trusted by the society, we tend to mutually create trust. Trust is built through reciprocity. In Chapter 10, Olli Kangas, Minna Ylikännö, and Mikko Niemelä analyse multifaceted associations between basic income and self-confidence. Furthermore, in the spirit of John Rawls, Amartya Sen and Martha Nussbaum, they also use survey data to determine whether basic income possibly enhances the capabilities required to be able to fully participate in society. Chapter 10 also concludes with some of the results from the earlier chapters by including health and financial stress in the multivariate models utilised in the analysis. It is also a conclusive chapter in a more philosophical sense in that, fundamentally, basic income is about trust more than anything else. The central question for functional societies is, to what extent should we or can we trust other people and societal institutions?

This central question partly defines how we think about basic income. If public opinion is against basic income, it is not feasible to implement it. Depending on the votes of the potential voters, politicians would not risk their political career in proposing something that had a lot of resistance among the public. However, if the majority of public opinion is for basic income, it may emerge in the political agenda and even end up being implemented. In Chapter 11, Miska Simanainen and Olli Kangas report results from opinion surveys collected just before and after the experiment. In addition to discussing the level of popular support for basic income in Finland, this chapter analyses how much citizens' financial insecurity, on the one hand, and political attitudes and perceptions of deservingness, on the other, explain popular opinion.

The evaluation of the experiment was not limited to registers or surveys; a vast number of face-to-face interviews were conducted among the recipients of basic income. For the qualitative analyses presented in Chapter 12, Helena Blomberg, Christian Kroll and Laura Tarkiainen have gone through hundreds of pages of transcribed text from almost a hundred interviews. Although the stories told are as many as there were interviewees, following the famous sociologist Hannah Arendt the researchers have been able to condense their analyses into three modalities: work, employment and labour.

The discussion on the role of public opinion regarding implementing basic income continues in the final chapter of the book (Chapter 14), where Olli Kangas analyses the feasibility of basic income in Finland, and whether the experiment increased the probability of implementation. If you decide to do what so many book readers do, and read the last lines of the book first, you will already know whether basic income is a feasible option for a new social policy model in Finland.

Every chapter in this volume looks at the basic income and the Finnish experiment from a different angle, and they have different stories to tell. The research group represents different scientific fields, which is a significant advantage on one hand, but, on the other hand, is reflected in how the individual articles are constructed and the story told. Keeping this in mind, the editors of the book, together with Edward Elgar Publishing, wish you a pleasant reading experience and hope you enjoy the journey as much as we did.

NOTE

1. Hämäläinen, K., Kanninen, O., Simanainen, M. and Verho, J. (2020), *Perustulokokeilun arvioinnin loppuraportti: Rekisterianalyysi työmarkkinavaikutuksista* [*The Final Evaluation Report on the Basic Income Experiment: Register-Based Analysis on Labour Market Effects*], Helsinki: VATT Institute for Economic Research, VATT Muistiot, 59.

2. The Finnish social security system: Background to the Finnish basic income experiment

Olli Kangas and Miska Simanainen

INTRODUCTION

All basic income experiments so far have been planned and implemented in national or local contexts. Thus, the questions posed in the experiments and the answers achieved are bound to time and place. To understand the motivations behind the experiments and the results achieved, we need familiarity with the institutional frameworks in which they occur. This also applies to the Finnish basic income experiment. In this chapter, we shed light on the context in which the experiment was planned, implemented, and carried out. The Finnish social protection system is comprehensive, and because of its comprehensiveness, it is complicated and difficult to describe in a simple way. We shall try anyway.

In its simplest form, the Finnish social security comprises three parts. The first part guarantees minimum income security for all Finnish residents (rather than citizens, as explained below). It includes 'basic level' social benefits paid either at a flat-rate or after means-testing based on personal or household income. The second part consists of income-related social insurance for those in employment. The third part of the system includes municipal social and health care services covering all residents from cradle to grave. (Kela, 2019).

In large part due to this comprehensiveness, the Finnish welfare state ranks top in the world in many aspects of economic and non-economic well-being. In Finland, shares of people at risk of poverty or social exclusion are among the lowest in the EU, for the total population and among all age groups. The income transfer system effectively lifts low-income people above the poverty line and equalises income differences (for example, Olafsson et al., 2019; Eurostat, 2020). Free or affordable public services just as effectively promote social inclusion through good quality education, health and social services, and public employment services, among many others.

Needless to say, comprehensive social protection has its costs. Finland's gross social spending is near 30 percent of its gross domestic product (data for 2019), second only to France among OECD countries. Two thirds of total social spending goes to cash benefits and the remainder to providing social and health services (OECD, 2020b).

High spending demands high tax rates. Total tax revenues correspond to 42 percent of the GDP compared with the OECD average of 20 percent (as of 2018). The main sources of revenue are taxes on income and profits (15 percent of GDP), taxes on goods and services (14 percent), and social security contributions (12 percent) (OECD, 2020c). In Finland, both the central government and local municipalities collect taxes to finance their duties.

In its comprehensiveness, the Finnish social security system is also complicated. For mainly bureaucratic reasons, people can become trapped in it and there may be several disincentives to try to find employment or accept job offers. There have been multiple attempts to simplify the system, but results have been poor. Not surprisingly, barriers to employment (for example because of high effective marginal and participation tax rates) and measures aimed at increasing labour force participation have been the main areas of interest. In a sense, the Finnish basic income experiment was just one episode in a never-ending quest for getting the unemployed to work.

In the interest of simplicity and concision, this chapter focuses on those social policy schemes that produce the income and bureaucracy traps and disincentives, touched upon above. That is, the focus is on the interplay between the various income-tested benefits, such as housing allowances, and social assistance combined with progressive taxation. Furthermore, some cash-for-care schemes create their own disincentives, particularly for women. Since basic income – at least in the Finnish context and policy discourse – is not to alter social, education, or health care services, we discuss provision of public services only cursorily.

The structure or this chapter is as follows: first we provide a brief and simplified description of the functional logic of the Finnish social security system, followed by a section describing benefits that target children and families. Some of these benefits are universal, such as child allowance, and do not contribute to income traps. However, some family benefits are income tested or are compensations for at home care work, such as the cash-for-care child home care allowance. These have ramifications, including negative impacts on the labour market behaviour of individuals. Since unemployed persons were the target group of the Finnish basic income experiment, the third section focuses on the structure of unemployment benefits and on last resort social assistance. Oftentimes, those who receive basic unemployment benefits also receive housing allowances and social assistance, which is problematic from the perspective of work incentives, as will be shown. The penultimate section describes the income and bureaucratic traps in the current income transfer system, and the final section concludes the central lessons from the previous sections.

THE DUAL STRUCTURE OF THE FINNISH INCOME TRANSFER SYSTEM

The Finnish system deviates from many other welfare states in two important ways. First, the minimum benefits are intended to guarantee basic security and a decent livelihood for every Finnish resident regardless of employment history. These flat-rate or income-tested benefits are mainly paid by the Social Insurance Institution of Finland (Kela), which also pays out basic social assistance benefits. Municipalities are responsible for supplementary and preventive social assistance and some cash-for-care schemes (Figure 2.1).

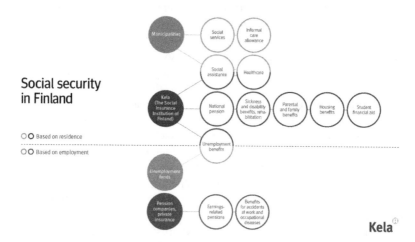

Figure 2.1   *The division of labour between residence-based and employment-based income transfer schemes in Finland*

As briefly noted above, entitlement to benefits is based on residency, rather than citizenship. The Constitution of Finland (731/1999) states:

> Those who cannot obtain the means necessary for a life of dignity have the right to receive indispensable subsistence and care. Everyone shall be guaranteed by the Act the right to basic subsistence in the event of unemployment, illness, and disability, and during old age as well as at the birth of a child or the loss of a provider. The public authorities shall guarantee for everyone, as provided in more detail by the

Act, adequate social, health, and medical services and promote the health of the population.

In that sense, some elements of basic income already exist in Finland.

Second, earnings-related benefits aim to guarantee the achieved consumption level if a claimant's income from employment ceases because of social risks such as illness, unemployment, disability, old age, and the like. The peculiarity of Finnish income transfer schemes is that there are no ceilings on benefits. Benefit amounts are wholly based on previous earnings. Furthermore, except for sickness insurance, all major forms of earnings-related social insurance are administered by either private insurance companies – as in the case of work accident insurance – or semi-private insurance institutions – as in the case of earnings-related pensions or voluntary unemployment funds providing earnings-related unemployment allowance. In the degree of corporatism in the administration of the social insurance system, Finland deviates from its Nordic neighbours.

Third, social security benefits and taxes and social security contributions are individual income based in Finland, as in the other Nordic countries (see Kautto, 2008; Kangas and Kvist, 2019), rather than household income based. Only in a very few schemes, such as housing allowance and social assistance transfers, is household income used as the basis for income-testing.

BENEFITS FOR CHILDREN AND FAMILIES WITH CHILDREN

Parents are entitled to the maternity or paternity allowance and the parental allowance for approximately four, two, and six months, respectively. The gross replacement rate is approximately 70 percent of income at the average income level. There is a minimum daily allowance (€724 per month as in 2020) available for parents with no or very low income.

The main child-related cash transfer is the child allowance, which is paid universally for every child below 16 years of age. The benefit amount is based on the number of children, and single parents receive higher benefits for each child.

Finland's dual system of early childhood care includes both day care service and a home care allowance in the form of a cash-for-care payment. Day care is a subjective right and is guaranteed for every child until they begin preschool at the age of six. The fees for public day care depend on the number of children in the family, the household's income, and the hours of care needed. The service is heavily subsidised and the fee ranges from €0 to €300 per month, per child (2020 data).

Kela pays out the widely used cash-for-care home care allowance for children under three years old who are not enrolled in municipal day care. The basic amount (€340 per month) is available for all regardless of family income. Low-income families can receive Kela's care supplement (about €180 per month). Some municipalities, mainly bigger towns, pay additional supplements. For example, the capital Helsinki paid about €250 extra per month for child home care in 2020. Thus, in Helsinki the home care subsidy in low-income families totalled to €770 per month.

Home care allowances and additional benefits paid by municipalities are incentives for mothers to stay at home and utilise the possibilities to stay at home given by the home care allowance (Kosonen and Huttunen, 2018). Almost all parents use the home care allowance, although use is gender biased and approximately 80 percent of the benefit periods are used by the mother. While the use of the care allowance is not linked to users' socio-economic characteristics, the duration of use is linked to parents' educational and family status. Mothers with higher educational attainment tend to collect the care allowance for shorter time periods than mothers with lower educational attainment. Furthermore, single mothers use it for longer periods than mothers with spouses (Haataja and Juutilainen, 2014; Räsänen et al., 2019).

In addition to family benefits, roughly 15 percent of Finnish households, receive a Kela-administered general housing allowance, another important income transfer for low-income families with or without children (Kela, 2020a). The allowance aims to decrease housing costs and secure adequate housing for low-income households. 70 percent of all the costs of housing allowance goes to single-person households, two-parent families with children and childless couples receive about 7 percent each, and single parents 16 percent of all the costs (Findikaattori, 2020).

Housing allowances compensate families for 80 percent of their qualifying housing costs, as determined by the number of household members and their municipality of residence. The gross income of the household members affects the amount of the housing allowance. Income exceeding the amount of the basic unemployment benefit tapers the amount of the housing allowance, and an earnings deduction of €300 made from every household member's salary or self-employment income brings the tapering rate to 33.6 percent, i.e., earnings of €100 decreases the allowance by around €34.

THE STRUCTURE OF THE FINNISH UNEMPLOYMENT PROTECTION SYSTEM

The duality of Finnish social security is also reflected in the unemployment protection system, which includes both 'basic' and income-related benefits, as shown in Figure 2.2.

There are two forms of basic unemployment income transfers, the basic allowance and the labour market subsidy, both of which are administered by Kela. They deliver the same gross monthly benefit amount (€734 in 2020) but differ in their eligibility criteria. Whereas the labour market subsidy is a means-tested benefit for those with little or no employment history, the basic allowance targets applicants who have employment records but are not members in voluntary unemployment funds (a requirement for receiving the income-related unemployment allowance). The gross income-loss compensation level in the earnings-related scheme is about 60 percent at the average income level of €3300 per month.

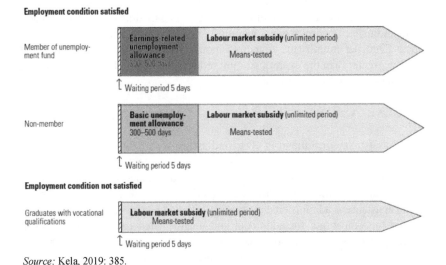

Source: Kela, 2019: 385.

Figure 2.2   The structure of the Finnish unemployment benefit system

In principle, all three forms of unemployment benefits are conditional. Recipients must be registered as unemployed jobseekers in the Employment and Economic Development Office, must permanently reside in Finland, be 17 to 64 years old, be fit to work, and be available for full-time work (Kela, 2020b). The basic unemployment allowance and the income-related benefit are payable for from 300 to 500 weekdays depending on the age and work history of the claimant (for a more detailed description, see Kela, 2020b).

All three benefits are paid after a five-day waiting period. There are specific regulations for those younger than 25 who have not completed their vocational education, including a five-month qualifying period prior to eligibility for labour market subsidy, and a requirement to seek education. During the five-month period, they are entitled to social assistance.

As shown in Figure 2.2, if unemployment continues longer than the maximum periods for the basic allowance or income-related benefits, the unemployed person qualifies for the labour market subsidy that has an unlimited duration. The labour market subsidy is an income-tested benefit. One's own income may reduce the amount of the subsidy (but not the spouse's income). If the unemployed person lives with his or her parents, the parent's income may also reduce the amount of the subsidy. Social benefits such as child and housing allowances and income support are exempted from income-testing, and income-testing is not applied when the unemployed person participates in employment promotion measures (Kela, 2019).

There is an adjustment system for income from part-time or incidental work. With 'adjusted unemployment benefits' [*soviteltu päiväraha*] work income up to €300 per month (the 'exempt amount') does not reduce benefits, but income greater than the exempt amount reduces the benefit by certain tapering percentages, usually 50 percent.

SOCIAL ASSISTANCE

Social assistance in Finland is classified as last-resort financial assistance. It comprises three parts: basic social assistance, supplementary social assistance, and preventive social assistance. Basic social assistance is paid by Kela to clients who fulfil the formal low-income criteria (Figure 2.1). Supplementary social assistance is administered by municipalities and, after stricter needs-testing, is paid to compensate for additional and unanticipated costs, such as broken washing-machines or expensive medication. Preventive assistance, also administered by the municipalities, is paid after more careful means and needs-testing to help the claimants cope with difficult life situations. Preventive assistance is case sensitive and depends on municipal decisions. Neither of the three forms of social assistance are time-limited. They are paid as long as eligibility conditions are met.

In principle, social assistance is means-tested and conditional. Recipients must be available for work and willing to accept job offers. If the claimant does not comply with the requirements, benefits can be cut by up to 40 percent for a maximum of two months. The sanctions applied in Finland are the most lenient among European countries (Eleveld, 2016; Penttilä and Hiilamo, 2017).

The problem with the Finnish basic benefits (for example the basic unemployment allowance or the labour market subsidy) is that their level is so low that in most cases persons living on these benefits are entitled to social assistance. If a household has low income and problems paying its housing costs, social assistance may cover the shortfall. In fact, social assistance is an important part of supporting housing among low-income households. About half of all the costs

The Finnish social security system 13

of basic social assistance go toward compensations for housing costs (Jauhiainen, 2019; Jauhiainen and Korpela, 2019). Hence, social assistance is supplementary and simultaneous to a number of other basic security transfers and is paid on top of the other benefits. When the decision on the Finnish basic income experiment was made, more than 90 percent of households receiving social assistance also received some other Kela-administered basic benefits (Kela, 2015).

Income- and means-tested programmes tend to create work disincentives. For example, the tapering rate in social assistance is 100 percent. The most severe disincentive problems are in cases where the income basket consists of multiple income-tested transfers. Then, effective participation tax rates will be high, creating disincentives for the unemployed to accept job offers. These problems are more fully described below.

INCOME TRAPS AND BUREAUCRATIC PROBLEMS

The combination of the home care allowance, the housing allowance, and social assistance is problematic for labour force participation rates. It generates high effective marginal tax rates, creating severe income traps for recipients in general and for single parents in particular. Compared with other Nordic countries, labour force participation rates of mothers with small children are low in Finland. Whereas the employment rate of mothers whose youngest child is 0 to 2 years of age is approximately 50 percent in Finland, it is approximately 80 percent in neighbouring Sweden. In contrast to the comparatively low employment rates among mothers with small children, the employment rate of mothers with older children (6 to 14 years of age) is approximately 90 percent, among the highest in the OECD (OECD, 2020a).

Progressive income tax, in turn, contributes to high participation tax rates, that is, the fraction of additional gross earnings lost to higher taxes or lowered benefits upon employment. According to the OECD's tax-benefit (OECD, 2020d) calculations, participation tax rates for unemployed people in Finland vary from 68 percent for single unemployed people without children to 79 percent for single parents with two children.

Figure 2.3 describes income formation in two typical cases of unemployment. The upper panel illustrates what happens to a single person when employment and income from work increases from zero to €2000 per month. In the lower panel, a corresponding situation is depicted for a single parent with one child. The horizontal axis represents wages obtained from employment, and the vertical axis shows changes in social benefits and the development of disposable income after taxes.

As the upper graph indicates, if a single person is unemployed (wage = 0 in the horizontal axis), his or her disposable income is about €1100 per month. Due to the adjusted labour market subsidy exempting work income up to €300 per month, work income up to that limit increases disposable income; thereafter, work income up to €500 per month does not increase disposable income at all, i.e., in this group the effective marginal tax rate is 100 percent. In the wage-income bracket of €600 to €2000, disposable income increases but only modestly.

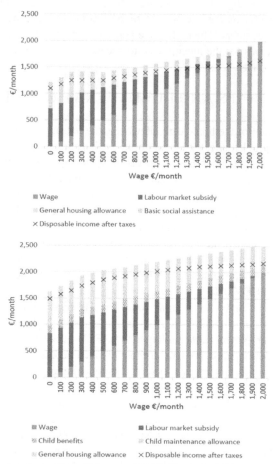

Note: The unemployed gets adjusted labour market subsidy, rent is €600 per month and lives in municipal category 3. Most of Finnish municipalities belong to that category. The rents housing allowance compensates depend on the municipality.

Figure 2.3   Composition of income formation of an unemployed person living alone and an unemployed single parent[1]

The lower part of the figure depicts the corresponding situation for a single parent. In this case, the disposable income while unemployed is about €1500 per month. If work income increases from €0 to €1000 per month, disposable income increases by €500, whereas a wage increase from €1000 to €2000 adds about €200 to the disposable income. Increases in the disposable income are smaller when possible child day care fees are included in the simulations.

High tax rates and net income that increases too slowly after receiving employment are one aspect of the incentive problem. If work does not pay or does not pay enough, unemployed people may choose to stay at home instead of obtaining employment. Additionally, eliminating the various bureaucratic traps that make unemployed people cautious about accepting short-term work offers has yet to be achieved. Owing to complicated eligibility criteria, and waiting periods during benefit handling processes, recipients may be averse to accepting job offers in general and offers for temporary and part-time jobs in particular.

CONCLUSIONS: THE (IM)POSSIBILITY OF ABOLISHING INCENTIVE TRAPS

The most common question we have answered since starting to plan the Finnish basic income experiment is, why did Finland implement a basic income experiment? Questioners to some extent familiar with the Finnish social security system have wondered, why not simply take the final step and implement universal basic income when there already seem to be elements of basic income in the Finnish income transfer system?

Indeed, in a sense Finland is already a basic income country. We have a universal income transfer scheme for all children younger than 17 years of age combined with free school meals and free school health care. All students have free study grants and free education, and basic pensions are paid to all elderly people who have not accrued an earnings-related pension or their pension is too low. Furthermore, labour market subsidies and social assistance have some resemblance to partial basic income. Benefits can be received indefinitely, and although benefits are conditional the sanctions (if they are applied) are among the most lenient in the European hemisphere. Thus, why not implement basic income? Why was an experiment needed?

As described above, the combination of taxes and means-tested benefits that are paid on top of each other too often lead to situations where income from employment increases disposable income very little or, in some cases, not at all. Sometimes, the net result can be even negative. During the three decades, consecutive governments of varying political compositions have attempted to solve these incentive problems, but without greater success.

16   *Experimenting with unconditional basic income*

The policy dilemma seems to be a mission impossible. In 2015, the Centre-Right government of Prime Minister Juha Sipilä wrote in its Governmental programme, quite out of the blue, that the government wanted to study whether basic income would solve the wicked (and for politicians also embarrassing) problem of persistently high unemployment and whether basic income would be an effective policy device to combat monetary and bureaucratic disincentives in the current Finnish income transfer system. Subsequent chapters in this volume give answers to that question.

NOTE

1. The unemployed has one child, gets adjusted labour market subsidy, the rent is €600 per month, and lives in municipal category 3. Day care fees are not included in the calculations. Source: SISU microsimulation model, Statistics Finland, the tax-benefit rules and parameters pertain to the year 2020.

REFERENCES

Constitution of Finland (731/1999), Unofficial translation in English available at https://finlex.fi/fi/laki/kaannokset/1999/en19990731.pdf) (retrieved 1 December 2020).

Eleveld, A. (2016), *Work-related Sanctions in European Welfare States: An Incentive to Work or a Violation of Minimum Subsistence Rights?* Amsterdam: The Amsterdam Centre for Contemporary European Studies, SSRN, Research Paper, 01.

Eurostat (2020), 'Income poverty statistics', Luxembourg: Eurostat, available at https://ec.europa.eu/eurostat/statisticsexplained/index.php?title=Income_poverty_statistics&oldid=440992#At-risk-of-poverty_rate_and_threshold (retrieved 8 December 2020).

Findikaattori (2020), 'General housing allowance: Recipient households', available at https://findikaattori.fi/en/table/110 (retrieved 20 December 2020).

Haataja, A. and Juutilainen, V. P. (2014), 'Kuinka pitkään lasten kotihoitoa? Selvitys äitien lastenhoitojaksoista kotona 2000-luvulla' ['How long child home care? A study of mothers' child home care spells in the 2000s']. Helsinki: Kela, Working Paper 58.

Jauhiainen, S. (2019), 'Toimeentulotuki ja asumisen kustannukset' [Social assistance and housing costs]. Presentation at Kela, 17 April 2019.

Jauhiainen, S. and Korpela, T. (2019), *Toimeentulotuen saajien elämäntilanne, asuminen ja työnteko* [*Circumstances, Housing and Employment of Social Assistance Recipients*], Helsinki: Valtioneuvoston selvitys-ja tutkimussarja 2019, 28.

Kangas, O. and Kvist, J. (2019), 'Nordic welfare states', in Greve, B. (ed.), *Routledge Handbook of the Welfare State*, London: Routledge, pp. 124–36.

Kautto, M. (2008), 'The Nordic countries', in Castles, F., Leibfried, S., Lewis, J., Obinger, H. and Pierson, C. (eds.), *The Oxford Handbook of the Welfare State*, Oxford: Oxford University Press, pp. 586–600.

Kela (2015), *The Second Expert Group for Evaluation of the Adequacy of Basic Social Security: Adequacy of Basic Social Security in Finland*, Helsinki: Kela, Working Papers 80/2015, pp. 2011–15.

Kela (2019), *Statistical Year Book 2018 of the Social Insurance Institution of Finland*, Helsinki: Kela.

Kela (2020a), *Kelan asumistukitilasto 2019* [*Kela Statistics on Housing Allowance 2019*], Helsinki: Kela.

Kela (2020b), 'Unemployment', Helsinki: Kela, available at https://www.kela.fi/web/en/unemployment (retrieved 7 December 2020).

Kosonen, T. and Huttunen, K. (2018), *Kotihoidontuen vaikutus lapsiin* [*The Impact of Home Care Allowance on Children*], Helsinki: Palkansaajien tutkimuslaitos ja VATT, Tutkimuksia 115/2018.

OECD (2020a), 'OECD Family data-base: Maternal employment rates', available at http://www.oecd.org/els/family/LMF1_2_Maternal_Employment.pdf (retrieved 6 December 2020).

OECD (2020b), *Social Expenditure – Aggregated Data*, Paris: OECD, available at https://stats.oecd.org/Index.aspx?DataSetCode=SOCX_AGG (retrieved 8 December 2020).

OECD (2020c), *Tax Administration*, Paris: OECD, available at https://www.oecd.org/tax/administration/ (retrieved 8 December 2020).

OECD (2020d), *The OECD Tax-Benefit Data Portal*, Paris: OECD, available at http://www.oecd.org/social/benefits-and-wages/data/ (retrieved 6 December 2020).

Olafsson S., Daly M., Kangas, O. and Palme, J. (eds.) (2019), *Welfare and the Great Recession: A Comparative Study*, Oxford: Oxford University Press.

Penttilä, R. and Hiilamo, H. (2017), 'Toimeentulotuen saajien sanktiointi euroopalaisessa vertailussa' ['Sanctions in European minimum income schemes'], *Yhteiskuntapolitiikka* 82 (3), 404–16.

Räsänen, T., Österbacka, E., Valaste, M. and Haataja, A. (2019), *Lastenhoidon tukien vaikutus äitien osallistumiseen työmarkkinoille* [*The Effect of Child Care Subsidies on Mothers' Labour Market Participation*], Helsinki: Kela, Sosiaali-ja terveysturvan raportteja 14.

3. Making of the Finnish basic income experiment

Olli Kangas

INTRODUCTION

The basic income experiment in Finland has received significant attention, generating considerable scientific, political and journalistic debate. For understandable reasons, attention has mainly focused on the possible outcomes of the experiment, but there has also been an abundance of speculations as to why the experiment was carried out in the first place, why the research setting was such as it was, and why the target population only consisted of unemployed people receiving a basic unemployment allowance or a labour market subsidy (see Chapter 2) from the Social Insurance Institution of Finland (Kela). The aim of this background chapter is to provide a narrative on how the planning process started and proceeded, and how the experiment was finally implemented within the complex Finnish social policy system.

De Wispelaere et al. (2019: 403) succinctly summarise what is necessary in designing basic income experiments: 'The experimental design of basic income trials will always require mastering the art of compromise'. It was indeed the case that planning of the Finnish experiment required various compromises. In contrast to all other basic income experiments, participation in the Finnish experiment was obligatory. Therefore, it had to be based on legislation, which made planning more complicated than would have been required if the experiment has been voluntary, as in many other previous experiments with basic income or negative income tax. Legal aspects of the experiment and the constitutional constraints are discussed in more detail in Chapter 4.

Many previous experiments have been driven by grassroots activism and other bottom-up initiatives, whereas in the Finnish case, the experiment was a top-down initiative of the Finnish government (however, see Danson, 2019). In subsequent sections of this chapter, we chronologically describe the planning process from when it began in the latter half of the year 2015 to the beginning of the experiment in 2017. The historical narrative begins with the government's decision to conduct the experiment and a description of what the government expected from the planning group. The first report was delivered to the government on 30 March 2016. The report evaluated the feasibility of full or partial basic income, participation income or negative income tax. We end the historical narrative at the point where a specific model was selected for use in the 2017–18 experiment. In the final section of this chapter, we highlight possibilities and obstacles in relation to conducting basic income experiments that are politically relevant.

THE GOVERNMENT'S ASSIGNMENT

The governmental programme of Prime Minister Sipilä's coalition cabinet (in force from 29 May 2015 to 6 June 2019) included a decision to have the basic income experiment. Whereas, in the Finnish version of a governmental programme, the government states briefly and boldly 'Toteutetaan perustulokokeilu' [a basic income experiment will be carried out], the English version says that the experiment would be a pilot study: 'A basic income pilot study will be performed' (Prime Minister's Office, 2015: 22).

In its budget proposal, the government reserved €20 million for the experiment covering two years, that is, from 2017 to 2018. The Prime Minister's Office launched a tender for designing the experiment (VNK/1413/48/2015), with a specific budget of €150 000 set aside. The planning budget was administrated by the Ministry of Social Affairs and Health, with the Minister of Social Affairs having the ultimate responsibility for the planning and implementation process of the experiment. Two other ministries were involved, namely the Ministry of Local Government and Public Reforms and the Ministry of Finance, to determine the appropriate tax model in the experiment.

The bid put forward by a multidisciplinary research consortium led by the Research Department at Kela won the tender. In addition to social scientists, statisticians, economists, and lawyers from Kela, economists from the VATT Institute for Economic Research, the Labour Institute for Economic Research, the University of Tampere, and the think tank Tänk were included in the planning that began in mid-October 2015.

The government's assignment comprised two parts. The first part required a feasibility report to provide the government with a general assessment of different basic income experimental models, including advantages and disadvantages, costs, and their distributional impacts if they were implemented at the national level. The second part required the preparation of a final model for the experiment.

The feasibility report sought to compile existing information, perform preliminary impact analyses, and outline a preliminary experimental design to be developed in the second part of the planning process. Based on the feasibility report, the government could decide how to proceed in terms of which one of the evaluated models should be selected for further elaboration. To enable this decision, the planning consortium had to specify the level of basic income (euros per month), make suggestions on how to integrate earnings-related benefits and different types of basic social security benefits (paid by Kela) into basic income, determine the taxation of the different models, consider constitutional aspects and European Union (EU) law, and evaluate outcomes in terms of poverty and income inequality. Determining the final model for experimentation was the task of the second planning report (final report). The planning group had to submit the preliminary report to the Ministry of Social Affairs and Health by 30 March 2016 and the final report by 15 November 2016. The experiment was planned to start on 1 January 2017.

The preliminary report (Kangas and Pulkka, 2016) was completed according to the timetable. In addition to the report, an appendix containing the results of extensive microsimulations made on different models was also submitted to the Minister (see Honkanen and Simanainen, 2016). The simulations investigated the incentive and income distribution effects of different typical family cases, as well as the economic costs for the national economy. Simulated calculations were used to determine how different levels of basic income could be financed, considering the savings resulting from the partial replacement of existing social security transfers and changes in the income tax system. In most calculations, current progressive income taxation was replaced by a simple flat-rate tax collected on income coming on top of basic income.

Simple flat-rate tax calculations were intended to provide a somewhat more realistic picture of the magnitude of tax rates that would be needed to finance the new system that would consist of basic income and transfers not replaced by basic income. We also simulated numerous combinations of flat tax rates and the current tax system, in which we also modified the existing tax system, applied a simple progressive tax scale, and simulated a scheme in which basic income was provided in the form of a negative income tax.

EVALUATION OF THE ALTERNATIVES FOR THE EXPERIMENT[1]

In response to the governmental assignment, we evaluated four different models: (1) full basic or pure basic income, in which everyone is paid the same amount of money, regardless of their situation or income, and where the amount of money is sufficiently high to replace most of the other income transfers; (2) partial basic income that would replace some basic security benefits, with most income-related social transfers remaining untouched to 'float' on top of basic income; (3) negative income tax, which is an income transfer scheme in which taxpayers pay income tax when their income exceeds a certain level, defined as the minimum level of income everyone in society should have, whereas, for those individuals whose incomes remain below that limit, the state pays financial support, that is, a negative income tax is provided to fill the gap between their actual income and the defined minimum income level; and (4) other possible models for experimentation, including participation income, which is conditional. In order to get it, the person should show some kind of activity, such as voluntary work in the third sector, care within a family, studies, or other forms of socially acceptable activities.

When evaluating the suitability of these four alternatives for experimentation, various aspects were considered, such as whether it was administratively possible to apply the model in question in the experiment, what kind of legislative changes the model would imply, and how it could be possible to integrate the model within current national or EU-level legislation, as well as the national economic and distributional costs involved if the model was fully implemented at the national level.

The main tools used to evaluate economic and distributional costs were microsimulations and typical case example calculations to determine how the total disposable income (consisting of social transfers, earnings, and taxes) of individuals or households would change when earned income increased. We sought to evaluate how different levels of basic income contributed to or eliminated monetary work disincentives. In the simulations, income from employment was gradually increased to see how income-tested social transfers diminished and how taxation increased, and to examine the (dis)incentive effect of such interaction in different models. We will start our narrative by discussing first the suitability of participation income and negative income tax for experimentation and then move on to discuss the suitability of full and partial basic income.

Participation Income and Negative Income Tax

In addition to unconditional models, several models have been proposed that resemble basic income, but which involve conditionality and obligations. The main principle in these proposals is that individuals can gain the right to basic income through being active. According to Anthony Atkinson (1996, 2014), the best-known developer of participation income, people in employment, job seekers, disabled people, and individuals involved in care work and in non-governmental organisations would be eligible for participation income.

The central and most challenging issue in relation to participation income is determining which types of activity can be interpreted as representative of proper participation, and which would be 'socially acceptable'. Any introduction of participation income would require a political debate about the conditions of participation. Furthermore, it could be difficult to define how much socially acceptable and important work individuals should do in return for monetary compensation. The identification and monitoring of beneficiaries if they comply with the agreed conditions might be problematic (for a discussion, see De Wispelaere and Stirton, 2007). We finally ruled out the participation income model because we considered it would be too difficult and bureaucratic to administratively screen the participants in the experiment effectively.

A negative income tax was advocated for in the US by Milton Friedman (for example, Friedman, 1962; see also Standing, 2017: 16) and, after gaining more widespread support, several experiments with negative income tax have been initiated (for example, Widerquist, 2018). Negative income tax is a social security and tax scheme based on income compensation by means of taxation when an individual's income remains below an agreed minimum level. The underlying philosophy of basic income and negative tax is different as well as the way of paying out the benefit, but the two models have rather similar distributional outcomes. Both models aim to guarantee minimum income and provide more incentives for work (Honkanen, 2014; van Parijs and Vanderborght, 2017: 32–40; Widerquist, 2018: 15–18). Thus, an experiment with partial basic income would also provide some information about the incentive effects of negative income tax (Honkanen, 2014).

An effective experiment involving a negative income tax would require an income register in relation to monthly income. Without such a register, it would be necessary to rely on people's self-reported income and there would be temptations to declare lower levels of earned income to maximise the level of negative income tax received. When planning the experiment and when it was running from 2017 to 2018, there was no such a register at our disposal. Such an income register become available in 2019. Given the unavailability of the required register at the time of the experiment, we opted not to proceed with a negative tax model.

Full Basic Income

Full basic income can be understood as a model in which a large proportion of other tax-financed and social insurance-based benefits is replaced. In practice, this would mean that the level of basic income would be higher than the current basic social security income (see Chapter 2). However, full basic income does not supersede all other social transfer benefits; for example, social assistance addressed to help people with special needs or in sudden unanticipated need situations is left intact (Standing, 2017: 83). The same applies to all social and health services.

We examined (dis)incentive effects of different models by simulating participation tax rates in situations where a previously unemployed individual becomes employed or starts working longer hours. For the sake of simplicity, we only present calculations for single individuals (Table 3.1). The participation tax rates listed in the table show to what extent taxes would increase, and current transfers would diminish, as work income rose. For example, if work income were to increase from €0 to €500 per month, the participation tax rate under the current social security and tax model would be 36.9 percent (Model 1). As the table shows, the participation tax rate would be substantially higher in both full basic income models (Models 2 and 3), apart from income increases of €1000 to €2000 per month.

Table 3.1   *Participation tax rates of an unemployed individual living alone in relation to the current model and basic income of €1000 and €1500 per month*

Change in wages	Model 1. Current legislation	Model 2. Basic income €1000/month	Model 3. Basic income €1500/month
€0 → €500	36.9%	73.4%	91.1%
€0 → €1000	51.7%	82.9%	85.1%
€0 → €2000	66.3%	71.4%	82.0%
€1000 → €2000	80.9%	60.0%	79.0%

Source: Kangas et al. (2016: 22)

High levels of basic income would naturally have significant effects on income distribution, and consequently, income inequality would substantially decrease. The Gini coefficient would fall from 26.4 to 21.7 at a basic income level of €1000 and to 17.9 at a basic income level of €1500, with the proportion of low-income households (at a poverty threshold of 60 percent of the national median income) falling from 14.1 percent to 9.5 percent or to 4.8 percent, respectively, and poverty among children falling from 13.2 percent to 9.4 percent or to 3.4 percent, respectively. Hence, our simulations corroborate the claim that relatively high full basic income would enhance more equal income distribution and substantially reduce poverty (for example, Mays, 2019; Standing, 2020).

The primary problem with such high levels of basic income is cost. At a basic income of €1000 per month, income transfers would be three times higher than in the current system; and at a basic income of €1500 per month, income transfers would be four times higher. Thus, such schemes would be difficult to implement economically and in terms of political feasibility.

Partial Basic Income

When evaluating economic and distributional outcomes of partial basic income, two different levels of benefit were used for benefit calculations, that

24   *Experimenting with unconditional basic income*

is, €550 and €750 per month, which were net payments, as tax was planned to be collected only on income coming on top of basic income. According to microsimulations at these two levels, the flat-rate tax collected on income exceeding basic income would be 43.0 percent and 50.5 percent, respectively, to cover all the extra costs caused by the implementation of basic income. In addition to those 'realistic' tax rates, we simulated the effects of 'unrealistic' tax rates, in other words, we used the current tax system on income from employment. Under the current tax system, a tax-free basic income of €550 would generate a budget deficit of approximately €11 billion, which corresponds to one-fifth of the state budget.

Table 3.2   *Participation tax rates of a single wage earner living alone and a single parent with two children in relation to the current model and basic income of €550 and €750 per month[2]*

Change in wages	Model 1. Existing legislation	Basic income of €550 and tax model on exceeding income		Basic income of €750 and tax model on exceeding income	
		Model 2. Flat-rate tax 43.0%	Model 3. Existing tax system	Model 4. Flat-rate tax 50.5%	Model 5. Existing tax system
Single person					
€0 → €500	36.9%	50.2%	47.5%	63.9%	38.5%
€0 → €1000	51.7%	63.6%	57.2%	74.0%	50.3%
€0 → €2000	66.3%	60.8%	51.1%	66.2%	44.2%
€1000 → €2000	80.9%	58.0%	44.9%	58.3%	38.2%
Single parent					
€0 → €500	29.3%	54.5%	28.8%	60.4%	27.7%
€0 → €1000	42.0%	64.7%	43.7%	72.8%	36.6%
€0 → €2000	70.3%	81.2%	64.6%	87.8%	59.9%
€1000 → €2000	98.7%	97.8%	85.6%	102.9%	83.1%

Source: Kangas et al. (2016: 30 and 32)

Regarding distributional outcomes, a basic income of €550 or €750 would not have any significant effect on income inequality, as the Gini coefficient would decline from 26.4 to 26.1 or to 24.2, respectively.

The work incentive structures concerning the two different levels of partial basic income and the two taxation systems are depicted in Table 3.2 in relation to two typical cases, namely, that of a single person living alone and a single parent. With this table, it is possible to compare the outcomes of the basic income schemes and the alternative tax models to current participation tax rates. It is also possible to see how the tax treatment (whether through

Making of the Finnish basic income experiment 25

a cost-neutral flat-rate tax or through the 'unrealistic' current tax system) of income exceeding basic income affects comparisons. The 'unrealistic' tax model could to some extent be made more realistic if a basic income scheme was not only financed through income tax but also through revenue derived from other sources such as a capital gains tax, and through narrowing the gap between more lenient taxation of capital and more progressive taxation on earned income, as well as through other alternative funding methods as proposed by advocates of basic income (for example, Standing, 2017: 129–54; Andrade et al., 2019; van Parijs and Vanderborght, 2017: 147–8).

With regard to single persons whose wages would increase from zero to €1000, they would be better off in the existing tax-benefit system (Model 1) compared with basic income schemes (Models 2 and 4), which would lead to higher participation tax rates than in the existing tax-benefit model. Only for higher income increases would basic income schemes perform better regardless of whether they were linked to the existing taxation system or to a flat-rate tax system. In the case of the single parent, basic income schemes (Models 2 and 4) with flat-rate taxes tended to produce higher tax disincentives than the existing system.

Basic Income and EU Legislation

One task specified in the governmental assignment was to study how basic income would fit within the context of EU-level legislation. This issue was discussed and analysed with social policy and legal experts. In principle, in the name of subsidiarity, social policies fall within the national domain and EU legislation could be considered as unlikely to affect the experiment, but since the government wanted to know what effects there might be in relation to fully implementing basic income in Finland we had to hypothetically consider all the possible EU consequences. EU-level considerations revolved around the questions of whether and how much basic income might entail engagement with EU legislation.

A simple schematic presentation provides clarification concerning these matters and how different levels of basic income are likely to involve the EU legislation (Figure 3.1 as modified from Kalliomaa-Puha et al., 2016). The horizontal axis depicts the form of financing (taxes versus social security contributions), and the vertical axis depicts the relevant EU legislation involved. The vertical axis roughly indicates the level of benefits. If the level of basic income is low enough, such that it would replace only tax-financed and income-tested or means-tested minimum benefits, it would likely remain a part of national decision-making without EU involvement. In contrast, at a basic income level ranging from €1000 to €1500 per month, basic income would automatically supersede a part of many social insurance schemes, and therefore, it would fall within the domain of the EU legislation.[3]

In principle, social security issues fall within national competence, but the EU regulation affects who is entitled to benefits as an employee, as a family member, etc. As shown in the lowest dark grey box in Figure 3.1, some schemes do not include such entitlement possibilities. The benefits from such schemes mostly comprise tax-financed programmes that do not involve strong claim rights and that are income- or means-tested, such as social assistance, housing allowance, and guarantee pension. As depicted in Figure 3.1, above these clearly national benefit schemes there are other transfer programmes whose position is not completely clear if they are exportable benefits or not, and finally, the highest, light-grey box includes those schemes that are definitely under the EU regulations and whose benefits are exportable from Finland to another countries.

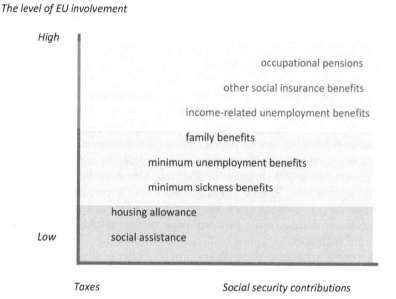

Figure 3.1   *The level and financing of benefits and the degree of the EU involvement in legislation*

Given these reservations, the planning group concluded that such high basic income levels were neither economically, institutionally or politically feasible (see Chapter 14). Furthermore, the higher the benefits, the more likely the benefits would be exportable to other countries, as social insurance-based benefits typically are. Therefore, rather than focusing on full basic income, planning concentrated on partial basic income. However, EU legislation still needed to be considered since, although the levels of the basic unemployment benefit and labour market subsidy are low and precisely the same, the former is an exportable benefit, whereas the latter is not (see for example, Tuovinen, 2020).

The aforementioned legislative issues raise questions concerning whether it is possible to implement basic income in a single EU member state, and of the role of national legislation vis-à-vis EU-level legislation. Fritz Scharpf (2000) is sceptical of the political feasibility of basic income in a single EU member state. According to him, fear of welfare migration decreases the viability of a universal scheme. In his response to Scharpf (2020), Philippe van Parijs (2000) discusses the possibilities of a Euro-Dividend in mitigating challenges to implementing basic income and, in his later publications (for example, van Parijs and Vanderborght, 2017: 235–41), he presents a more detailed proposition for further discussion about the level (€200 per individual per month) and financing (possibly through an EU-wide corporate tax or a 'Europeanised' Value Added Tax) for such a Euro-Dividend.

THE IDEAL EXPERIMENTAL SETTING AND STEPS TOWARDS THE EXPERIMENTATION MODEL

Following the ideas in the previous negative income experiments in the US, the feasibility report recommended that different levels of basic income (€550, €600, and €700 per month, tax free) and different tax levels (40, 45, and 50 percent, respectively) linked to those benefit levels should be applied. Furthermore, the American examples showed that a purely local experiment may be problematic. If different kinds of internal or external economic shocks were to hit the municipality where the experiment was running, the experiment would be significantly compromised, and it would be impossible to determine to what extent any changes were caused by the intervention (basic income) or by those shocks. Therefore, the planning group recommended that the starting point of the Finnish experiment should consist of representative nationwide random sampling and saturated local experiments with more intensive take-up rates to capture various interactions and community effects. Special groups, such as the self-employed, low-income earners and other forms of bogus employees would have their own weighted samples. Each of these experimental groups would have their own control groups identical to the experimental groups.

The experiment was to be obligatory to avoid selection bias. Because the government's assignment entailed studying the employment effects, younger people (expected to be mainly studying and who have their own 'basic income' in the form of a free study grant) and older people (who already have their own

28 *Experimenting with unconditional basic income*

'basic income' in the form of pensions) were to be left out of the sampling frame. The €20 million set aside for the experiment was calculated to be sufficient for a sample of 1500 persons. To increase the sample size, it was initially planned that the payment of several basic security benefits administrated by Kela would be changed to resemble the unconditional payment of basic income so that the number of participants could be increased to 10 000. However, due to bureaucratic obstacles, this plan could not be followed. Moreover, efforts to obtain an additional €10 million from the Finnish Innovation Fund Sitra also failed. Thus, the experiment had to be based on a budget of €20 million, which reduced the ambitions of the original plans and narrowed possibilities in relation to determining the final model.

Steps Towards the Experimentation Model

According to the governmental plan, the final model for experimentation had to be ready by 15 November 2016 and the experiment was expected to start at the beginning of 2017. This timetable was completely unrealistic. Within a timeframe of one and half months, it would have been impossible to pass the relevant legislation on the experiment, plan the sample, develop the platform to pay out the benefits, inform the participants, and educate the social security administration on how to answer the multiple possible questions and requests for further clarifications arising from those people included in the experiment. Passing relevant legislation, in terms of initial preparation through to the presentation of a governmental bill via public hearing, parliamentary committee debates, and parliamentary votes until its final promulgation by the President, takes time, usually considerably more than half a year, which was all that finally was available for the planning consortium. Therefore, we had to start all practical preparations immediately in the spring of 2016 before any political approval of the experimental model had been obtained. There were many open questions and very few answers.

The situation was further complicated in that coordination at the state level did not work very well. Tensions within and between administrative sectors made planning challenging. The lack of a coordinated view concerning which kinds of major administrative or social policy reforms were planned for the period 2017–18 caused additional problems for the practical design of the experiment. Two such reforms were of importance. First, in early 2017, basic social assistance was transferred from municipalities and centralised to Kela. Kela's information and communication technologies (ICT) service became primarily engaged in implementing that massive reform, which raised a question as to whether resources would be available for use in planning an ICT platform for the basic income experiment. Second, the Finnish Tax Administration was planning to reform its register system at the beginning of

Making of the Finnish basic income experiment 29

2018. Whereas the first reform did not ultimately harm the planning or implementation of the experiment, the second reform had more serious implications. The Tax Administration withdrew from the planning of the tax model for the experiment due to a lack of resources, and the Ministry of Finance refused to give extra resources for planning. Because the government insisted that the experiment must begin in 2017, the experiment had to be based on the existing taxation.

The planning group confronted a limited experimental budget and an unrealistic time frame. It soon became clear that the experiment the planning group proposed in the feasibility report could not commence by 1 January 2017. Therefore, in May 2016, the Minister of Social Affairs suggested that the experiment could start as a pilot (as said in the English version of the government's programme), with the unemployed getting their 'basic' flat-rate benefits from Kela as a target group. Several practical considerations made this option appealing and feasible. Updated data on unemployed persons and their bank accounts were already centrally located and easily available in Kela's registers, whereas income-related benefits were paid by voluntary unemployment funds (Chapter 2) and inclusion of those unemployed would have been administratively difficult and time consuming to handle. Furthermore, in the Kela-based experiment, it was possible to increase the number of persons included in the experiment. As long as the unemployed were unemployed and getting their unemployment benefits from Kela, benefits could be unconditionally paid from Kela's budget as if they were basic income and, until the claimants found employment, their basic income could be paid from the experimental budget of €20 million.

The research group recommended that the experiment should be based on random nationwide sampling and that participation should be obligatory. The motivation for the first decision was to avoid issues arising from internal or external economic or other shocks that might have varying local effects (as discussed above). This decision meant that it was not possible to study various community effects, which has been a major criticism against randomised nationwide experiments (for example, Standing, 2017, 2020; Widerquist, 2018).

Intensive planning regarding the relevant legislation and all the practical issues began in Kela in late May 2016. The pre-existing Kela ICT platform used to pay out ordinary unemployment benefits was modified and tailored to accommodate basic income payments. The major challenge involved determining the appropriate legislation for the experiment, and it was not always easy to adapt the scientific conceptualisations of the planning group with the social policy reality as regulated by complex legal regulations (see for example, Torry, 2020: 253–72). In this process, 'mastering the art of compromising' became essential. It soon became clear that it would be impossible

30 *Experimenting with unconditional basic income*

within the given time frame to integrate the research groups' ideas on different levels of taxes and different levels of basic income and devise appropriate legislation. Because legislation strongly conditioned the practical design and content of the experiment, a close analysis of the relevant legislative constraints is required, which is undertaken in Chapter 4 by Anna-Kaisa Tuovinen.

Parliamentary Discussion on the Basic Income Experiment Bill Reveals Party Positions

The government submitted its bill (HE 215/2016) on a basic income experiment to parliament on 20 October 2016. The parliamentary debates were vigorous and revealed differences in opinion between the political parties (PTK 106/2016 vp). The experiment and its design received criticism from the Social Democrats and the Conservatives, both traditionally opposed to basic income in Finland (Andersson and Kangas, 2005; Koistinen and Perkiö, 2014). The Social Democrats criticised the design of the experiment, which was claimed to be poorly prepared. The Social Democratic MPs further demanded that the experiment should be postponed until the updated income register on monthly income was working effectively, which would enable a better and more effective experiment to be undertaken.

In a similar way, the Conservatives, although part of the coalition government that initiated the experiment, claimed that there was no point in experimenting with basic income as it was not a viable policy option in promoting employment and that it would become too expensive as a policy programme. Instead, Finland should learn from the British Universal Credit Model and develop the country's social policy in that direction. A Conservative MP compared basic income with Linus's Great Pumpkin in the Peanuts cartoon, noting sarcastically that: 'The Great Pumpkin comes and solves all problems'. Additionally, the Conservatives criticised the experimental design for the same reasons as the Social Democrats.

Criticism also came from the ranks of the Green Party and the Left Alliance, both of which were normally vehement supporters of basic income. They found fault with the decision to focus solely on the unemployed, that the basic income would be exempt from tax, and with the high cost of the system. The Greens agreed that the experiment was a good step but claimed that it concentrated too much on employment effects and neglected other important aspects of basic income.

A representative of the Left Alliance rhetorically summarised her opinion as follows: 'This is a partial basic income experiment in the same sense as a fork is a partial meal. This does not mean that this would be a bad experiment. It is only wrongly named'. According to her, the experiment concerned employment rather than basic income. This criticism echoed that of many basic income advocates outside Finland. The most positive views in the parliamentary debates were expressed by members of the Prime Minister's Centre Party and the Finns Party, the third party in the Sipilä coalition government. Both these parties agreed that there were problems with the experiment but they emphasised that the experiment needed to be seen as a pilot for better experiments, as a precedent for large-scale field experiments, and as a start in creating a culture more willing to undertake experiments and produce evidence-based policymaking, which were the objectives of the Sipilä centre-right government (see, Experimental Finland, 2020).

Despite the criticisms expressed, all the members of parliament voted for the experiment in the final parliamentary session on 20 December 2016, apart from the five members of the Christian Democratic Party (CD) who voted against the experiment. The CD is a vehement supporter of the British Universal Credit Model. Once passed in Parliament, the president promulgated the Act on Basic Income Experiment (1528/2016) on 29 December 2016, just three days before the basic income experiment was due to start.

The Basic Income Experiment Act Defines the Research Design

According to the Basic Income Experiment Act, the purpose of the experiment was to obtain information on the effects of basic income on the labour market behaviour of those persons participating in the experiment, as well as to determine other possible effects of basic income. The Ministry of Social Affairs and Health was to lead and direct the implementation of the basic income experiment, and Kela became responsible for the practical implementation of the Act.

The target population of the experiment comprised those who, in November 2016, were receiving basic unemployment benefits or labour market subsidies (see Chapter 2) from Kela and who were aged between 25 and 58 years. Out of that target population, Kela had to randomly select a sample of 2000 persons to be included in a treatment group receiving basic income. Random sampling was performed in such a way that everyone in the target group had an equal opportunity to be selected into the treatment group. Kela had to publish the programme used for sampling before the start of the experiment. Those in the target population not included in the treatment formed a control group, which meant that, at the beginning of the experiment, there were two identical groups, namely, the treatment group and the control group.

Kela had to inform those who were selected for the treatment group of their obligatory participation in the experiment. Furthermore, Kela had to provide their names and social security numbers to the Tax Administration and to municipalities concerned, to enable the experiment to proceed.

The amount of tax-free basic income was set at €560. Basic income was paid without any testing or conditions attached on the second banking day of each month directly to the recipient's account. The amount of basic income remained the same throughout the experiment, and it was not reduced in relation to any other income the participant may have had. Participants who found work during the experiment continued to obtain basic income. Basic income was exempt from taxes, which meant there were no further consequences for the participants' taxation. The existing tax model was applied to income coming on top of basic income, which created a monetary incentive to find employment. In the case of a single person, the participation tax rate (i.e., when moving from unemployment to employment) with monthly wages of €1000 or €2000 would decrease by 18 percentage points and 28 percentage points, respectively. In the case of an unemployed person with dependent children, the decreases were smaller (approximately 13 and 25 percentage points, respectively) (Hämäläinen et al., 2020).

Basic income replaced other income transfers (for example, unemployment, sickness, and rehabilitation benefits) lower than €560. If a recipient's existing bundle of income transfer was higher than €560, Kela had to pay the difference between the actual level of the benefit and the basic income. For example, if a claimant's previous benefits (consisting of unemployment benefit, housing allowance, and social assistance) totalled €960, Kela paid the basic income plus the difference of €400. If the participants had unemployment benefits that exceeded the amount of basic income, they had to apply them separately, and then they had to comply with the conditions that were defined for those extra benefits. Approximately 40 percent of the treatment group had such conditions (Hämäläinen et al., 2020). Therefore, for those individuals, the experiment was not fully unconditional. However, the basic income of €560 per month was paid unconditionally.

The Act also regulated the collection of information. Data on the persons involved in the experiment and on those in the control group were stored in a basic income experiment register kept by Kela. The information in the register can be combined with other Kela-based registers as well as registers administered by other authorities. This possibility to combine different registers gives extraordinary possibilities for further analyses.

CONCLUSION

The making of the basic income experiment in Finland involved a process that operated within a severely limited time frame and which confronted numerous other constraints. Throughout the process, there were moments of inspiration, 'perspiration' and desperation. Compared with the inspiratory expectations of the experiment and given the optimal experimental design outlined in the

Making of the Finnish basic income experiment 33

preliminary feasibility report, the proposed bill and final act were a great disappointment for many, in a similar fashion to the services of the mouse who was a tailor to the cat in the old fairy tale.

There were limitations given that the sample only consisted of unemployed people who were receiving basic unemployment benefits. Some of these individuals were long-term unemployed people whose rights to income-related benefits had expired, some of them were suffering from illness, and some of them were young people without previous work experience. Thus, when evaluating the results, it is important to bear in mind that the target group of the experiment consisted of specific kinds of unemployed. Because the experiment was implemented at the national level, we could not study possible community and interaction effects and, because there was only one model applied, we could not distinguish between possible effects due to unconditionality versus those effects due to the economic incentives (see Simanainen and Kangas, 2018).

Despite these limitations, the Finnish basic income experiment was unique in several respects. Since the motivation behind the governmental directive initiating the experiment was to study whether basic income was effective in promoting employment and in eliminating work disincentives, it was appropriate to concentrate on unemployed people and seek to determine the extent to which they react to monetary incentives. The experiment was a large-scale, national, randomised experiment. Participation in the experiment was obligatory to avoid selection bias. The treatment and control groups were identical at the beginning of the experiment. This research setting and good registers allowed us to draw causal conclusions concerning the possible effects of basic income on employment.

Both in national and international discussions, there has often been criticism that the experiment could not show any significant or stronger employment effects. As shown in Chapter 6, employment is strongly conditional on an individual's health, age and education. As such, basic income does not make people younger or increase their level of education, but basic income may make them feel better (Chapters 7, 8 and 10). Finnish registers offer comprehensive data on various aspects of human life and facilitate longitudinal analyses. Therefore, it is possible to carry out more detailed register-based cross-sectional and longitudinal analyses and corroborate or falsify the results presented in this volume.

We substantially agree with Karl Widerquist's (2018: 64) summary of the Finnish experiment:

> ...although the study is not designed to examine how a large [universal basic income] UBI would affect a large cross section of the public, it is well designed to

examine how a small UBI would affect people currently on unemployment benefits. And that kind of study can reveal a great deal of useful information.

In subsequent chapters, there is indeed a great deal of information presented, which, it is hoped, the reader will find useful.

NOTES

1. This section is based on the English version of the feasibility report 'From idea to experiment – Report on universal basic income experiment in Finland'. Helsinki: Kela Working papers 106 | 2016. The feasibility report was prepared by a research and planning consortium consisting of Olli Kangas, Ville-Veikko Pulkka, Miska Simanainen, Pertti Honkanen, Markus Kanerva, Tapio Räsänen, Anna-Kaisa Tuovinen, Kari Hämäläinen, Jouko Verho, Ohto Kanninen and Jani-Petri Laamanen (Kangas et al., 2016).
2. The effects of housing allowance, social assistance, and adjusted unemployment benefit and childcare fees are taken into consideration in the calculations.
3. In this context, the most important pieces of EU legislation are Regulations 883/2004 and 987/2009 on the coordination of social security systems and implementation of that coordination, Regulation 492/2011 on the freedom of movement for workers, and Directive 2004/38/EC on the right of citizens of the Union and their family members to move and reside freely within the territory of the Member States (Kalliomaa-Puha et al., 2016).

REFERENCES

Act on The Basic Income Experiment (1528/2016; available in Finnish at https://finlex .fi/fi/laki/alkup/2016/20161528) [retrieved 15 December 2020].

Andersson, J. O. and Kangas, O. (2005), 'Universalism in the Age of Workfare. Attitudes to basic income in Sweden and Finland', in Kildal, N. and Kuhnle, S. (eds), *Normative Foundations of the Welfare State: The Nordic Experience*, London: Routledge, pp. 112–29.

Andrade, J., Crocker, G., and Lansley, S. (2019), 'Alternative Funding Methods', in Torry, M. (ed.), *The Palgrave International Handbook of Basic Income*, London: Palgrave Macmillan, pp. 177–90.

Atkinson, A. (1996), 'The Case for a Participation Income', *Political Quarterly* 67 (1), 67–70.

Atkinson, A. (2014), *Inequality: What Is To Be Done?* Cambridge MA: Harvard University Press.

Danson, M. W. (2019), 'Exploring Benefits and Costs: Challenges of Implementing Citizen's Basic Income in Scotland', in Delsen, L. (ed.), *Empirical Research on and Unconditional Basic Income in Europe*, Cham: Springer, pp. 81–108.

De Wispelaere, J. and Stirton, L. (2007), 'The Public Administration Case against Participation Income', *Social Service Review*, September, 523–49.

De Wispelaere, J., Halmetoja, A. and Pulkka V. V. (2019), 'The Finnish Basic Income Experiment: A Primer', in Torry, M. (ed.), *The Palgrave International Handbook of Basic Income*, Cham: Palgrave Macmillan, pp. 389–406.

Making of the Finnish basic income experiment 35

European Commission Regulations 883/2004 and 987/2009 on the coordination of social security systems and implementation of the coordination.

European Commission Regulation 492/2011 on the freedom of movement for workers and Directive 2004/38/EC.

Experimental Finland (2020), 'Nothing Ventured – Nothing Gained', Helsinki: Prime Minister's Office, available at https://kokeilevasuomi.fi/en/frontpage?p_p_id=fi _yja_language_version_tool_web_portlet_LanguageVersionToolMissingNotificat ionPortlet&_fi_yja_language_version_tool_web_portlet_LanguageVersion ToolMissingNotificationPortlet_missingLanguageVersion=1 (accessed 20 December 2020).

Friedman, M. (1962), *Capitalism as Freedom*, Chicago: University of Chicago Press.

HE215/2016 [Governmental Bill], 'Hallituksen esitys eduskunnalle laeiksi perustu-lokokeilusta' ['Governmental Bill on Basic Income Experiment'], available at https://www.eduskunta.fi/FI/vaski/KasittelytiedotValtiopaivaasia/Sivut/HE_215+ 2016.aspx (accessed 10 December).

Honkanen, P. (2014), 'Basic Income and Negative Income Tax: A Comparison with a Simulation Model', *Basic Income Studies* 9 (1–2), 119–35.

Honkanen, P. and Simanainen, M. (2016), *Ideasta kokeiluun? Esiselvitys perustu-lokokeilun toteuttamisvaihtoehdoista. Liite 1. Perustulohankkeen mikrosimulointit-uloksia [From an Idea to an Experiment – Preliminary Report on alternatives for basic income experiment. Appendix 1. Results from Microsimulations in the Basic Income Project]*, Helsinki: Valtioneuvosto, Valtioneuvoston selvitys- ja tutkimusto-iminnan julkaisusarja 13/2016.

Hämäläinen, K., Kanninen, O., Simanainen, M. and Verho, J. (2020), *Perustulokokeilun arvioinnin loppuraportti: Rekisterianalyysi työmarkkinavaikutuksista [The final evaluation report on the basic income experiment: Register-based analysis on labour market effects]*, Helsinki: VATT Institute for Economic Research, VATT muistiot 59.

Kalliomaa-Puha, L., Tuovinen, A-K., and Kangas, O. (2016), 'The Basic Income Experiment in Finland', *Journal of Social Security Law*, 23 (2), 74–87.

Kangas, O. and Pulkka, V-V. (eds) (2016), *Ideasta kokeiluun? – Esiselvitys perustu-lokokeilun toteuttamisvaihtoehdoista [From an Idea to an Experiment – Preliminary Report on alternatives for basic income experiment]*, Helsinki: Finnish Government, Valtioneuvoston selvitys ja tutkimustoiminnan julkaisusarja 13/2016.

Kangas, O., Pulkka, V-V., Honkanen, P., Hämäläinen, K., Kanerva, M., Kanninen, O., Laamanen, J-P., Räsänen, T., Simanainen, M., Tuovinen, A-K., and Verho, J. (2016), *From Idea to Experiment: Report on Universal Basic Income Experiment in Finland.* Helsinki: Kela, Working papers 106, available at https://helda.helsinki .fi/bitstream/handle/10138/167728/WorkingPapers106.pdf (accessed 3 December 2020).

Koistinen, P. and Perkiö, J. (2014) 'Good and Bad Times of Social Innovations: The Case of Universal Basic Income in Finland', *Basic Income Studies*, 9 (1), 25–57.

Mays, J. (2019), 'Social Effects of Basic Income', in M. Torry (ed.), *The Palgrave International Handbook of Basic Income*, London: Palgrave Macmillan, pp. 73–90.

Prime Minister's Office (2015), *Finland, a Land of Solutions: Strategic Programme of Prime Minister Juha Sipilä's Government*, Helsinki: Prime Minister's Office.

PTK 106/2016 vp [Diary of parliamentary discussion].

Scharpf, F. (2000) 'Basic Income and Social Europe', in Van der Veen, R. and Groot, L. (eds), *Basic Income on the Agenda*, Amsterdam, Amsterdam University Press. pp. 155–60.

Simanainen, M. and Kangas, O. (2018), 'What Experiments in Finland Can Tell Us About Basic Income?' *The Political Quarterly*, 14 March 2018, available at https://politicalquarterly.blog/2018/03/14/what-experiments-in-finland-can-tell-us-about-basic-income/ (accessed 26 November 2020).

Standing, G. (2017), *Basic Income: And How We Can Make It Happen*, London: Pelican Books.

Standing, G. (2020), *Battling Eight Giants: Basic Income Now*, London: Tauris.

Torry, M. (2020), *Citizen's Basic Income: A Multidisciplinary Approach*, Cheltenham: Edward Elgar Publishing.

Tuovinen, A-K. (2020), 'Sosiaaliturvauudistuksen keskeisiä kysymyksiä EU-oikeuden valossa' ['Central questions of social security reform in the light of EU-legislation'], Helsinki: Kela, Research blog, available at https://tutkimusblogi.kela.fi/arkisto/5619 (accessed 26 November 2020).

van Parijs, P. (2000), 'Basic Income at the Heart of Social Europe', in van den Veen, R and Groot, L. (eds), *Basic Income on the Agenda*, Amsterdam: Amsterdam University Press, pp. 161–9.

van Parijs, P. and Vanderborght, Y. (2017), *Basic Income. A Radical Proposal for Free Society and Sane Economy*, Cambridge, MA/London: Harvard University Press.

VNK/1413/48/2015, 'Valtioneuvoston päätöksentekoa tukevan selvitys- ja tutkimus-toiminnan hakuilmoitus 2015' ['Announcement of application for investigation and research activities in support of Government decision-making 2015'], available at https://vnk.fi/documents/10616/1277483/Hakuilmoitus.pdf (accessed 30 November 2020).

Widerquist, K. (2018), *A Critical Analysis of Basic Income Experiments for Researchers, Policymakers, and Citizens*, London: Palgrave Macmillan.

4. Constitutional preconditions for the Finnish basic income experiment

Anna-Kaisa Tuovinen

LEGISLATION ENABLING THE EXPERIMENT

The Finnish basic income experiment was planned and conducted as a mandatory experiment to avoid selection biases and obtain statistically generalisable and reliable results (HE 215/2016 vp). It appears to have been the very first basic income experiment in the world based on mandatory participation and a randomised nationwide sample (2000 persons). An experiment of this kind could not have been implemented without amendments to the social security legislation. Therefore, this chapter examines, albeit rather briefly, the constitutional preconditions for the legislation governing the Finnish basic income experiment.

The rule of law is a fundamental principle of democratic society. The Constitution of Finland (731/1999) requires, among other things, that '[t]he exercise of public powers shall be based on an Act. In all public activity, the law shall be strictly followed' (Section 2.3) and that 'the principles governing the rights and obligations of private individuals and the other matters that under this Constitution are of a legislative nature shall be governed by Acts' (Section 80.1). Owing to these constitutional provisions, individuals cannot be compelled to participate in an experiment in the absence of relevant legislation. Hence, participation in the basic income experiment was made mandatory by law for those who were selected as part of the treatment group via random sampling. This group received the basic income benefit during the course of the experiment in 2017–18 (henceforth, the treatment group).

In addition, the right to social security is not only a human right, but also a fundamental right guaranteed under the Constitution of Finland: '[e]veryone shall be guaranteed by an Act the right to basic subsistence in the event of unemployment, illness, and disability and during old age as well as at the birth of a child or the loss of a provider' (Section 19.2).

The treatment group comprised 2000 persons who were recipients of the basic unemployment allowance or labour market subsidy in November 2016.

As the right to unemployment benefits is a fundamental right that is guaranteed by law (Unemployment Security Act, 1290/2002), replacing the normal unemployment benefits with basic income required legislation enacted by the Parliament. The outcome was the Act on the Basic Income Experiment (1528/2016) – a piece of legislation enabling the experiment.

ASSESSING EXPERIMENTATION LEGISLATION IN FINLAND

The function of the Constitution is not only to enable the exercise of public powers but also to set the necessary limitations for it. In Finland, the Constitutional Law Committee of the Parliament is obliged to issue statements on the constitutionality of legislative proposals and their compliance with international human rights treaties (Section 74 of the Constitution; see also Tuori, 2011).[1] When it comes to the constitutionality of experimentation legislation, the Constitutional Law Committee has evaluated several government bills concerning different societal experimentation projects in recent decades.

It is important to note that societal experiments often require deviation from the principle of equal treatment. However, the Constitutional Law Committee has ruled that the principle of equality does not constitute an impediment to experimentation legislation and that, in an experiment, people may be treated differently from others, within certain limits. During past decades, the Constitutional Law Committee has established the criteria for legislation regulating a societal experiment. (Rautiainen, 2019; Tuovinen, 2017.) Based on the Committee's praxis, the Ministry of Justice issued a 'guide for drafters of legislation enabling experimentation projects in society' in late 2018 (Ministry of Justice, 2020). In accordance with these guidelines, the following criteria must be met by an experimentation legislation (Ministry of Justice, 2020; Rautiainen, 2019; Tuovinen, 2017):

1. *Acceptable objective*: The objective of an experiment is to obtain evidence-based information for future decision-making. It is assessed especially in light of the fundamental rights system. An experiment must not violate the fundamental rights of any individual; otherwise, the objective of the experiment would be deemed unacceptable. Although the principle of equality is a fundamental right, deviating from it may be possible if the experiment has an acceptable objective.
2. *Legislative requirements*: In terms of the regulation of fundamental rights and deviation from other legislation during an experiment, provisions regulating an experiment must be enacted by the Parliament. This means that detailed criteria for selecting participants and/or the area where the

experiment will be conducted (or criteria for determining the area) as well as the scope of the experiment must be based on an act.

3. *Proportionality principle*: The experimentation legislation must be proportionate to its objective, and only necessary deviations from other legislation are acceptable. An experiment is necessary when the information obtained by the experiment cannot be achieved when applying other less-invasive means. No one should obtain an undue advantage from an experiment. That is, the proportionality criterion is not fulfilled if there are unreasonable differences between the treatment group and those not participating in the experiment.

4. *Non-discrimination principle*: The experimentation legislation must be non-discriminatory, for instance, in relation to the criteria for selecting participants. However, differences in treatment based on person-related causes (e.g. age) may be justified when there is an acceptable reason, so long as it is not arbitrary.

5. *Temporary validity*: The experimentation legislation must be temporary. The act may be in effect only for a limited, rather short period of time that is necessary for obtaining reliable results from the experiment.

6. *Evaluating the results*: The examination and analysis of the results of an experiment must be accurately planned and organised.

THE BASIC INCOME EXPERIMENT IN LIGHT OF THE CONSTITUTIONALITY REVIEW

In its statement concerning the government bill on the basic income experiment, the Constitutional Law Committee focused on three key dimensions: equality and proportionality, regulation by laws, and clarity of regulation. In addition, the Committee clearly pointed out that in an experiment based on mandatory participation, it is prohibited to reduce the level of social security benefits for the participants (PeVL 51/2016 vp: 5).

Equality and Proportionality

The idea of controlled experiments is that persons subjected to an experiment are treated differently from others in order to measure the effects of an intervention. Therefore, the target population must be divided into at least two groups: a treatment group and a control group. The basic income experiment placed those in the treatment group in a different position from persons in the control group as well as people outside of the experiment. For this reason, the government bill on the basic income experiment had to be assessed in light of the equality provision of the Constitution (PeVL 51/2016 vp: 2).

The Constitution of Finland states that '[e]veryone is equal before the law. No one shall, without an acceptable reason, be treated differently from other persons on the ground of sex, age, origin, language, religion, conviction, opinion, health, disability or other reason that concerns his or her person' (Section 6, subsections 1–2). The list in this provision is the core of the non-discrimination principle, but it is not exhaustive. This means that, without an acceptable reason, it is prohibited to treat persons differently based on any other person-related reason such as wealth, family relations, pregnancy, sexual orientation, or residence. (HE 309/1993 vp: 43–4.) The provisions of equal treatment and non-discrimination limit the discretion of the legislator, but the latter more than the former (Rautiainen, 2019: 205).

In line with the government bill, the Constitutional Law Committee held that the random sampling method provides an equal opportunity for each person in the target population to enter the treatment group. This means that in random sampling, there is no different treatment based on person-related reasons; otherwise, it would not be random. Hence, only the general equality provision of the Constitution was applicable in this regard. The Committee held that the experiment complies with Section 6.1 of the Constitution because the objective of the experiment – to study the effects of basic income in society – was acceptable. (PeVL 51/2016 vp: 3.)

However, the bill on the basic income experiment included some person-related limitations in terms of defining the target population based on age and unemployment status. The Constitutional Law Committee held that, taking into consideration the objectives of the experiment, there were acceptable reasons for the differing treatment (PeVL 51/2016 vp: 3). That is, the Constitutional Law Committee accepted that the societal objectives of the basic income experiment were acceptable in light of the fundamental rights system. Regarding other fundamental rights, the basic income experiment was especially aimed at simultaneously securing the right to work (Section 18) and the right to social security (Section 19).

In addition, the principle of proportionality had to be taken into consideration in the assessment of the constitutionality of the experiment. In an experimentation, the principle of proportionality requires that '[d]ifferences in the treatment of those who do and those who do not participate in a given experimentation project must not be unreasonable' (Ministry of Justice, 2020). In other words, experimentation must be necessary and proportionate to its objective, and people should not be put in unreasonably different positions; only reasonable differences are acceptable. When assessing the level of the basic income in the experiment (that is, its cumulative effect), the Constitutional Law Committee noted that persons in the treatment group were in significantly better positions than others. However, the Committee held that the experiment fulfilled the proportionality requirement because the experiment was temporary and the objective of the experiment was acceptable in light of the fundamental rights system. (PeVL 51/2016 vp: 3–4.)

Regulation by Law and Clarity of Regulation

In the government bill, it was proposed that 2000 participants would be selected by random sampling (HE 215/2016 vp: 7). The Constitutional Law Committee noted that the treatment group could not be defined solely by the (random sampling) software code;[2] the legislative requirements stipulate that the criteria for selecting the participants in an experiment must be provided for by law. In addition, the Committee held that the software code must be made public before completing the selection. (PeVL 51/2016 vp: 5.) These remarks were added to the Basic Income Experiment Act (Section 5) by the Social Affairs and Health Committee of the Parliament (StVM 42/2016 vp; Rautiainen, 2019: 207). Thus, in accordance with Section 5 of that Act, the random sampling had to be conducted in such a way that it provided an equal opportunity for each person in the target population to enter the treatment group.

One of the justifications for the basic income experiment was that the current social security legislation can be considered very complex from the perspective of the beneficiary. Therefore, the beneficiary is not always able to assess, for example, the effect of small earnings on certain benefits. (PeVL 51/2016 vp:5; HE 215/2016 vp: 5.) The Constitutional Law Committee emphasised that special attention should be paid to clear and precise regulation, especially in the context of fundamental rights regulation. In its previous statements, the Constitutional Law Committee required that persons concerned should be able to apply the provisions affecting their daily lives and livelihoods without difficulty. (PeVL 51/2016 vp: 5.) This aspect was of significant relevance in the basic income experiment, and the Social Affairs and Health Committee of the Parliament also highlighted this aspect in its own report. It stated that informing the treatment group about the experiment and its effects on the beneficiary's rights and duties was of utmost importance (StVM 42/2016 vp: 7).

Prohibition against Reducing the Social Security Benefit Levels of the Participants

The government bill on the basic income experiment was based on the idea that the level of benefit(s) for participants in the basic income experiment should not be lower than that for people outside the experiment (HE 215/2016 vp: 10). In its statement, the Constitutional Law Committee emphasised that the basic income experiment must not reduce the current social security benefits of persons selected for the treatment group (PeVL 51/2016 vp: 5). The Committee ruled that the experiment was acceptable when the individuals involved in the experiment were entitled to a benefit level that was at least commensurate with normal benefits (PeVL 51/2016 vp: 3). In other words, in an experiment based on mandatory participation, there is a prohibition against reducing the social security benefits or legal protections of participants. It is important to take this principle into account when assessing the acceptability of an experiment. The Committee was of the opinion that this principle should be clearly laid down in the Act on the Basic Income Experiment (PeVL 51/2016 vp: 5).

However, the Act was passed in the Parliament without this kind of explicit provision. This was because the Social Affairs and Health Committee of the Parliament noted that when coordinating basic income with other social security benefits, the beneficiary of basic income should never receive less income than he/she would get without basic income (i.e. compared with receiving the normal unemployment benefit). Therefore, the Social Affairs and Health Committee held that it was not necessary to enact this separately. (StVM 42/2016 vp: 5.) That is, for those who previously received unemployment benefits with, for instance, a child increase (supplement), it was necessary to apply separately for the child increase in order to maintain the same benefit level. Nonetheless, the principle highlighted by the Constitutional Law Committee materialised de jure, in one way or another. The question of whether it materialised de facto is an empirical one. In the following chapters, the empirical results of the Finnish basic income experiment are described and analysed.

NOTES

1. A short introduction to the Committees of the Parliament and how they work is available at https://www.eduskunta.fi/EN/valiokunnat/Pages/default.aspx (accessed 28 December 2020).
2. The software code refers to the sampling algorithm used to conduct the randomisation in December 2016, i.e. random selection of the treatment group from the target population. The sampling algorithm is available in Finnish at https://www.kela.fi/web/en/random-sample-algorithm-used-in-the-basic-income-experiment (accessed 28 December 2020).

REFERENCES

Act on The Basic Income Experiment (1528/2016), Available in Finnish at https://finlex.fi/fi/laki/alkup/2016/20161528 (accessed 28 December 2020).
The Constitution of Finland (731/1999), Unofficial translation in English available at https://finlex.fi/fi/laki/kaannokset/1999/en19990731.pdf (accessed 28 December 2020).
HE 309/1993 vp. The government bill on amending the fundamental rights provisions of the constitutions (available in Finnish at https://www.eduskunta.fi/FI/vaski/HallituksenEsitys/Documents/he_309+1993.pdf) (accessed 28 December 2020).

Constitutional preconditions for the Finnish basic income experiment

HE 215/2016 vp. The government bill on the Basic Income Experiment Act (available in Finnish at https://www.eduskunta.fi/FI/vaski/HallituksenEsitys/Documents/HE_215+2016.pdf) (accessed 28 December 2020).

Ministry of Justice (2020), 'Guide for drafters of legislation enabling experimentation projects in society', available in English at http://kokeiluohje.finlex.fi/en/ (accessed 28 December 2020).

PeVL 51/2016 vp. The Constitutional Law Committee Statement – HE 215/2016 vp, available in Finnish at https://www.eduskunta.fi/FI/vaski/Lausunto/Documents/PeVL_51+2016.pdf (accessed 28 December 2020).

Rautiainen, P. (2019), 'Kokeilulainsäädäntö ja sen perustuslailliset reunaehdot' [Experimental legislation and its constitutional constraints], *Lakimies*, 2, 192–220.

StVM 42/2016 vp. The Social Affairs and Health Committee Report – HE 215/2016 vp, available in Finnish at https://www.eduskunta.fi/FI/vaski/Mietinto/Documents/StVM_42+2016.pdf (accessed 28 December 2020).

Tuori, K. (2011), 'Judicial constitutional review as a last resort', in Campbell, T., Ewing, K.D. and Tomkins, A. (eds), *The Legal Protection of Human Rights: Sceptical Essays*, Oxford: Oxford University Press, pp. 365–91.

Tuovinen, A-K. (2017), *Perustuslainmukainen perustulokokeilu. Perustulokokeilun arviointia perustuslain ja kansainvälisten ihmisoikeussopimusten valossa [The Constitutional Framework for the Basic Income Experiment. Assessing the Basic Income Experiment in Light of the Constitution and International Human Rights Treaties]*, Helsinki: Kelan tutkimus, Työpapereita 114/2017.

Unemployment Security Act (1290/2002), Available in Finnish at https://finlex.fi/fi/laki/ajantasa/2002/20021290 (accessed 28 December 2020).

5. Evaluation of the experiment

Signe Jauhiainen, Olli Kangas, Miska Simanainen and Minna Ylikännö

INTRODUCTION

The aim of the Finnish basic income experiment was to provide information for the coming social security reforms and to test a new type of social security benefit that would better meet the challenges of the future labour market. From the outset, the idea was to run a randomised controlled trial that could be reliably evaluated.

Randomised controlled trials have been used in medicine for several decades to examine the effects of various medicines. In addition, randomised controlled trials have become widespread in development economics, and they have extended over the social sciences. Randomised controlled trials conducted in natural settings are often called field experiments. Randomised controlled trials are utilised in cases where it is unclear what the actual effect would be and whether a treatment, such as development programmes, is effective (Gerber and Green, 2012; Glennerster and Takavarasha, 2013). Trials can also be informative for policy implementation because costs and risks are significantly lower in an experiment organised in a small scale than in a full-scale implementation process (Haynes et al., 2012).

In real life, we cannot observe both outcomes for the same individual simultaneously with and without treatment. In other words, we cannot observe the counterfactual. Units of the target group, such as individuals or villages, are divided into groups in a randomised controlled trial. The assignment to the treatment and control groups is random, ensuring that the average effect of the treatment can be evaluated. The treatment and control groups have no systematic differences affecting the results, which imitates the counterfactual. In addition, the effects of external factors, such as economic fluctuations, can be excluded. As a result, randomised controlled trials allow causal inferences to be made. When the treatment and control groups are identical at the beginning of the experiment, the observed difference between the groups is attributed to the treatment (Gerber and Green, 2012; Glennerster and Takavarasha, 2013; Haynes et al., 2012).

In the case of the Finnish basic income experiment, the group that received basic income was randomly assigned from the entire target group. The treatment group would suffer from selection without the random assignment. If the treatment group was participating on a voluntary basis, the group would be biased, probably consisting of more active individuals. The randomised controlled trial and these two groups provide an excellent basis for the evaluation of the Finnish basic income experiment. Naturally, several practical matters emerged in the evaluation process, and the aim of this chapter is to describe the process. Nevertheless, the experiment provided information that would not have been yielded without the experiment.

The evaluation comprises several studies that explored the experiment and basic income from different perspectives with a rich set of data sources. First, the employment effect of basic income was evaluated using a register-based statistical analysis. Second, possible impacts of the experiment on subjective well-being were analysed by examining survey data collected towards the end of the experiment. Third, a qualitative study based on many in-depth interviews with basic income recipients described the details of everyday life in relation to basic income. Finally, the media coverage of the basic income experiment and public opinion on basic income were analysed in two additional studies.

This chapter is organised as follows. First, the evaluation process and data sources are described. Then, we consider the possible pitfalls of the data collection and evaluation process. Finally, the lessons learned from this process are summarised.

EVALUATION PROCESS

A randomised controlled trial consists of several phases. Planning (see Chapter 3) and implementation phases are followed by an evaluation. From the outset, scientific evaluation of the Finnish basic income experiment was part of the project since the aim was to provide empirical evidence for future social security reforms. The evaluation and data collection phases for research purposes had been designed in the planning phase prior to implementation. The research ethics committee of the Social Insurance Institution of Finland (Kela) had also conducted an ethical review of the survey and interview protocols before starting the evaluation phase. The committee emphasised accurate information letters, voluntary participation in the data collection, good data management practices, regulations on archiving and reusing the data.

The evaluation process started in 2018 when the survey was conducted, and register data from the first year of the experiment (i.e. 2017) were collected. The preliminary report (Kangas et al., 2019) was published in February 2019

46

Experimenting with unconditional basic income

shortly after the end of the experiment. Employment effects from the first year of the experiment and preliminary survey results on well-being were presented in the report. The results of the entire experiment period were not available due to time lags in the availability of register data. Some of the registers provided real-time data. Benefit payments could have been observed instantly. However, registers on employment and income were available for research purposes not before the second half of 2019.

After the preliminary report, the research team continued with further survey data analysis. Several indicators of survey data were examined more thoroughly. The register data from the entire duration of the experiment were collected, and the employment effect was analysed. Qualitative interviews were conducted after the experiment. The final report (Kangas et al., 2020) was published in Finnish in May 2020, containing all sub-studies of the evaluation. In addition, the VATT Institute for Economic Research has reported results on employment, participation in active labour market policy measures, benefit take-up, and income in two separate reports (Hämäläinen, Kanninen, Simanainen and Verho, 2019; 2020). Eventually, register data will be available via Statistics Finland and the survey data via the Finnish Social Science Data Archive.

The evaluation of the basic income experiment was conducted by the Social Insurance Institution of Finland (Kela) together with the VATT Institute for Economic Research, University of Turku, University of Helsinki, Labour Institute for Economic Research, the Finnish Association for Mental Health, and think tank Tänk. Some of the institutions and researchers participated in the planning phase, but new researchers joined the evaluation team. The Ministry of Social Affairs and Health funded and steered the evaluation project.

SEVERAL DATA SOURCES

Register Data and Employment Effects

The focus of interest in the evaluation was how basic income affects employment. In Finland, the extensive register data on income, benefit recipiency, and use of public services provide fruitful possibilities to carry out register-based analyses. Registers enable analysis before, during, and after the experiment since they are collected frequently and stored permanently. All individuals permanently residing in Finland are identified by their individual identity (ID) code in all official registers. Therefore, separate administrative registers can be easily linked with this ID code, and new research can be carried out after the experiment. Register data collection does not rely on individuals' possibilities or motivation to participate in the data collection process. All 2000 participants in the basic income experiment and the entire control group of 173 000 persons

Evaluation of the experiment   47

were included in the register data because the administrative registers are statutory and are compiled in any case.

Register data from Kela, Finnish Centre for Pensions (ETK), local Employment and Economic Development Offices, Finnish Tax Administration, and the Population Register Centre were collected (Table 5.1). These registers contain information on general demographic variables, receipt of social security payments, employment, income, and participation in active labour market policy measures. Eventually, an accurate and detailed database was compiled, including both treatment and control groups.

Table 5.1   Register data sources and their contents

Register	Data
Social Insurance Institution (Kela)	Target population of the experiment
	Basic income payments and spells
	Social security benefits
Finnish Centre for Pensions (ETK)	Employment spells
Local Labour Offices	Registration as a job seeker
	Participation in active labour market policy
	measures
Finnish Tax Administration	Income from employment
	Other taxable income
Population Register Centre	Demographic variables

The target population was randomly assigned to the treatment and control groups, which enabled the identification of the causal effect of basic income on selected outcomes. The evaluation was designed prior to the experiment, and the outcome variables were selected in the pre-analysis plan, RCT ID: AEARCTR-0002095 (Hämäläinen, Kanninen and Verho, 2019). The analysis was documented in this plan to increase reliability and to avoid problems of testing several outcome variables. Testing multiple outcomes increases the risk of obtaining statistically significant effects by accident. The primary outcome was the number of days in employment between 1 November 2017 and 31 October 2018. Secondary outcomes were annual earnings, take-up of social security benefits, and enrolment in employment services. Owing to the multiple testing, the results of the secondary outcomes are less reliable (Hämäläinen et al., 2020).

According to the results, the employment effect was modest. Basic income increased employment for six days over a one-year period (Hämäläinen et al., 2020). The employment effect was somewhat heterogeneous. When the effect was estimated for sub-groups, the basic income increased employment the most in groups of foreign language speakers and families with children.

48 *Experimenting with unconditional basic income*

In addition, the participants remained as customers of local Employment and Economic Development Offices and participated in active labour market policy measures almost as actively as prior to the experiment, although basic income was unconditional.

Well-being Indicators Measured in Target Group Survey

Official registries do not capture some aspects that are relevant in understanding basic income and its effects, for example, subjective well-being and the personal experience of participating in the experiment. In order to capture some of these more subjective aspects, a survey was carried out. The survey focused on social and financial well-being, subjective health, trust and confidence as well as attitudes towards basic income. For example, life satisfaction is a relevant factor of overall well-being, and health is a determinant of employment. Aspects of well-being are prominent in basic income discussions. Analysing health and well-being indicators was also highlighted by the parliamentary committee during the law-making process.

For comparative purposes, questions from international and large national surveys of well-being were chosen for our survey (European Social Survey, the International Social Survey Programme, the European Union Survey on Income and Living Conditions, and the Regional Health and Well-being Study ATH). Thus, the questions used in the survey had been mainly approved in previous studies, and we have plenty of comparative data. The survey results on health and well-being, financial well-being, bureaucracy, trust, confidence, and opinions on basic income are reported in this book.

The survey was targeted at 2000 recipients of basic income and at a sample of 5000 persons in the control group. These individuals were contacted with an information letter about the survey following the survey, which was conducted through a phone interview from October–December 2018. In total, 3970 persons out of 7000 were reached, and 1633 agreed to participate in the survey; in total, 586 were from the treatment group, and 1047 were from the control group (Table 5.2). Participation in the survey was entirely voluntary for both groups. The response rate was low, being 31 percent in the treatment group and 20 percent in the control group, which is not exceptional in survey studies.

Owing to the low response rate, we cannot exclude the possibility of attrition and non-response bias. Individuals speaking a foreign language as their mother tongue as well as those in age categories under 45 years were underrepresented (Table 5.2). Around 25 percent of the target group spoke a foreign language as their mother tongue, whereas the proportion of this group was more than 10 percentage points lower in the survey data. In the target group, the proportion of individuals 45 years or older was less than 40 percent, but in the survey the proportion was over 40 percent.

Evaluation of the experiment   49

Table 5.2   Demographic characteristics of the target group, survey respondents and in the re-weighted survey data

	Target group		Respondents		Respondents (re-weighted)	
	Treatment	Control	Treatment	Control	Treatment	Control
Labour market subsidy	87.2%	84.6%	85.2%	83.2%	86.9%	83.6%
Woman	47.8%	47.5%	47.6%	48.2%	48.1%	45.6%
Age:						
–34	33.5%	35.1%	31.6%	28.7%	33.4%	35.8%
35–44	27.5%	27.1%	25.4%	23.8%	27.3%	27.0%
45–	39.1%	37.7%	43.0%	47.5%	39.3%	37.2%
Married	35.0%	34.1%	31.6%	33.4%	33.7%	33.6%
Foreign language	24.6%	25.4%	13.3%	9.6%	23.1%	24.6%
Number of observations	2000	173222	586	1047	586	1047

Due to the non-response-bias, the survey data were re-weighted with a response probability model. Personal characteristics, such as gender, age category, marital status, mother tongue, unemployment benefit, and region of residence, were included in the model, and weights were calculated.

Background variables of the target group, survey respondents, and re-weighted data are presented in Table 5.2. The background variables show that the re-weighted data are similar to the original target group. The re-weighted data were used in all analyses included in this book.

Other Data Sources

More in-depth information was collected via face-to-face interviews after the experiment. By collecting interview data, we can answer some of the unanswered questions and understand unexpected results yielded by other sub-studies. The interview invitation and informed consent form were delivered to 988 basic income recipients after the end of the experiment. In total, 106 informed consent forms were returned, and 81 participants were interviewed between February and June 2019. Interviews were semi-structured, enabling participants to freely discuss several themes and their own experiences. The three main themes were: (1) general life situation and well-being; (2) unemployment, work, and bureaucratic encounters; and (3) experiences as a basic income experiment participant. Chapter 12 illustrates how labour, work, and action modalities are reflected in participants' own experiences.

We were also interested in the media coverage of the Finnish basic income experiment both internationally and nationally, in particular, how Finnish and the international media have framed the Finnish basic income experiment. The data contain 348 online news articles published in Finnish online newspapers and 48 news articles published in international online newspapers from 2016 to 2019. Many of the articles are short but include extensive reportage, editorials, columns, and opinion pieces. The selected articles, which were from internationally well-known media outlets, were mainly published in English. The study on media coverage is reported in Chapter 13.

As the interest was also in the opinions on basic income, we conducted two phone surveys from February–March 2020. In both surveys the survey sample was representative of the total Finnish population. The two population surveys explored the support for basic income in Finland by collecting data that complement previous opinion surveys. Chapter 11 describes how income inadequacy, insecure employment relations, and attitudes to societal problems are associated with the propensity to support or oppose basic income in Finland.

ASSESSING THE EVALUATION STUDY

The Finnish basic income experiment was designed as a randomised controlled trial. Randomisation enables the avoidance of several pitfalls, but field experiments are not conducted in a laboratory environment. When evaluating an experiment, we need to keep in mind that several factors can affect the results. Experiments have also encountered criticism. Economic trends occurring simultaneously with the experiment also affect the results. GDP and employment rate increased in Finland during the experiment, but we can assume that this trend affected both the treatment and control groups, which is an advantage in nationwide experiment.

In randomised controlled trials, non-compliance and partial compliance are possible threats (Gerber and Green, 2012; Glennerster and Takavarasha, 2013). In other words, individuals randomly assigned to the treatment group may not participate or participate only partially in the programme. In those cases, exposure to the treatment decreases in the treatment group, hindering the benefits of randomisation. In the Finnish basic income experiment, individuals allocated to the treatment group were not allowed to opt out since participation was obligatory. Some statuses, such as receiving a pension or moving abroad, disallowed the basic income payments, but the number of these cases was small. By the end of the experiment, only 94 individuals had discontinued their participation, but everyone else received a monthly basic income. Due to obligatory participation and a small number of discontinuations, non-compliance did not pose a problem in the evaluation of this experiment.

Evaluation of the experiment 51

Another threat in evaluation is attrition, which means that the outcome cannot be measured for all participants because some refuse to take part in the data collection process (Gerber and Green, 2012; Glennerster and Takavarasha, 2013). In this experiment, the primary outcome was observed from the register data that contained all individuals in the treatment and control groups and thus did not suffer from attrition. Attrition is a more significant problem when the survey data are at stake.

The response rate of the survey was low, 31 percent in the treatment group and 20 percent in the control group, indicating that we cannot exclude problems caused by attrition. The two groups are randomly assigned in the register data, but this is not the case with the survey data. A low response rate reduces comparability of the treatment and control groups. However, it is possible to analyse and correct attrition by linking survey data with registers that contain objectively measured covariates. As described above, the survey data were re-weighted, but the survey results need to be interpreted with caution. We compared two groups and avoided making causal claims when interpreting the results. Eventually, the survey data contained subjective indicators of health and well-being that complemented the evaluation and allowed us to observe different aspects of basic income.

The experiment itself may have affected the participants in several ways (Glennerster and Takavarasha, 2013; Widerquist, 2018). Individuals in the treatment group were aware that they were participating in the basic income experiment since they received an information letter at the beginning of the experiment. In addition, the payment date of benefits changed. The control group was not informed about the experiment, but they could have found out since the information on the target group criteria was publicly available. The basic income experiment gathered significant media attention, and a small number of participants gained publicity in several news articles. However, the research team avoided contacting the participants during the experiment to ensure that the participants were not reminded of the experiment. The aim was to investigate the effect of basic income, not the effect of participating in this experiment. An information letter on the experiment was delivered to the treatment group in December 2016, and the survey was conducted from October–December 2018, taking place at the end of the experiment. No other contacts occurred.

The treatment group knew that they were participating in the study. Therefore, they might have changed their behaviour and acted differently because they were under evaluation. This phenomenon is called the Hawthorne effect (Glennerster and Takavarasha, 2013; Widerquist, 2018). The aim of the experiment, which was to improve employment, was announced publicly. Therefore, it is possible that the treatment group knew what the expectation was. For example, if they were thankful for being in this experiment and wanted to promote basic income, they might have increased their job search effort. From the register data, we learned that the employment effect was eventually modest. The survey data might have been distorted by the same Hawthorne effect, and the survey itself might have affected their behaviour and responses. Interestingly, the in-depth interviews provided insight into the experiences of the basic income recipients; thus, we are able to gain some insight into how the participants felt that they were affected by the experiment.

This experiment cannot provide evidence on general equilibrium effects or community effects. In addition, the two-year duration of the experiment was predetermined, and the participants were aware of this fact. After this experiment, we do not know what would happen in the labour market between employers and employees if the basic income was implemented in Finland. The number of participants was limited, and these participants were located around the country. The two-year duration does not allow the evaluation of the long-term effects of permanent implementation of basic income.

Community effects have been emphasised in basic income literature (Widerquist, 2018). Regional experiments would have provided more information about the effects of basic income on the local labour market and regional economy. When basic income is experimented or implemented in a community, there are also feedback effects. These feedback effects can either similarly affect or counteract the effects at the individual level. In the evaluation of this experiment, we analyse the effects of basic income at an individual level.

Activation Model

Introducing the activation model in 2018 was a major policy reform during the experiment, and it affected the target group asymmetrically by increasing the conditionality of the unemployment benefits. This is not in accordance with the standard principles of field experiments. In addition, the activation model sparked a major public debate on conditionality and working while receiving an unemployment benefit. Basic income and conditional unemployment benefits are, to some extent, opposite social security models, although they both aimed to increase employment, particularly in the Finnish context. The activation model was abolished at the end of 2019.

According to the activation model, an unemployed individual had to either find employment for 18 hours in a three-month observation period, receive entrepreneurial income of at least €241, or participate for five days in a training course or other services offered by the employment offices. If the condition was not met, the unemployment benefit was cut by 4.65 percent for the next three months. The control group was affected by the activation condition if they received an unemployment benefit. In contrast, basic income remained unconditional. Individuals receiving only a basic income did not have to meet the conditions, and the basic income was not cut. Some of the basic income recipients applied and received unemployment benefits, especially child and activation supplements. At the end of the first year of the experiment, the share of those in the control group who applied for unemployment benefit was about 63 percent, and in the treatment group the share was around 47 percent (Hämäläinen, Kanninen, Simanainen and Verho, 2019 and 2020). The activation model affected these participants and supplements.

The activation model might have affected the results in several ways, thus complicating the interpretation of the results. On the one hand, the possible employment effect of basic income would be reduced if the conditionality increased employment in the control group. On the other hand, the activation model encouraged participation in active labour market policy measures. Due to the lock-in effect, increased participation in these measures could also reduce the job search effort and employment of the control group.

The employment effects of both the activation model and basic income were modest. The results showed that the employment of the control group did not increase above that of the treatment group (Hämäläinen et al., 2020), and the employment effect of the activation model on the unemployed receiving a basic unemployment benefit and labour market subsidy was small (Kyyrä et al., 2019). The survey was conducted in autumn 2018; thus, we cannot exclude the role of the activation model in those results. The treatment group knew that they were better off, which might have increased their well-being, whereas the activation model might have negatively affected the well-being of the control group.

LESSONS LEARNED

The Finnish basic income experiment showed that it is possible to plan, implement, and evaluate a nationwide randomised controlled trial. The randomised controlled trial, and especially this experiment, has some caveats because the setting was not ideal. The planning phase was substantial, but still, the time frame was limited. However, the experiment has several features accompanied by multiple datasets, which enable scientific evaluation. This experiment has already provided information on basic income that would have been impossible to obtain otherwise.

The experiment was planned together with ministries and policymakers. Therefore, some choices were not based on scientific principles but were a compromise between practical and scientific arguments. Constitutional preconditions and budgetary constraints also needed to be considered. In Finland, this experiment was the first field experiment in which participation was obligatory. Therefore, many practicalities and legislative matters were

54 *Experimenting with unconditional basic income*

dealt with for the first time, as described in Chapter 4. Planning and conducting a field experiment entails public servants and policymakers having knowledge on experiments.

In this book, we present a variety of sub-studies that evaluate the Finnish basic income experiment. This chapter aims to describe the process of scientific evaluation, several data sources, as well as the strengths and weaknesses of the research design. Thus, the results presented can be interpreted from different perspectives.

REFERENCES

Gerber, A. and Green, D.P. (2012), *Field Experiments: Design, Analysis, and Interpretation*, New York: W.W. Norton & Company.

Glennerster, R. and Takavarasha, K. (2013), *Running Randomized Evaluations; A Practical Guide*, Princeton: Princeton University Press.

Hämäläinen, K., Kanninen, O. and Verho, J. (2019), 'Finnish Basic Income Experiment', AEA RCT Registry, available at https://doi.org/10.1257/rct.2095-4.0 (accessed 11 December 2020).

Hämäläinen, K., Kanninen, O., Simanainen, M. and Verho, J. (2019), *Perustulokokeilun ensimmäinen vuosi* [*First Year of the Basic Income Experiment*], Helsinki: Valtion taloudellinen tutkimuskeskus, VATT Muistiot 56.

Hämäläinen, K., Kanninen, O., Simanainen, M. and Verho, J. (2020), *Perustulokokeilun arvioinnin loppuraportti: Rekisterianalyysi työmarkkinavaikutuksista* [*Final Report of the Basic Income Experiment: Register-based Analysis on Labour Market Effects*], Helsinki: Valtion taloudellinen tutkimuskeskus, VATT Muistiot 59.

Haynes, L., Service, O., Goldacre, B. and Torgerson, D. (2012), 'Test, learn, adapt: Developing public policy with randomised controlled trials', Cabinet Office, Behavioural Insights Team, available at https://assets.publishing.service.gov.uk/government/uploads/system/uploads/attachment_data/file/62529/TLA-1906126.pdf (accessed 15 December 2020).

Kangas, O., Jauhiainen, S., Simanainen, M. and Ylikännö, M. (eds). (2019), *The Basic Income Experiment 2017–2018 in Finland: Preliminary Results*, Helsinki: Ministry of Social Affairs and Health, Reports and Memorandums 2019: 9.

Kangas, O., Jauhiainen, S., Simanainen, M. and Ylikännö, M. (eds). (2020), *Suomen perustulokokeilun arviointi* [*Evaluation of the Finnish Basic Income Experiment*], Helsinki: Ministry of Social Affairs and Health, Reports and Memorandums 2020: 15.

Kyyrä, T., Naumanen, P., Pesola, H., Uusitalo, R. and Ylikännö, M. (2019), *Aktiivimallin vaikutukset työttömiin ja TE-toimistojen toimintaan* [*The Effects of the Activation Model on the Unemployed and TE Offices*], Helsinki: Valtion taloudellinen tutkimuskeskus, VATT Tutkimukset 189.

Widerquist, K. (2018), *A Critical Analysis of Basic Income Experiments for Researchers, Policymakers, and Citizens*, Cham: Palgrave.

6. Basic income and employment

Minna Ylikännö and Olli Kangas

INTRODUCTION

In the Finnish basic income experiment, the main interest was in its employment effects. The centre-right government of Prime Minister Juha Sipilä (2015–19) wanted to know whether the provision of basic income would reduce bureaucracy, income traps, and other disincentives linked to the present social security system (see Kangas and Pulkka, 2016; De Wispelaere et al., 2019; Chapter 2 above), thus boosting labour supply and increasing employment.

The target group of the experiment consisted only of unemployed jobseekers (see Chapter 3). This is not the first time that the unemployed are direct targets of measures to increase labour supply. Since the 1950s, elements of active labour market policies (ALMPs) have been gradually introduced in Finnish employment policies. Most social benefits given are intended to activate the benefit recipients in their job search. This policy paradigm culminated in the activation model implemented at the beginning of 2018.

The same government that implemented the two-year basic income experiment introduced the activation model in the middle of the experiment. The activation model introduced a set of stricter criteria for all unemployed persons in Finland who were receiving unemployment benefits. Within a three-month surveillance period, unemployed jobseekers had to work for 18 days, take part in active labour market services for five days, or earn income from their own business to avoid a 4.65 percent cut in unemployment benefits during a three-month surveillance period.

Owing to massive criticism from citizens and trade unions, the newly-elected centre-left government, the Social Democratic Party, with leader Antti Rinne as Prime Minister, abolished the activation model at the beginning of 2020.[1] The emphasis of the government, now led by Prime Minister Sanna Marin, is more carrot than stick when promoting active citizenship. Considering the strong path dependence in policymaking, it is still unlikely that conditionality in the current unemployment benefit system would radically decrease.

The path dependence was however broken, but only for two years in the Finnish basic income experiment. In the experiment, 2000 unemployed individuals were selected to receive unconditional income transfer of €560 per month. This means that these 2000 people were free of screening, which effectively categorises people into deserving and undeserving – a process typical in today's social security system and criticised by the proponents of basic income to be an unjust way of delivering social benefits. According to these proponents, citizens have a subjective right to decent livelihood in the form of basic income. They claim that basic income also boosts small-scale self-employment and other economic activities; thus, by giving protection against social risks, basic income boosts alternative activities beneficial for the functioning of the societies.

In this chapter, we discuss and analyse the relationship between basic income and employment. We ask whether basic income enhances employment and the re-employment possibilities, and measure them through self-assessments on work ability and confidence in finding new work. Work ability is a prerequisite for re-employment, and confidence in finding work is a subjective assessment of overall re-employment possibilities considering both labour supply and demand considerations.

We start with a short review of the theoretical discussion on the topic and discuss the results from previous basic income experiments. Thereafter, we will analyse findings from the Finnish basic income experiment. We briefly discuss the results of the register study (see also Hämäläinen et al., 2019, 2020a, 2020b), after which we will focus on analysing the survey data collected from the participants of the Finnish basic income experiment (for an outline of the data, see Chapter 5). In the final part of the chapter, we review the data analysis and its policy implications.

ENCOURAGEMENT TO WORK OR SEDUCTION TO LAZINESS?

When discussing basic income, questions around labour supply and incentives to work inevitably arise. Sceptics argue that unconditional social benefits eventually deteriorate work morale. This idea can be found in all activation policies targeted at the unemployed and those at risk of unemployment. On the other hand, advocates of basic income have more faith in humankind, with some placing their full trust in the goodness and wisdom of human beings. According to them, basic income not only frees people from low-quality jobs but also enables them to make (only good) choices in their lives that eventually increase well-being and life satisfaction.

As usual, the truth about human behaviour can be found somewhere in between these views. Unconditional income without expectations of any kind of compensation – that is, labour in some form – could certainly encourage some to exploit the possibility of freeing themselves from work. However, studies on what drives people suggest that most human beings have a need to acquire more than what is needed for mere existence, beyond providing for their families and learning new skills (Lawrence and Nohria, 2001). Thus, free money that covers only the minimum standard of living would not satisfy those needs.

Of course, not all are lucky enough to have the capability to acquire more income or a higher status in society. Different segments of the population can, either occasionally or on a long-term basis, experience difficulties in finding work and earning a decent income in the labour market. The stricter the criteria for receiving social benefits, and the more barriers to employment, the higher the risk for an individual to be excluded from the labour market and – in the worst-case scenario – from society.

Automation and 'robotisation' is already starting to exclude those with less capabilities and an ever-increasing number of workforces from the labour market, adding to challenges faced in the labour market and, by extension, the social security systems. From this perspective, the results from basic income experiments such as the Finnish one should be of particular interest to policy makers and others involved in reforming current systems for social protection.

Employment Effects of Other Basic Income Experiments

Societal experiments are implemented in specific cultural contexts, and therefore each basic income experiment is unique with its own goals and purposes (Widerquist, 2013; Van Parijs and Vandeborght, 2017: 138–44; Standing, 2020: 87–199). In developing economies, these goals typically relate to poverty, health, education, overall social security, emancipation, and empowerment of girls and women (for example, Davala et al., 2015; Davala, 2020). For example, the world's largest basic income experiment in Kenya had been designed to study poverty alleviation and income distribution effects (Widerquist, 2013: 63–4).

In the Basic Income Grant project conducted in the region of Otjivero-Omitara of Namibia in 2007–09, the aim was to study whether basic income can reduce persistently high levels of income inequality (Haarman et al., 2020). Standing (2020: 91) summarises the results from the Namibian experiment as follows: 'Basic income resulted in improved health, nutrition, sanitation, schooling, and economic activity, with several indicators of strong emancipatory effect for women, disabled and minorities'.

It is one thing to carry out basic income experiments in poorer developing economies, where any social benefit introduced will eventually lead to better income and well-being. It is another thing to carry out such experiments in

58   *Experimenting with unconditional basic income*

modern economies with developed and often quite complicated social security systems, where any policy implication is difficult to predict. For example, if the motivation for the experiment is to increase employment (as it usually is), introducing a simple social benefit in a complex system may not make life for the recipients of social security any simpler or increase their incentives to accept work by reducing high effective marginal tax rates (see Chapter 2).

As in the Finnish basic income experiment, employment effects were of great interest in the negative income experiments implemented in the United States in the 1960s and the 1980s: the New Jersey experiment (running 1968 to 1972), the Rural Income Maintenance Experiment (1970 to 1972), the Seattle–Denver Income Maintenance trial (1970 to 1980), and the Gary Income Maintenance Experiment (1971 to 1974). Alongside employment effects, these voluntary experiments were also designed to study the completion of education, educational results, dissolution of marriages, and consumption patterns. With regard to employment, results from these experiments were mixed. Overall, labour supply decreased, with the decrease being more significant among women with children and younger adults. The explanation is that mothers stayed longer at home with their small children and youngsters stayed longer in school. (Widerquist, 2013).

Canada has experimented with basic income on two occasions. In 1974, the Manitoba provincial government introduced a social experiment called the Canadian Guaranteed Annual Income. Also in this experiment, the employment effects were of interest. The results of Hum and Simpson (1991, 1993, 2001) and Prescott et al. (1986) showed a small decrease in working hours among benefit recipients. It is debatable, however, whether this was caused by the unconditional social benefit or the fact that the (voluntary) participants knew that the experiment was only temporary and would eventually end. Furthermore, Calnitsky (2016), based on a survey collected in the town of Dauphin in 1976, found that when compared with conventional social security with means-testing, the experimented annual income caused less stigma.

In 2017, policymakers in Ontario in Canada decided to experiment with basic income among a few thousand recipients of Ontario Works, or Ontario Disability Support Program benefit recipients. They wanted to study the effects of poverty, inequality, and a complicated social security system. However, the experiment was cancelled in 2019 by the newly-elected provincial government, which underlies the highly political nature of basic income.

In the Netherlands, a new model for delivering last-resort social assistance was investigated in order to determine whether decreasing conditionality in the social security system would end up increasing employment and overall activity of benefit recipients. In six Dutch cities, instead of delivering 'money after distrust', those in need for last resort financial aid were given 'money for trust', that is, unconditional social benefit comparable to basic income. At the same time, a more dignifying way of treating these people in the public administration was investigated (Muffels and Gielens, 2019).

Although the Dutch experiment was not a basic income experiment, the idea behind it was practically the same: to challenge the prevailing discourse that the stick works better than the carrot in creating incentives to supply labour, even amongst the most disadvantaged of the population. Its evaluation report, *Sociaal en Cultureel Planbureau* (2019), criticized the Dutch politicians for being too strong in their belief in the power of sanctions to increase labour supply when they introduced the 'crown jewel' of the activation policies, the 2015 participation law (*participatiewet*).

It is not that sanctions are never effective. For some unemployed jobseekers, imposed sanctions may be necessary to incentivise them towards the labour market. However, to accept work, one has to be fit enough to perform the tasks at work. According to the OECD (2020a: 41), one-third of those weakly attached to the labour market in Finland had health problems. In their cluster analysis, OECD (2020a: 46) found a group of unemployed living in rural areas with no recent work experience, and among them, 61 percent had health problems limiting their ability to work.

Hence, the question of activation cannot be approached only from the income transfer perspective. When trying to find the most effective measures for enhancing employment, we need to acknowledge that a number of the unemployed face multiple barriers to employment, including health problems, and lack of skills and recent work experience (OECD, 2020a).

RESEARCH SETTING

In the Finnish basic income experiment, the main interest was in the employment effects of an unconditional social benefit. In the evaluation of the experiment, based on administrative register data, the number of days at work was compared between the receivers of basic income (treatment group) and the control group. According to the results, the former committed more days at work during the experiment, but the difference compared with the controls was modest (Hämäläinen et al., 2019, 2020a, 2020b).

When the first results for the employment effects were published, a media and political debate broke out: 'Disappointing results!'; 'Last nail in the coffin of basic income!'; 'The basic income experiment failed!' Thus, for those who expected to see positive employment effects, the results indicated that basic income is not a proper solution when reforming social security systems. If the adherents of basic income were waiting for a landslide victory, they were disappointed, although the results were, in a sense, positive as well-being increased while employment neither increased nor decreased (Kangas et al., 2020).

60 *Experimenting with unconditional basic income*

Although administrative registers have indisputable benefits for evaluating the effects of societal experiments, they are not able to tell the whole story of the people who participated in the experiment – their motivations, aspirations, and orientations in life. In this chapter, we go beyond register data and numbers of days at work. By utilising the survey data, we aim to provide a richer picture of the relationship between basic income and employment. When striving for evidence-based policymaking in reforming social security systems, we emphasise the need for multiple sets of data offering different viewpoints on experimented social policy models, such as basic income.

In the Finnish experiment, recipients of basic income were randomly selected from all unemployed jobseekers who received either basic unemployment allowance or labour market subsidy from the Social Insurance Institution of Finland (Kela) in November 2016. In the two years before the experiment, 20 percent of them had been unemployed during the entire period from 2015 to 2016 and 76 percent had been unemployed for more than one year (Hämäläinen et al., 2020b: 14). Thus, most probably at the beginning of the experiment, many of the recipients of basic unemployment benefits had one or more barriers to employment, including health conditions and reduced ability to work (for example, OECD, 2020a).

Research Questions, Variables Used and Methods

In this chapter, we ask whether basic income enhances employment and re-employment possibilities, which we measure using self-assessments on work ability and confidence in finding new work.

In the results section, we first describe those who found employment and those who did not find employment despite receiving basic income. We are also interested in how those employed found work. Thereafter, we continue to analyse the ability to work of those in the experiment and how it is connected to their employment. Finally, we analyse and compare self-ratings between the treatment and control groups on confidence in finding new work and how they relate to actual employment.

The dichotomous variable 'employed' pertains to those respondents who stated in the survey that they were either employees or self-employed. Out of all employed respondents, as many as 94 percent were employees and the rest were self-employed.

Work ability was measured by the following question: 'Let's assume that the top rating we can give your ability to work is 10. How would you rate your ability to work on a scale of 0 to 10, where zero is very poor ability to work and 10 is excellent ability to work?' Confidence in finding employment was measured by the following question: 'If you are currently unemployed or were to become unemployed, do you think that you would find work corresponding

Basic income and employment 61

to your qualifications and experience within 12 months?' Respondents could answer 'yes', 'no' or 'I do not know'. In the subsequent binary logistic regressions, the third option is omitted.

Furthermore, for the regression analysis, we recoded the variable on ability to work into five categories instead of 11. In the first category, we combined the first three (0–2) categories of the original variable into one. Likewise, for the next four categories, we combined two categories of the original variable into one (3–4 = 2nd category; 5–6 = 3rd category; 7–8 = 4th category; and finally, 9–10 = 5th category). Occasionally, we refer to the original scale.

We start by describing how these variables and labour market statuses are distributed among basic income recipients (treatment group) and the control group. Thereafter, we run separate regression models, one for employment and one for confidence in finding employment. The independent variables included gender, age, level of education, family structure, and the degree of urbanisation of the municipality of residence. To visualise the connection between ability to work, the treatment (getting basic income), employment, and confidence in finding employment, we run general linear models and present estimated marginal means in two graphs. The estimated marginal means tell the mean response for each factor, adjusted for other background variables included in the model.

RESULTS

According to the survey, 35 percent of the recipients of basic income reported having employment at the end of 2018 compared with 28 percent in the control group. These numbers are higher and the differences between the treatment and control groups slightly larger than in the register study (27 percent and 25 percent, respectively) (Hämäläinen et al., 2019, 2020a, 2020b). While the survey only describes the cross-sectional situation at the end of the experiment, we do not know for how long the employed had been in employment during the experiment.

Of those who were employed by the end of the experiment, a vast majority (66 percent) were working full-time and the rest 34 percent were working part-time. In principle, part-time work is less common in Finland (15 percent) than the average of 17 percent in many other industrialised OECD countries (OECD, 2020b). Furthermore, part-time work in Finland is concentrated mainly in the retail and service sectors. With this in mind, the share of part-time workers is surprisingly high.

For some, working part-time may be a preferable solution in their current life situation; for others, it is involuntary, indicating difficulties in getting work with full hours. Part-time work can facilitate the transition to an open labour market for those who have been outside the labour market, whether they have been unemployed or taking care of the children at home. An underdeveloped part-time labour market may thus be a major barrier to employment. Indeed, when asked about it in the survey, as much as 67 percent of those working part-time expressed their wishes to get full-time work.

When asked about how the respondents had found work, contacts given by the public employment services (PES) available at the Employment and Economic Development Offices were the most common route to employment in the control group (28 percent), whereas this figure was lower in the treatment group. In the treatment group, the most common way back to the labour market was by making direct contact with the employer (32 percent of those who were employed). Nonetheless, PES remained an important way to find work for basic income receivers (20 percent), which emphasises the importance of well-functioning employment services for job seekers. In the Finnish experiment, recipients of basic income were not excluded from the PES, and quite a large share of them had registered themselves as clients at the Employment and Economic Development Offices (Hämäläinen et al., 2019, 2020a, 2020b).

What Explains Employment?

There is a positive and significant association between basic income (treatment) and employment (sig. = 0.007). In this respect, the results are in line with those from the register-based evaluation of the experiment. However, the association loses its statistical significance when controlling for gender, age, level of education, household structure, municipality of residence, and ability to work (Table 6.1). In Table 6.1, coefficients for treatment and for those background variables that got significance are presented.

According to the results, receiving basic income did not quite significantly contribute to finding employment; coefficients for municipality of residence were also found to be insignificant. On average, males have somewhat better possibilities of finding employment than women. Not surprisingly, education increases the probability of employment. The probability of employment among groups with only basic education compared with those with the highest educational attainment was less than 40 percent ($\exp(\beta) = 0.399$). The coefficient of the size of the household is also significant in the model. The respondents who lived alone had the lowest probability of being employed ($\exp(\beta) = 0.459$). Of those who belonged to the treatment group and were living alone, 74 percent were without employment and 62 percent of them were men.

Basic income and employment   63

Table 6.1   *Results of logistic regression for probability to be employed in the end of the experiment*

	Coefficient	Sig.	Exp(β)
Treatment	0.202	0.107	1.224
Woman	−0.262	0.034	0.769
Age		0.018	
25–35	0.535	0.015	1.707
36–45	0.198	0.385	1.219
46–55	0.497	0.026	1.644
55+		ref	
Education		0.000	
1 Basic	−0.918	0.000	0.399
2 Vocational	−0.281	0.094	0.755
3 High school	−0.434	0.074	0.648
4 College	−0.219	0.374	0.803
6 Applied university	0.091	0.670	1.095
7 University degree		reference	
Size of the household		0.000	
1 person	−0.779	0.000	0.459
2 persons	−0.297	0.191	0.743
3 persons	−0.078	0.747	0.925
4 persons	0.072	0.769	0.930
5+ persons		reference	
Ability to work		0.000	
1 (in original scale 0–2)	−2.751	0.000	0.064
2 (in original scale 3–4)	−2.904	0.000	0.055
3 (in original scale 5–6)	−1.454	0.000	0.234
4 (in original scale 7–8)	−0.389	0.003	0.638
5 (in original scale 9–10)		reference	

Condition for Employment is Ability to Work

In addition to proper skills and education, one important precondition for employment is the ability to work. Those who received basic income for two years rated their ability to work on average better than the control group. 45 percent in the treatment group and 39 percent in the control group indicated in the original 0 to 10 scale that their ability to work is 9 or higher.

In the regression analysis, the ability to work significantly explains employment. In all categories of work ability, the probability of employment is significantly lower than in the reference category 5; that is, those who in the original scale evaluated their ability to work to be either 9 or 10. This is in line with the recent *Faces of Joblessness* report by the OECD (2020a), which states that health problems are one of the main barriers to employment in Finland. The report concludes that, 'compared to other OECD countries, a large proportion of Finland's jobless report poor health as a barrier to employment'. In its report, the OECD suggests that, in particular, mental health problems of joblessness should be paid more attention when developing active labour market policies.

A closer look at the interaction between the treatment variable (receipt of basic income) and ability to work shows that for those who had low ability to work (lower than 4 points in the original scale), the treatment had no effect, whereas on higher levels we observe a positive association (Figure 6.1). The result indicates that, at least in the Finnish experiment, basic income made it easier for those who had better ability to work to find work. However, for those who suffered from physical or mental health problems (possibly associated with low skills, see Table 6.1), unconditional social benefit alone was not sufficient to increase labour supply; in addition to decent level of income security, this group of unemployed individuals would need health, employment, and social services.

Our interpretation is that basic income is hardly more than another form of social transfer for those with cumulative social and health problems. These people do not benefit from the abolishment of all conditions in the income transfer system; they need affordable and accessible services designed with a multidisciplinary approach to help them find their way back to the labour market and live a more meaningful life.

Although most of the basic income recipients were unemployed at the end of the experiment, our findings indicate that re-employment possibilities were better for the treatment group than for the control group, who rated themselves lower in their ability to work. In the subsequent section, we take a look at respondents' confidence in finding employment and how that confidence is related to a number of those background factors used in Table 6.1.

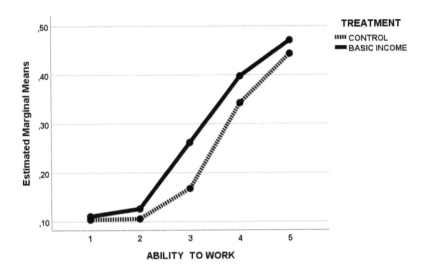

Figure 6.1   Estimated marginal means for employment at the end of the experiment, treatment and ability to work

Basic Income and Confidence in Re-employment

Even the most motivated unemployed jobseekers may find re-employment difficult due to various employment barriers such as lack of suitable jobs, health problems, or lack of sufficient occupational skills. The previously published results from the evaluation of the basic income experiment show that overall well-being at the end of the experiment was significantly higher among the basic income recipients than the controls (Kangas et al., 2019, 2020). We can reasonably assume that with better well-being and a higher ability to work, it is easier to be re-employed. Of course, better health or well-being do not comfort much if, after dozens of job applications, one is still unemployed. That said, the precondition for seeking employment is that the person in question still believes in her or his possibilities to be employed.

In the survey, we asked the respondents to evaluate their employment possibilities within the coming year if they were currently unemployed or if they would become unemployed from their current job. Not surprisingly, the employed respondents were more confident in finding work than unemployed respondents. Whereas 81 percent of the currently employed believed that they would find employment, if they now became unemployed, the corresponding share was 51 percent among the currently unemployed. Furthermore, basic income recipients were significantly more confident in their re-employment opportunity than the control group (69 and 56 percent, respectively).

Table 6.2   *Confidence in finding work corresponding to one's qualifications and experience within 12 months. Logistic regression results*

	Coefficient	Sig.	Exp(β)
Treatment	0.466	0.001	1.593
Employed	0.904	0.000	2.469
Age		0.000	
25–35	0.945	0.000	2.572
36–45	0.653	0.003	1.921
46–55	0.521	0.013	1.684
56+		reference	
Ability to work		.000	
1 (in original scale 0–2)	−1.950	0.000	0.142
2 (in original scale 3–4)	−1.924	0.000	0.146
3 (in original scale 5–6)	−1.174	0.000	0.306
4 (in original scale 7–8)	−0.605	0.000	0.546
5 (in original scale 9–10)		reference	

As shown in Table 6.2, treatment significantly explains confidence in finding work. The probability of believing in their possibilities in finding work was 1.6 times higher (exp(β) = 1.593) among those who received basic income, compared with the controls. Consequently, the probability of believing in their possibilities in finding work was 2.5 times higher (exp(β) = 2.469) among those in employment, compared with the unemployed. Less surprisingly, age significantly decreases confidence in finding work as does lower work ability. Other background variables were not very significantly associated with the dependent variable.

As with work ability and employment, Figure 6.2 shows an interesting interaction between confidence in finding work and ability to work. This has an important bearing on the discussion in the division of labour between benefits in cash and benefits in kind in helping people to believe in their possibilities to find employment and thus attracting them back to the labour markets. When self-rated ability to work was low, there was no difference in confidence levels between the treatment and control groups, whereas among those who regarded their work ability as good or very good (values 7 to 10 in the original work ability scale), confidence in finding employment was higher among the treatment group. These results further emphasise the importance of health and rehabilitation services, not just for the unemployed but for every citizen.

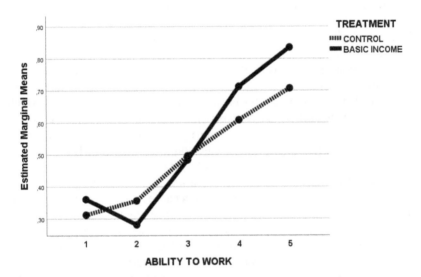

Figure 6.2   *Estimated marginal means for confidence in finding employment, treatment and ability to work*

Although the mechanisms behind employment and tackling barriers to employment are complicated, our results show that there is positive correlation between basic income, employment and confidence in finding work among those with better self-rated ability to work. In the survey, we also asked the respondents whether they had had an opportunity to do meaningful work or improve the material standard of living within the past two years; that is, during the basic income experiment (see also Chapter 10). Basic income recipients answered 'yes' more often to both questions than those in the control group.

DISCUSSION

One key motivation behind basic income is that it is said to give possibilities for people to open new avenues in their lives and to switch careers. Since basic income provides basic security and reduces economic risks, it is seen as a facilitator for starting new small-scale businesses by providing economic support during the formative years of the business and also minimising shame if the business fails (for example, Nooteboom, 2013: 213).

Furthermore, proponents of basic income regard it as a social policy model for societies where wage labour or dependent employment disappears (Gilber et al., 2020). However, in that respect, our story is much about stability. Basic income contributed to some extent in finding employment, but many of those who were unemployed at the beginning of the experiment had the same status at the end of the experiment. We also did not find any dramatic differences in the employee or self-employed statuses between the treatment and control groups.

There are several reasons for this rather static picture. First, the target group of the experiment consisted of unemployed persons receiving flat-rate unemployment benefits from the Social Insurance Institution of Finland, which means that many of them had an experience of lengthy unemployment spells. Second, the recipients of basic income knew from the very first payment of the benefit that the experiment would end after two years. Knowledge of the finality of the unconditional monthly payment inevitably affected their behaviour. Third, income transfers, which are provided in the form of basic income or in more traditional income maintenance systems, are not enough if an unemployed person faces multiple barriers to employment, including health problems. As shown above, while basic income had a positive association with employment among those unemployed who had better health, there was no such association among those who had low work ability.

Based on our results and the results presented in other chapters of this book, we can argue that freeing people from screening and the financial stress linked to the sanctioning of social benefits increases their well-being, therefore creating better conditions for learning new skills and acquiring jobs they are motivated to do (see also Kangas et al., 2020). This phenomenon is visible in the higher levels of confidence in finding employment among the treatment groups compared with the controls.

Unfortunately, the two-year experiment was not long enough to reliably observe the long-term effects on the employability of the recipients or employment effects of basic income more generally. Needless to say, receiving basic income does not suddenly give the recipients better education, better health, or remove other possible hindrances to employment. In a society with basic income, positive or negative changes in employment are conditional on the same factors that influence labour supply and demand in systems without basic income.

Furthermore, when health problems form a barrier to employment, as we have shown, the conditionality of a social benefit is not a relevant issue. To enhance re-employment possibilities and further activation of citizens, services are needed. In Finland, the Employment and Economic Development Offices offer services to unemployed jobseekers, as well as municipal health and social services, and education services. The emphasis in these services is in the transition towards more intensified multidisciplinary work in a customer-oriented manner. Decent economic security is necessary, but is not a sufficient condition for re-employment. Income transfers must be accompanied by a wide array of services to improve the employability of those who have multiple barriers to employment.

REFERENCES

Calnitsky, D. (2016). '"More normal than welfare": the Mincome experiment, stigma, and community experience', *Canadian Review of Sociology* 53(1), 26–71.

Davala, S. (2020), 'Pilots, evidence and politics: The basic income debate in India', in Torry, M. (ed.), *The Palgrave International Handbook of Basic Income*, Cham: Palgrave Macmillan, pp. 373–87.

Davala, S., Jhabvala, R., Mehta, S. K. and Standing, G. (2015), *Basic Income. A Transformative Policy for India*, London: Bloomsbury.

De Wispelaere, J., Halmetoja, A. and Pulkka V-V. (2019), 'The Finnish basic income experiment: A primer', in Torry, M. (ed.), *The Palgrave International Handbook of Basic Income*, Cham: Palgrave Macmillan, pp. 389–406.

Gilber, R., Huws, U. and Yi, G. (2020), 'Employment market effects of basic income', in Torry, M. (ed.), *The Palgrave International Handbook of Basic Income*, Cham: Palgrave Macmillan, pp. 47–72.

Haarman, C., Haarman, D. and Nattrass, N. (2020), 'The Namibian basic income grant pilot', in Torry, M. (ed.), *The Palgrave International Handbook of Basic Income*, Cham: Palgrave Macmillan, pp. 357–72.

Hämäläinen, K., Kanninen, O., Simanainen, M. and Verho, J. (2019), *Perustulokokeilun ensimmäinen vuosi* [*The First Year of the Basic Income Experiment*], Helsinki: VATT Institute for Economic Studies, VATT Muistiot 80.

Hämäläinen, K., Kanninen, O., Simanainen, M. and Verho, J. (2020a), 'Perustulokokeilun työllisyysvaikutukset' ['Employment effects of the basic income experiment'], in Kangas, O., Jauhiainen, S., Simanainen, M. and Ylikännö, M., *Suomen perustulokokeilun arviointi* [*Evaluation of the Finnish Basic Income Experiment*], Helsinki: Ministry of Social Affairs and Health, Raportteja ja muistioita 2020: 15, pp. 32–49.

Hämäläinen, K., Kanninen, O., Simanainen, M. and Verho, J. (2020b), *Perustulokokeilun arvioinnin loppuraportti: Rekisterianalyysi työmarkkinavaikutuksista* [*The Final Evaluation Report on the Basic Income Experiment: Register-Based Analysis on Labour Market Effects*], Helsinki: VATT Institute for Economic Research, VATT Muistiot 59.

Hum, D., and Simpson, W. (1991), *Income Maintenance, Work Effort, and the Canadian Mincome Experiment*, Ottawa: Economic Council of Canada.

Hum, D., and Simpson, W. (1993), 'Economic response to a guaranteed annual income: Experience from Canada and the United States', *Journal of Labor Economics* 11(1, Part 2), 263–96.

Hum, D., and Simpson, W. (2001), 'A guaranteed annual income: From Mincome to the millennium', *Policy Options* 22(1), 78–82.

70   *Experimenting with unconditional basic income*

Kangas, O. and Pulkka, V-V. (eds.) (2016), *Ideasta kokeiluun? – Esiselvitys perustulokokeilun toteuttamisvaihtoehdoista* [*From an Idea to an Experiment – Preliminary Report on Alternatives for Basic Income Experiment*], Helsinki: Finnish Government, Valtioneuvoston selvitys ja tutkimustoiminnan julkaisusarja 13/2016.

Kangas, O., Jauhiainen, S., Simanainen, M. and Ylikännö, M. (eds.) (2019), 'Perustulokokeilun työllisyys- ja hyvinvointivaikutukset: Alustavia tuloksia Suomen perustulokokeilusta 2017–2018' ['The basic income experiment 2017–2018 in Finland: preliminary results'], Sosiaali- ja terveysministeriö, Raportteja ja muistioita 2019: 19.

Kangas, O., Jauhiainen, S., Simanainen, M. and Ylikännö, M. (eds.) (2020), *Suomen perustulokokeilun arviointi* [*Evaluation of the Finnish Basic Income Experiment*], Helsinki: Ministry of Social Affairs and Health, Raportteja ja muistioita 2020: 15.

Lawrence, P. R. and Nohria, N. (2001), *Driven: How Human Nature Shapes Our Choices*, San Francisco: Jossey-Bass.

Muffels, R. and Gielens, E. (2019), 'Job search, employment capabilities and well-being of people on welfare in the Dutch "participation income" experiments', in Delsen, L. (ed.), *Empirical Research on and Unconditional Basic Income in Europe*, Cham: Springer, pp. 109–38.

Nooteboom, B. (2013), 'Basic income as a basis for small business', in Widerquist, K., Noguera, J., Vanderborght, Y. and De Wispelaere, J. (eds.), *Basic Income. An Anthology of Contemporary Research*, Chichester: Wiley-Blackwell, pp. 210–15.

OECD (2020a), *Faces of Joblessness in Finland – A People-centred Perspective on Employment Barriers and Policies*, Paris: OECD.

OECD (2020b), 'Part-Time Employment Rates', available at https://data.oecd.org/emp/part-time-employment-rate.htm (accessed 2 December 2020).

Prescott, D., Swidinsky, R., and Wilton, D. A. (1986), 'Labour supply estimates for low-income female heads of household using Mincome data', *Canadian Journal of Economics* 19(1), 34–141.

Sociaal en Cultureel Planbureau (2019), *Eindevaluatie van de Participatiewet* [*Final Evaluation of the Participation Act*], Den Haag: Sociaal en Cultureel Planbureau.

Standing, G. (2020), *Battling Eight Giants: Basic Income Now*, London: Tauris.

Van Parijs, P. and Vandeborght, Y. (2017), *Basic Income: A Radical Proposal for a Free Society and Sane Economy*, Cambridge MA and London: Harvard University Press.

Widerquist, K. (2013), 'What (if anything) can we learn from the negative tax experiments?', in Widerquist, K., Noguera, J., Vanderborght, Y. and De Wispelaere, J. (eds.), *Basic Income. An Anthology of Contemporary Research*, Chichester: Wiley-Blackwell, pp. 216–29.

7. Subjective health, well-being and cognitive capabilities

Miska Simanainen and Annamari Tuulio-Henriksson

INTRODUCTION

The existence of the relationship between poverty and poor health has been known for ages, although the actual mechanisms that connect poverty to health have not been well understood. A growing body of literature indicates that unemployment (which often goes hand in hand with poverty) can pose substantial health risks by negatively affecting, in particular, the mental health, psychological well-being and cognitive capabilities of those who experience it (for example, Acevedo et al., 2020; Wahrendorf et al., 2019; Wanberg, 2012; Pelzer et al., 2014; Van der Noordt et al., 2014; Kim and von dem Knesebeck, 2016). Moreover, we know that the psychological, social and economic dimensions of well-being are strongly interconnected. Unemployment usually leads to a lack of financial resources, and financial resources serve as an important determinant of well-being (Paul and Moser, 2009). Unemployment can also decrease life satisfaction and happiness by means other than income, such as reducing social participation (Kunze and Suppa, 2017). From a practical perspective, whether we can govern the complex relationship between poverty and well-being through a policy action is an important question.

Unconditional cash transfers (UCT) are one potential group of policy instruments for organising social security. UCTs are regular cash transfers that are paid without screening for eligibility and without income-testing or means-testing. Earlier studies have indicated that the introduction of a UCT policy could improve population health. For example, Forget (2011) reports positive results from a Canadian experiment with a guaranteed annual income. Another body of evidence suggests that UCTs may improve some health outcomes in low and middle-income countries, although the relative effectiveness of UCTs and conditional cash transfer programmes (CCT) remains uncertain (for example, Costello et al., 2003; Davala et al., 2015; Pega et al., 2017).

Assuming the findings from previous studies indicate a causal link between UCTs and better health and well-being, multiple causal mechanisms could be in play depending on the health outcomes measured. For example, increases in household disposable income could be a key explanation for behavioural changes that lead to positive health outcomes, e.g. via better nutrition or increased use of health services. On the other hand, the unconditional nature of UCT payments could potentially reduce income insecurity as reflected in different subjective measures of well-being, such as life satisfaction. Interestingly, in their observational study Zuelke et al. (2018) found that the negative impact of unemployment on depression risk could not be explained solely by differences in material and social resources. The result points to a potential association between benefit type (means-tested versus non-means-tested) and elevated depression risk.

There are only a limited number of empirical studies available covering the effects of UCTs on health and well-being in developed countries. However, in a recent review of studies on instruments similar to UTCs, Gibson et al. (2020) found UCTs could potentially positively affect mental health. In this chapter, we contribute to this mostly unexplored field of research by analysing the health outcomes of a survey study conducted during the Finnish basic income experiment (2017–18), a randomised field experiment with a particular UCT policy called basic income. In the experiment, 2000 unemployed individuals were paid €560 monthly for two years without income-testing or means-testing and almost without any screening for eligibility. We study how the treatment group (receiving basic income) differs from the control group (not receiving basic income) regarding their subjective health, mental distress, and cognitive capabilities in the end of the experiment. We also reflect on the findings of previous studies on UCTs and basic income and provide a basis for further research on the health outcomes of the Finnish basic income experiment.

The structure of this chapter is as follows. First, we briefly discuss the concept of well-being and the motivation for our multidimensional approach. Second, we describe how the dimensions are operationalised in the survey questionnaire to measure well-being. Thereafter, we present the results and, in the final section, we summarise our findings and discuss their quality and relevance.

MULTIDIMENSIONALITY OF WELL-BEING

According to the World Health Organization (WHO), health is 'a state of complete physical, mental, and social well-being and not merely the absence of disease or infirmity' (WHO, 2001a). When we ask a person how they perceive their health, the answer represents their own point of view and particular life situation. Two individuals suffering from the same illness may give surprisingly different answers. For example, individuals with illnesses may evaluate their state of health as very good if they are receiving medical treatment and, as a result, are not facing any major decline in their level of performance.

Well-being is a highly multidimensional concept that can be approached from the point of view of clinical or subjective health, quality of life, or social and economic impact on living conditions, for example. For individuals, self-actualisation, social interaction, happiness, and social capital are all important elements of well-being. Accordingly, the WHO defines mental health as 'a state of well-being in which an individual realizes his or her own abilities, can cope with the normal stresses of life, can work productively, and is able to make a contribution to his or her community' (WHO, 2001b).

During the last few decades, researchers have increasingly shown interest in the subjective dimensions of well-being (for example, Veenhoven, 2004; Layard, 2006). In addition to the objective living conditions and economic resources that individuals need when pursuing their personal goals, subjective perceptions of state of health and life satisfaction are more often being considered relevant indicators of well-being. Yet another line of research concentrates on health-related, social, psychological, and other capabilities of individuals as the core determinants of personal and societal well-being (for example, Sen, 1993).

In our study on the potential effects of the Finnish basic income experiment on health and well-being, we accept the multidimensionality of the concept of well-being and incorporate measures on different dimensions. We explore the potential impact of receiving UTCs on the subjective health, life satisfaction, mental distress, social isolation, and cognitive capabilities of the treatment group. To provide a comprehensive picture of the state of health of the participants, we also investigate the use of health services and the existence of a self-reported, prolonged illness.

DATA AND METHODS

In the empirical analysis of our study, we utilise data from a telephone survey conducted during the Finnish basic income experiment. In the questionnaire, different dimensions of well-being chosen for the analysis, i.e. subjective health, life satisfaction, mental distress, social isolation, and cognitive capabilities were operationalised with standard question patterns that have been used and validated in earlier studies (for more information on the survey, see Chapter 5).

In the survey, subjective health was measured with the question, 'How would you describe your health generally?' Five response items were available: 'very good', 'good', 'fair', 'poor' and 'very poor'. In addition, state of health was measured with a question about the existence of a long-term illness, impairment, or mental health issue that complicates the daily life of the respondent. The existence and the level of impediment caused by the disease was evaluated with response categories 'yes', 'very much so', 'yes, to some extent' and 'no'. We mapped the use of health services by separately asking the number of visits respondents made to a public health care nurse or physician, hospital physician, dentist, or other health care provider.

General life satisfaction was evaluated on a scale from zero ('extremely dissatisfied') to ten ('extremely satisfied'). This particular survey question has also been used in the European Social Survey (ESS, 2018).

Mental distress was evaluated using the five-item Mental Health Index (MHI-5) (Berwick et al., 1991). The index's five distinct questions focus on respondents' subjective mental state during the past month. The dimensions of mental well-being evaluated include nervousness, inability to cheer up, calmness, melancholy, and happiness. Subjective feelings were measured on a six-item scale: 'all the time', 'most of the time', 'much of the time', 'some of the time', 'rarely' and 'not at all'.

The survey also included two distinct screening questions for depression. In the first, respondents were asked if, over the last 12 months, they had experienced a period of at least two weeks during which they were predominantly sad, downcast or depressed. In the second, respondents was asked if they had experienced a period during which they predominantly lacked interest in most of the things that usually bring them enjoyment, such as hobbies, work or other. The evaluation was based on a dichotomous scale with values 'yes' or 'no'. In previous studies, these questions were shown to reliably screen for clinical depression (Arroll et al., 2003).

Social aspects of well-being were surveyed by asking how often the respondents felt lonely ('never', 'very rarely', 'sometimes', 'quite often', 'all the time'). The last dimension of well-being analysed in the study concerned the cognitive capabilities of the respondents. They were asked to describe their recent experiences with memory, concentration, and the ability to learn new things (cp. Troyer and Rich, 2002). The evaluation was based on a five-item scale with the values 'very good', 'good', 'satisfactory', 'poor', 'very poor' (and 'cannot say').

We analysed the survey data by comparing the distributions and summary statistics of the responses of the treatment and control groups. The analysis of group differences was complemented by calculating appropriate tests of statistical significance (t-test and chi-squared test) and interpreted at 5% significance level. To make the analysis more robust, a logistic regression model was estimated for the study variable on mental distress (MHI-5 index). The regression analysis was performed with two model specifications. The first model included treatment indicator, age and gender as explanatory variables,

Subjective health, well-being and cognitive capabilities 75

while the second model also included indicators of employment status during the experiment and of respondents' health.

Employment status was inferred from the survey question 'How did you find the jobs you have had since the beginning of 2017?' If a respondent provided an answer to the question ('responded to a job advertisement', 'contacted an employer directly', 'received a referral from the employment office') they were given a positive indicator value for being employed during the experiment. The interpretation of the positive indicator value is that the respondent had at least some work since the beginning of the experiment. Health status, on the other hand, was measured with the previously described study question, 'Do you have a long-term illness, impairment, or mental health issue that complicates your daily life?'

In most cases, we report the results for different study variables as response distributions. Response categories were combined where relevant. In the telephone interview, a 'cannot say' option was offered to respondents with each survey question. A relatively small number of respondents chose this answer, varying from 0.0 percent to 7.0 percent for the questions analysed here. It is not meaningful to include the 'cannot say' answers in the outcome variable on mental distress (MHI index) and so we have omitted them from the regressions. The data were analysed with the R programming tool.

RESULTS

Health, Use of Health Services, and Life Satisfaction

In the treatment group, 58.5 percent evaluated their state of health as good or very good. In the control group, the proportion was 51.4 percent. Those who evaluated their health status as moderate constituted a relatively larger proportion in the control group (32.1 percent) than in the treatment group (27.9 percent). In the treatment group, 13.4 percent considered their health poor or very poor compared with 16.0 percent in the control group. The differences between the groups were almost statistically significant, and the biggest difference in percentage points was observed among those who reported good or very good state of health (Table 7.1, A).

Compared with the treatment group, a larger proportion of the control group reported having a disease, disability or mental disorder that caused hindrance to daily life (Table 7.1, B). In the treatment group, more than half did not report any disease, disability or mental disorder.

Table 7.1 (C) also reports visits to health care services by the treatment and control groups. The differences between the groups are not statistically significant. Both in the treatment and control group, some 40 percent visited a nurse or public health care physician three or more times during the previous

76   *Experimenting with unconditional basic income*

two years. In both groups, over three quarters had visited a hospital physician or used other health services fewer than three times in the same period. Respectively, almost three quarters had visited a dentist no more than twice.

In addition to the subjective state of health and the use of health services, a measure of life satisfaction was included in the survey. The average value of life satisfaction on a scale from zero to ten was 7.3 for the treatment group and 6.8 for the control group (t-test, $p<0.001$). Approximately 1 percent of the treatment group were extremely dissatisfied with their lives, while in the control group, the proportion was about 2 percent. In the treatment group, over 9 percent were extremely satisfied with their lives, compared with 7 percent in the control group. The difference between the group averages was statistically significant.

Mental Distress, Depressive Symptoms and Social Isolation

Table 7.2 reports the response distributions of separate questions (A.1–A.5) of the MHI-5 index that measures mental distress. Persons in the treatment group reported feeling sad and downcast less often than those in the control group (A.4). In addition, the treatment group reported a higher level of ability to cheer up than the control group (A.2). For other individual questions, we observed no statistically significant differences between the groups. In the treatment group, a greater proportion reported being happy most or all of the time than in the control group, although neither difference was statistically significant.

The MHI-5 index is formed by rescaling the sum of the five separate responses (from 5–30 to 0–100). A dichotomous measurement for clinically significant mental distress was formed using a threshold of 52 points. Respondents who receive no more than 52 points are classified as having clinical mental distress. In the study, we classified persons in the treatment and control groups according to the criteria. Based on this measure, 17 percent of the treatment group and 24 percent of the control group suffered from clinically significant mental distress (A.6).

According to the responses to the screening questions for depression, about one third of the control group reported experiencing depression during the previous year that lasted at least two weeks. In the treatment group, the proportion was approximately one fifth. In addition, more than one third of the control group reported experiencing a period of at least two weeks during which their ability to enjoy or find interest in their usual pursuits declined significantly. In the treatment group, approximately one quarter reported similar experiences. (Table 7.2, B.1–B.2)

Social isolation provides yet another measure of well-being or, more correctly, a dimension of well-being that is both affected by other dimensions

Subjective health, well-being and cognitive capabilities 77

Table 7.1   *Response distributions of survey questions on (A) self-evaluated state of health; (B) existence and level of impediment of a disease, disability or mental disorder; and (C) usage of health services during the previous two years*

	Treatment group, N=586	Control group, N=1047	χ^2-test, p-value
(A) State of health			0.051
Very good	16.3%	11.4%	
Good	42.2%	40.0%	
Moderate	27.9%	32.1%	
Poor	9.5%	12.3%	
Very poor	3.9%	3.7%	
Cannot say	0.4%	0.3%	
(B) Do you have a disease, disability or mental disorder that hinders daily life?			0.026
Yes, with significant hindrance	13.3%	14.9%	
Yes, with some hindrance	31.6%	37.5%	
No	55.1%	47.7%	
(C.1) Visits to public health care nurse			0.070
0–2 times	52.2%	51.6%	
≥3 times	40.7%	43.4%	
Cannot say	7.1%	5.1%	
(C.2) Visits to public health care physician			0.744
0–2 times	56.8%	56.6%	

	Treatment group, N=586	Control group, N=1047	χ^2-test, p-value
≥3 times	38.7%	40.4%	
Cannot say	4.5%	3.0%	
(C.3) Visits to hospital physician			0.616
0–2 times	78.2%	76.9%	
≥3 times	18.1%	21.1%	
Cannot say	3.7%	2.9%	
(C.4) Visits to dentist			0.385
0–2 times	72.8%	69.8%	
≥3 times	25.3%	29.0%	
Cannot say	1.9%	1.2%	
(C.5) Visits to other health care services			0.607
0–2 times	72.9%	73.7%	
≥3 times	22.9%	23.5%	
Cannot say	4.1%	2.9%	

of well-being (e.g. mental distress) and a contributing factor itself (the effect of loneliness on mental well-being) (for example, Beutel et al., 2017). The persons in the treatment group reported experiencing less loneliness than those in the control group. The difference was statistically significant (Table 7.2, C). However, in both groups, experiences of continuous loneliness were rare, and over half rarely or never experienced loneliness.

Memory, Learning and Ability to Concentrate

Cognitive capabilities may serve as important mediators of the impact of a UCTs on the well-being of individuals and on their ability to improve their

Subjective health, well-being and cognitive capabilities   79

Table 7.2   *Response distributions of survey questions on (A) mental distress (individual MHI-5 items and clinically significant mental distress); (B) experiences of depression and inability to enjoy or be interested in things during the previous year; and (C) experiences of loneliness*

	Treatment group, N=586	Control group, N=1047	χ^2-test, p-value
(A.1) I have been very nervous over the last 4 weeks			0.162
All the time	1.8%	2.3%	
Most of the time	3.6%	6.1%	
Much of the time	7.5%	9.0%	
Some of the time	22.2%	25.0%	
Rarely	36.8%	34.9%	
Not at all	27.5%	22.1%	
Cannot say	0.5%	0.6%	
(A.2) I felt so low that nothing could make me feel better over the last 4 weeks			0.003
All the time	1.1%	0.9%	
Most of the time	1.9%	4.5%	
Much of the time	4.2%	5.9%	
Some of the time	12.2%	14.2%	
Rarely	19.1%	22.4%	
Not at all	60.4%	48.5%	
Cannot say	1.2%	1.5%	
(A.3) I felt peaceful and calm over the last 4 weeks			0.161

	Treatment group, $N=586$	Control group, $N=1047$	χ^2-test, p-value
All the time	13.4%	10.8%	
Most of the time	42.2%	40.6%	
Much of the time	16.2%	15.0%	
Some of the time	17.2%	17.4%	
Rarely	7.6%	11.4%	
Not at all	2.6%	4.2%	
Cannot say	0.8%	0.6%	
(A.4) I felt sad and downcast over the last 4 weeks			0.003
All the time	1.5%	2.9%	
Most of the time	3.4%	5.1%	
Much of the time	6.7%	7.5%	
Some of the time	15.2%	21.0%	
Rarely	28.2%	29.8%	
Not at all	42.7%	31.4%	
Cannot say	2.3%	2.3%	
(A.5) I have been happy over the last 4 weeks			0.073
All the time	14.3%	10.1%	
Most of the time	36.9%	33.7%	
Much of the time	16.5%	16.7%	
Some of the time	16.7%	20.2%	

	Treatment group, $N=586$	Control group, $N=1047$	χ^2-test, p-value
Rarely	10.4%	12.3%	
Not at all	3.6%	5.8%	
Cannot say	1.6%	1.2%	
(A.6) Clinical mental distress (based on MHI-5)	16.5%	24.0%	0.001
(B.1) I have experienced depression			<0.001
Yes	22.3%	32.4%	
No	76.3%	65.0%	
Cannot say	1.5%	2.5%	
(B.2) I have experienced an inability to enjoy			<0.001
Yes	24.4%	35.9%	
No	72.3%	62.4%	
Cannot say	3.3%	1.8%	
(C) I experience loneliness			0.032
Never or rarely	58.7%	51.3%	
Sometimes or pretty often	38.6%	44.2%	
All the time	2.3%	4.4%	
Cannot say	0.5%	0.1%	

personal living conditions. For example, Mullainathan and Shafir (2013) discuss the process of cognitive 'bandwidth scarcity', where lack of resources impedes sound decision-making and potentially results in negative health

82   *Experimenting with unconditional basic income*

outcomes. Earlier empirical case studies (Forget, 2011; Pega et al., 2017; Zuelke et al., 2018; Gibson et al., 2020) motivated us to ask if cognitive bandwidth scarcity could be tackled, at least in part, with a UCT policy. CCTs and especially means-tested benefit schemes may cause confusion through poorly understood and complex eligibility and payment rules and welfare sanctions that potentially create new difficulties in the daily lives of benefit recipients. UCTs on the other hand, should provide foreseeable income security via regular, non-means-tested and non-tapered monthly payments.

We found statistically significant differences between the treatment and control groups for all three self-evaluative survey questions concerning cognitive capabilities (Table 7.3). The treatment group evaluated memory functioning, learning new things, and ability to concentrate more positively than the control group. In both groups, less than 10 percent reported having poor or very poor capabilities. The results on cognitive capabilities are in line with the treatment group's consistent outperformance of the control group on different dimensions of well-being.

Sensitivity of the Results: Unemployment and Mental Distress

A growing body of literature indicates that unemployment poses a substantial health risk to individuals by negatively affecting their mental health, psychological well-being, and cognitive capabilities (for more, see Acevedo et al., 2020; Wanberg, 2012; Kim and von dem Knesebeck, 2016). Wahrendorf et al. (2019) conclude that adverse employment histories are associated with poor subsequent health functioning. A systematic review by Van der Noordt et al. (2014) demonstrates that employment is beneficial for health, particularly in terms of depression and general mental health. Moreover, Pelzer et al.'s (2014) findings suggest that depressive syndromes result from, rather than cause, unemployment. In general, unemployment is linked to decreased subjective well-being (Brown et al., 2003).

We were motivated to control for employment status by the evidence of association and potential causal relationship between employment status and mental well-being shown in the above-mentioned studies. A register study showed only a slight employment effect in the Finnish experiment (Hämäläinen et al., 2020). However, the high non-response rate of the survey study raises doubts about the balance of the study groups regarding relevant covariates of mental health. To analyse the sensitivity of the presented results for potential over-representation of employed and healthier participants, we regress clinically significant mental distress over the treatment indicator and take employment and the existence of a long-term health impediment as additional controls. We assume that the existence of a long-term health impediment

Subjective health, well-being and cognitive capabilities   83

Table 7.3   *Response distributions of survey questions on memory functioning, ability to learn new things, and ability to concentrate*

	Treatment group, N=586	Control group, N=1047	χ^2-test, p-value
Memory			0.001
Very good	22.0%	16.1%	
Good	48.8%	46.1%	
Satisfactory	21.9%	28.3%	
Poor	5.8%	7.7%	
Very poor	0.9%	1.8%	
Cannot say	0.6%	0.0%	
Learning			<0.001
Very good	23.8%	16.7%	
Good	49.8%	46.2%	
Satisfactory	20.7%	27.1%	
Poor	4.2%	7.7%	
Very poor	0.5%	1.8%	
Cannot say	0.9%	0.4%	
Ability to concentrate			<0.001
Very good	16.1%	10.3%	
Good	51.9%	47.4%	
Satisfactory	24.3%	29.6%	

	Treatment group, N=586	Control group, N=1047	χ^2-test, p-value
Poor	6.4%	9.4%	
Very poor	1.1%	3.2%	
Cannot say	0.1%	0.2%	

Table 7.4   *Regression results on clinically significant mental distress*

	Coefficient (basic income)	p-value	Odds ratio
Clinically significant mental distress			
model 1	−0.47	0.0014	0.63
model 2	−0.34	0.0297	0.71

Note: In model 1, explanatory variables include the treatment indicator (receiving basic income), age and gender. In model 2, the existence of a long-term disease and employment status are also controlled.

is not affected by participation in the experiment. However, we consider the effect of the health status on subjective well-being plausible.

We tested the stability of the observed difference in mental distress between the treatment and control groups using two logistic regression models. The explanatory variables in the first model included the treatment indicator, age at the beginning of the experiment (age groups 25–34, 35–44 and 45–59 years). The second model also included the state of health (existence of a long-term disease) and employment (being employed during the experiment). In both models, a statistically significant coefficient was estimated for the treatment indicator (receiving basic income) (Table 7.4).

DISCUSSION AND CONCLUSIONS

In this article, we analysed the self-reported evaluations of participants in the Finnish basic income experiment regarding their state of health, use of health care services, mental distress, and cognitive capabilities. The treatment group receiving basic income reported higher life satisfaction, better health, less mental distress and depression, and stronger cognitive capabilities regarding memory, ability to learn new things, and ability to concentrate than the control group not receiving a basic income. Health and employment status were relevant explanatory factors for the difference in mental distress observed in the data. However, the difference between the treatment and control group remained statistically significant even when employment status and health were controlled.

It seems possible that receiving basic income partially reduced the treatment group's economic difficulties and feelings of insecurity caused by unemployment. As a result, this may have increased the mental well-being of the treatment group relative to the control group. An improvement in the perceptions of economic security may have empowered the treatment group in coping with the challenges of daily lives and provided a better sense of direction in life. On the other hand, the analysis showed that employment was a relevant explanatory factor for the differences in mental distress between the groups. It is important to note that, in the experiment, basic income payments also worked as earnings supplements. Relatively greater mental well-being in the treatment group may have resulted from the additional economic resources the experiment provided for those who found a job during the two-year follow-up period.

The results regarding health outcomes are in line with previous studies indicating a positive association between UCT reforms and better mental well-being, although most existing evidence comes from developing countries (for example, Ruckert et al., 2018). In addition to complementing the body of evidence on mental distress, our study provides new and interesting evidence on the association between receiving basic income and improved cognitive capabilities in the context of developed countries. Individuals' cognitive capabilities play a vital role in present-day information societies. Scarcity of cognitive resources impedes sound decision-making, and this hindrance may have a negative effect on health outcomes (Mullainathan and Shafir, 2013). Policy actions that could potentially reduce bandwidth scarcity are worth further analysis and experimentation.

From the Canadian MININCOME field experiment, Forget (2011) reports a reduction of 8.5 percent in the hospitalisation rate of treatment group relative to control group for accidents and injuries and mental health. Their study also found that treatment group's contacts with physicians declined, especially for mental health. In their systematic review of UCT studies in low and middle-income countries Pega et al. (2017) found that UCTs did not increase the use of health services but did potentially improve some health outcomes. However, the evidence on the relative effectiveness of UCTs and CCTs remains very uncertain (Pega et al., 2017).

In our analysis, the use of health services does not differ between the treatment and control groups, but the analysis of subjective health outcomes indicates a potentially positive effect of basic income. In order to find stronger evidence on the potential effects of the Finnish experiment on health behaviour and health outcomes, a register study covering all the subjects of the experiment should be conducted.

It is worth noting that, based on survey data, both the treatment and the control groups used health care services quite rarely. Similarly, a register study by Lappalainen et al. (2018) found that long-term unemployed individuals use health care services infrequently. The result is societally relevant considering that some half of the individuals in the target group had a prolonged disease causing hindrance in their daily lives.

This study has several limitations that need to be taken into account when interpreting the results. First, the definition of well-being we use concentrates mostly on psychological aspects, ignoring social and economic dimensions. We did, however, control for employment status in our analysis of mental distress. The results of the modelling exercise verified the relevance of employment in explaining mental well-being. On the other hand, even when employment was controlled, a positive association between participation in a UCT experiment and mental well-being was observed.

Second, the data used in the analysis included answers from only 31 percent of participants that were contacted. In the sample of the control group, the response rate was roughly 20 percent. Low and unbalanced response rates raise possibilities of selection bias in the comparisons. We have tried to correct for the possible unrepresentativeness of the samples by weighing the data. However, the results should still be evaluated with caution, and we should avoid any causal conclusions. It is possible that our results indicating higher levels of psychological well-being in the treatment group can be explained by differences between the groups that could not be controlled in the analysis. Here again, a further register study on the Finnish experiment is essential for filling in the knowledge gaps.

In sum, the participants in the basic income experiment receiving a UCT seemed to feel mentally better than those who remained in the existing tax-benefit framework. The treatment group reported less mental distress, depression, downcast, or loneliness than the control group. In addition, the treatment group experienced higher level cognitive capabilities than the control group. The differences were consistently observed when comparing the response distributions of the groups on several different survey measures. The evidence suggests that a UCT policy could help improve beneficiaries' mental well-being, possibly by providing a greater control over their lives in and out of work. Looking ahead, further research on the health outcomes of the Finnish experiment, utilising both administrative registers and survey data, will deepen our understanding of the potential of a UCT programme for improving health outcomes. It will also, we hope, shed light on the complex mechanisms that connect UCTs to the health and well-being of the beneficiaries in a developed welfare state.

REFERENCES

Acevedo, P., Mora-Urda, A. I. and Montero, P. (2020), 'Social inequalities in health: duration of unemployment unevenly effects on the health of men and women', *European Journal of Public Health*, 30(2), 305–10.

Arroll, B., Khin, N. and Kerse, N. (2003), 'Screening for depression in primary care with two verbally asked questions: cross sectional study', *BMJ*, 327(7424), 1144–6.

Berwick, D. M., Murphy, J. M., Goldman, P. A., Ware, J. E., Barsky, A. J. and Weinstein, M. C. (1991), 'Performance of a five-item mental health screening test', *Medical Care*, 29(2), 169–76.

Beutel, M. E., Klein, E. M., Brähler, E., Reiner, I., Jünger, K., Michal, M., Wiltink, J., Wild, P. S., Münzel, T., Lackner, K. and Tibubos, A. N. (2017), 'Loneliness in the general population: prevalence, determinants and relations to mental health', *BMC Psychiatry*, 17(1), 1–7.

Brown, D. W., Balluz, L. S., Ford, E. S., Giles, W. H., Strine, T. W., Moriarty, D. G., Croft, J. B. and Mokdad, A. H. (2003), 'Associations between short- and long-term unemployment and frequent mental distress among a national sample of men and women', *Journal of Occupational and Environmental Medicine*, 45(11), 1159–66.

Costello, E. J., Compton, S. N., Keeler, G. and Angold, A. (2003), 'Relationships between poverty and psychopathology: a natural experiment', *JAMA*, 290(15), 2023–9.

Davala, S., Jhabvala, R., Standing, G. and Mehta, S. K. (2015), *Basic Income: A Transformative Policy for India*, London: Bloomsbury.

European Social Survey ESS (2018), 'ESS9 Source Questionnaires', available at https://www.europeansocialsurvey.org/docs/round9/fieldwork/source/ESS9_source _questionnaires.pdf (accessed 12 November 2020).

Forget, E. L. (2011), 'The town with no poverty: the health effects of a Canadian guaranteed annual income field experiment', *Canadian Public Policy*, 37(3), 283–305.

Gibson, M., Hearty, W. and Craig, P. (2020), 'The public health effects of interventions similar to basic income: a scoping review', *Lancet Public Health*, 5(3), 165–76.

Hämäläinen, K., Kanninen, O., Simanainen, M. and Verho, J. (2020), *Perustulokokeilun arvioinnin loppuraportti: Rekisterianalyysi työmarkkinavaikutuksista* [*The Final Report on the Evaluation of the Basic Income Experiment: Register Analysis on Labour Market Effects*], Helsinki: VATT Institute for Economic Research, VATT Muistiot 59, available at http://urn.fi/URN:ISBN:978-952-274-259-9 (accessed 18 December 2020).

Kim, T. J. and von dem Knesebeck, O. (2016), 'Perceived job insecurity, unemployment and depressive symptoms: a systematic review and meta-analysis of prospective observational studies', *International Archives of Occupational and Environmental Health*, 89(4), 561–73.

Kunze, L. and Suppa, N. (2017), 'Bowling alone or bowling at all? The effect of unemployment on social participation', *Journal of Economic Behavior & Organization*, 133, 213–35.

Lappalainen, K., Mattila-Holappa, P., Yli-Kaitala, K., Hult, M. and Räsänen K. (2018), 'Pisimpään työttömänä olleet käyttävät vähiten terveyspalveluja' ['Those who have been unemployed for the longest use health services the least'], *Suomen lääkärilehti* [*Finnish Medical Journal*], 42, 2421–6.

Layard, R. (2006), *Happiness: Lessons from a New Science*, London: Penguin Books.

Mullainathan, S. and Shafir, E. (2013), *Scarcity: Why Having Too Little Means so Much*, New York: Times Books.

Paul, K. and Moser, K. (2009), 'Unemployment impairs mental health: meta-analyses', *Journal of Vocational Behavior*, 74(3), 264–82.

Pega, F., Liu, S. Y., Walter, S., Pabayo, R., Saith, R. and Lhachimi, S. K. (2017), 'Unconditional cash transfers for reducing poverty and vulnerabilities: effect on use of health services and health outcomes in low- and middle-income countries', *Cochrane Database of Systematic Reviews*, 11.

Pelzer, B., Schaffrath, S. and Vernaleken, I. (2014), 'Coping with unemployment: the impact of unemployment on mental health, personality, and social interaction skills', *Work*, 48(2), 289.

Ruckert, A., Huynh, C. and Labonté, R. (2018), 'Reducing health inequities: is universal basic income the way forward?' *Journal of Public Health*, 40(1), 3–7.

Sen, A. (1993), 'Capability and well-being', in Sen, A. and Nussbaum, M. C. (eds.), *The Quality of Life*, Oxford: Clarendon Press, pp. 30–52.

Troyer, A. K. and Rich, J. B. (2002), 'Psychometric properties of a new metamemory questionnaire for older adults', *Journals of Gerontology, Series B, Psychological Sciences & Social Sciences*, 57(1), 19–27.

Van der Noordt, M., IJzelenberg, H., Droomers, M. and Proper, K. I. (2014), 'Health effects of employment: a systematic review of prospective studies', *Occupational and Environmental Medicine*, 71(10), 730–6.

Veenhoven, R. (2004), 'Subjective measures of well-being', in McGillivray, M. (ed.), *Human Well-being*, London: Palgrave Macmillan, pp. 214–39.

Wahrendorf, M., Hoven, H., Goldberg, M., Zins, M. and Siegrist, J. (2019), 'Adverse employment histories and health functioning: the CONSTANCES study', *International Journal of Epidemiology*, 48(2), 403.

Wanberg, C. R. (2012), 'The individual experience of unemployment', *Annual Review of Psychology*, 63, 369–96.

WHO (2001a), *Basic Document*, 43rd Edition, Geneva: World Health Organization.

WHO (2001b), Strengthening mental health promotion, *Fact Sheet, 220*, Geneva: World Health Organization.

Zuelke, A. E., Luck, T., Schroeter, M. L., Witte, A. V., Hinz, A., Engel, C., Enzenbach, C., Zacharie, S., Loeffler, M., Thiery, J., Villringer, A. and Rieder-Heller, S. G. (2018), 'The association between unemployment and depression – results from the population-based LIFE adult-study', *Journal of Affective Disorders*, 235, 399–406.

8. Financial well-being in basic income experiment

Maarit Lassander and Signe Jauhiainen

INTRODUCTION

The potential impact of income distribution on different aspects of well-being is a timely issue to consider when discussing the future of social policies in many European countries (Senik, 2009; Jakab, 2012; Blomgren et al., 2017) and current hardships facing these societies (Ståhl and MacEachen, 2020). Our aim in this chapter is to discuss how basic income is related to financial well-being. Basic income is often assumed to increase people's sense of security, intrinsic motivation, and empowerment when their monthly income is guaranteed, which in turn can affect various well-being outcomes (Forget, 2011).

Understanding the mechanisms and different aspects of financial well-being has also become increasingly important in societies where socially provided financial safety nets are lacking and where personal financial planning is needed, even in traditional welfare states (Smith, 2015). The burden of mental and physical ill-health lies on a significant percentage of population and the social costs of health inequities are rising (Jakab, 2012; Marmot et al., 2012). Income is considered the most important social determinant of health, and income inequality is associated with lower well-being, but the specific models of income distribution have been difficult to assess (Ngamaba et al., 2018). Financial problems at the individual level are reflected in communities in terms of safety and collective well-being (Layard et al., 2008). Basic income has been proposed to foster more cooperative, less competitive, interconnections within societies. These societies would be based on trusting and cooperative relationships, offering an antidote to increasing inequalities (Mays, 2019).

Better personal financial management can reduce credit risk and increase financial stability and employment productivity (Diener, 2000). Financial well-being has also been linked to individual experience of well-being (Van Praag et al., 2003; Kahn and Pearlin, 2006), whereas long-term indebtedness has been linked to depressive symptoms (Hojman et al., 2016) and the likelihood of early retirement (Blomgren et al., 2017). Stress caused by financial instability affects not only individuals but also families and communities, for example through decreasing labour productivity and increasing physical health problems (Kim and Garman, 2003).

A well-established theoretical framework for understanding financial well-being springs from Maslow's (1943) hierarchy of needs, which separates short-term acute needs (food and housing) from longer-term security enhancing needs (saving for retirement, investing in the family's future) (Xiao and Noring, 1994). This separation of needs is still useful, as it facilitates understanding of how financial difficulties can detract from considering long-term, more advanced goals. On the other hand, Maslow's hierarchy has been challenged in situations where individual values and priorities affect the order of hierarchical needs (Kenrick et al., 2010). In addition, not all approaches to financial well-being are needs-based. For example, standard of living surveys (Johansson, 1973) emphasise resources that add to material well-being. Measurement of well-being has involved two influential traditions (Diener and Biswas-Diener, 2002) that have focused on either: (1) objective well-being, i.e. resources enabling individuals to pursue their personal goals, e.g. access to housing, clean water, education, or reasonable income (Sen, 1993), and (2) the subjective experience of fulfilling one's needs (Erikson, 1993). A third perspective has been advocated by Sen (1993), who emphasised the role of basic capabilities and functioning, varying from good health to self-respect and social integration, as the basis of well-being.

Another theory that has been supported and replicated across numerous studies proposes that raising the income of all does not increase the happiness of all (Easterlin, 1995), and that men on low income seem to benefit most from an income increase (Zyphur et al., 2015). A third approach to financial well-being involves engaging with eight dimensions of wellness identified by Swarbrick and Yudof (2015), one of which is financial well-being specifically. The model used in that approach is based on the concept of physical and psychological wellness of individuals.

As discussed earlier, in Chapters 3 and 5, the Finnish basic income experiment was a randomised controlled trial (RCT) that has the potential to offer some indications of connections between intervention and measured variables, even if further research is needed to draw conclusions. To the best of our knowledge, the Finnish basic income experiment was the first national experiment with obligatory participation, which enables exploring the relationship between basic income and subjective financial well-being (SFWB). This study offers promising findings and motivates further research endeavours.

In this chapter, we discuss the following questions in relation to the Finnish basic income experiment:

1 How are unemployment and SFWB related?
2 How did the receivers of basic income and the control group differ in their experience of SFWB?

In this chapter, we review previous literature on SFWB to provide an overview and we discuss how SFWB and basic income are related. Our empirical analysis focuses on Research Question 2. We analyse the difference in the experienced financial situation and subjective financial well-being between treatment and control groups. These indicators were measured in a survey conducted in autumn 2018. The survey data are described in more detail in Chapter 5. Owing to the low response rate and possible non-response bias, the data were re-weighed. The treatment and control groups in this chapter refer to those individuals in these groups who responded to the survey. In this chapter, we also utilise data derived from the administrative register of the Social Insurance Institution of Finland (Kela). This register contains information on receiving social assistance, which is an indicator of both low income and of having no savings. An individual is defined as a social assistance recipient if he or she is a member of a household that has received social assistance at least once during 2018.

Our results indicate that basic income may be related to subjective financial well-being and a person's experienced financial situation. However, we also acknowledge the potential psychological effect of being included in an experiment that attracted positive media attention (further discussed in Chapter 5). Nevertheless, our findings are in line with the results from the Canadian basic income experiment (e.g. Forget, 2011, 2013).

The structure of this chapter is as follows. We begin by defining the concept of SFWB, proceed to review previous relevant research, and discuss the financial well-being of the unemployed. We then analyse the experienced financial situation in treatment and control groups. We show the results of the SFWB indicators in treatment and control groups and validate the results in a regression analysis. Finally, we conclude and discuss our findings.

DEFINING FINANCIAL WELL-BEING

The measurement of subjective financial well-being (SFWB) reflects the development of subjective versus objective measures in the well-being literature. In recent decades, psychologists, economists, and social scientists have all become increasingly interested in subjective dimensions of well-being (SWB) (e.g. Veenhoven, 2002; Keyes, 2006; Layard et al., 2008). As the relationality of perceived well-being seems to be better captured with subjective measures, these measures have been gaining ground (Veenhoven, 2002; Keyes, 2006; Cooke et al., 2016), while it is still understood that certain basic levels of objective well-being (e.g. food and shelter) are necessary for SWB (Maslow, 1943; Sen, 1993; Diener and Biswas-Diener, 2002). Health status has been found to be strongly related to subjective well-being when examined using multidimensional measures in developed countries (WHO, 2008).

Some definitions of financial well-being utilise both objective and subjective indicators, and some focus on either objective or subjective well-being (Brüggen et al., 2017). Objective indicators provide information about the situation and subjective indicators measure an individual's evaluation of a situation. Self-reported evaluation is crucial when considering outcomes. Arber et al. (2014) demonstrated in a longitudinal study that SFWB mediates income-related health outcomes. Chou et al. (2016) proposed that SFWB is linked to physical pain mediated through a sense of control. Subjective measures enable individuals to evaluate the experience of their own financial situation through both cognitive and affective reactions (Diener, 1984). Subjective measures are also better equipped to examine non-financial effects (e.g. societal attitudes toward wealth). Individuals facing a similar financial situation can experience it in very different ways, depending on expectations, environment, social status, and opportunities. The need for financial security in any particular life stage and the ability to live with uncertainty are also noteworthy factors in relation to experienced well-being (Kim and Garman, 2003; Malone et al., 2010), and basic income may strengthen resilience in the face of adverse life events (Haagh, 2019).

There are a few definitions of financial well-being that have been proposed over the past decade. Brüggen et al. (2017) define financial well-being as the *perception of being able to sustain current and anticipated desired living standards and financial freedom.* A similar definition has been introduced by Netemeyer et al. (2018), dividing financial well-being in (1) a manageable level of stress over current finances, and (2) a sense of security about achieving future financial goals. Zyphur et al. (2015) conclude that financial well-being includes subjective financial stress, financial manageability, and future prospects. Chou et al. (2016) refer to financial well-being as involving experienced economic security in the present and in the foreseeable future. Based on these definitions, a consensus seems to exist that financial well-being can be defined by the subjective evaluation of (1) present financial situation (stress and manageability), and (2) future expectations. These notions appear to be linked to the discussion that has arisen around subjective well-being and the capabilities approach, focusing on the basic capabilities needed for living a reasonable life (Sen, 1993).

SFWB is influenced by demographic factors (age, gender, family structure and level of education) (Joo and Grable, 2004; Malone et al., 2010). Other factors to be noted are financial awareness and capability (Shim et al., 2009; Vosloo et al., 2014), financial attitudes (Norvilitis et al., 2003), personal traits and values (Gutter and Copur, 2011), and financial behaviour (Joo and Grable, 2004; Shim et al., 2009). Societal factors that can have an impact include the labour market situation, inflation, and interest rates (O'Neill et al., 2005). Personal and professional peer groups can also affect how individuals perceive their situation compared with others (Ferrer-i-Carbonell, 2005; Dolan et al., 2008). If the experience of financial well-being cannot be reduced to objective indicators (income level) or behavioural modes (financial management), we are then faced with the question of what should be measured.

SFWB among the Unemployed

The Finnish basic income experiment participants were long-term unemployed. Unemployment affects not only access to income but also mental health (Paul and Moser, 2009). Unemployment decreases life satisfaction and happiness (e.g., Winkelmann and Winkelmann, 1998; Lucas et al., 2004; Layard et al., 2008; Winkelmann, 2009) and several dimensions of well-being (e.g., Goul Andersen, 2002; Paul and Moser, 2009; Kunze and Suppa, 2017). It seems that the longer unemployment lasts, the more it affects well-being in terms of life satisfaction and psychological distress, and the effects may be permanent even if the individual in question is eventually employed (Goul Andersen, 2002; Knabe et al., 2010). Long-term unemployment also leads to a reduced likelihood of employment over time and adds to the disadvantages of vulnerable social groups. The risk of long-term unemployment is higher for low-skilled persons and occupations, single parents, migrants, and disabled persons. It has also been shown that women, older people, and permanently employed persons are more affected by long-term unemployment (Heidenreich, 2015).

SWB is highly sensitive to the effects of unemployment, leading to significant reduction (Brown et al., 2003), but there is no comparable evidence on SFWB. However, it is known that unemployment can severely decrease self-efficacy and effective decision-making as well as increase vulnerability to stress. In addition, the effect of income on well-being is greater at lower levels of income (Van Praag et al., 2003; Layard et al., 2008). Therefore, it is of paramount importance to find solutions that can enhance the SFWB of the unemployed, not only to promote better mental and physical health but also to increase the likelihood of meaningful employment in the future.

RESULTS

Experienced Financial Situation

In our survey, basic income recipients and members of the control group were asked how they experienced their household's income nowadays. The given

94 *Experimenting with unconditional basic income*

alternatives were: (1) living comfortably, (2) coping, (3) finding it difficult, and (4) finding it very difficult on present income. The question was phrased similarly to that in the European Social Survey (ESS) to enable comparison with a representative sample. The outcomes and comparative data are presented in Table 8.1.

The basic income recipients experienced their financial situation as better than those in the control group when the whole sample was analysed. Of the basic income recipients, 13 percent felt that they were living comfortably and 47 percent felt that they were coping. Of the control group, 8 percent felt that they were living comfortably and 44 percent felt that they were coping. A total of 40 percent of the basic income recipients had some level of difficulty getting by compared with 48 percent among the control group members.

In the linked data, we were able to analyse two sub-groups according to their receipt of social assistance. It was necessary to examine these two groups separately since the proportion of social assistance recipients was smaller in the treatment group (29 percent) than in the control group (43 percent). Social assistance recipients encounter financial difficulties more often than those who do not receive social assistance. A significant difference between the basic income recipients and those in the control group was observed in the sub-group not receiving social assistance. The difference between the treatment and control groups was very small when social assistance recipients were compared. In fact, the basic income recipients seemed to evaluate their financial situation as very difficult slightly more often than those in the control group. The proportion of those who stated that, on their income, life was difficult or very difficult was nearly the same.

Comparative data from the Finnish sample of the ESS are presented in Table 8.1. In the ESS data, financial difficulties were reported as less frequent than in our survey data. The financial situation of the basic income recipients and those in the control group resembled the situation of the unemployed looking for jobs.

Measuring SFWB in the Basic Income Experiment

In line with the definitions of SFWB discussed, we examined the subjective experience of financial stress, the current financial management, evaluation of the capability to make rational financial decisions (financial freedom), and preparedness in terms of financial emergency funds (securing future). These measures are loosely based on the Swarbrick and Yudof (2015) dimension of financial wellness. Little is known concerning the effects of basic income on SWB in relation to public health, even if such effects might be considered potentially more consistent than labour market effects (Gibson et al., 2020).

Financial well-being in basic income experiment 95

Table 8.1   Proportions of self-reported feeling about household's income nowadays

	Social assistance	Living comfortably (%)	Coping (%)	Finding it difficult (%)	Finding it very difficult (%)
Treatment group		13	47	28	12
Control group		8	44	32	15
n = 1614					
Treatment group	Yes	6	34	34	26
Control group	Yes	5	33	41	21
Treatment group	No	16	53	25	7
Control group	No	11	52	27	10
n = 1524					
ESS 2018					
All		29	59	9	3
Paid work		34	58	7	1
Unemployed, looking for job		17	45	25	14
Unemployed, not looking for job		12	34	23	32

There is some evidence of the effects of basic income on subjective well-being. The data analysed 30 years after collection showed that basic income had significant effects on the use of mental health services and accident-related health visits, which decreased by 10 percent (Forget, 2011, 2013). In an unconditional cash transfer experiment in Malawi, schoolgirls were 38 percent less likely to experience psychological distress than those in the control group (Baird et al., 2011). Studies from sub-Saharan Africa also point to some moderately positive health and quality of life outcomes (Owusu-Addo et al., 2018), with an ongoing experiment in Kenya currently being reviewed to assess the effects of basic income on depression. These findings have yet to be replicated, and there are no similar studies available on the effects of basic income on SFWB.

This is in an unchartered territory of research, which is likely to become of increasing interest.

The findings concerning SFWB obtained from the Finnish basic income experiment are presented in Table 8.2. Most respondents were at least occasionally stressed over finances. This was unsurprising, considering that the participants were mainly receiving a low income.

Table 8.2   Response proportions of subjective financial well-being (SFWB) in the treatment and control groups

	Group	Never (%)	Rarely (%)	Sometimes (%)	Always (%)	χ^2-test, p-value
I have financial worries.	Treatment	14	13	47	26	0.011
	Control	11	13	41	34	
My financial situation is under control and I can pay my bills on time.	Treatment	1	6	20	72	0.000
	Control	4	12	25	59	
I can make reasonable financial decisions.	Treatment	20	24	35	21	0.059
	Control	23	29	30	18	
I have an emergency fund.	Treatment	41	13	18	27	0.006
	Control	47	16	17	20	

When comparing the basic income recipients and the control group, we noticed that in terms of financial stress, the basic income recipients seemed to be significantly less stressed by financial matters, but the differences were small (after combining the sometimes/always response categories for the basic income group (73 percent) and the control group (75 percent)). Among the basic income recipients, 26 percent reported being always worried about financial matters, whereas, among the control group, the figure was 34 percent. Many respondents in both groups (47 percent of the basic income recipients and 41 percent of the control group) were sometimes worried about financial matters. A total of 14 percent of the basic income recipients were never worried about financial matters compared with 11 percent of the control group.

Financial distress/stress has been contrasted with SFWB in some studies, but it is worth noting that it is a far more specific concept. Financial stress refers to the current situation where an individual finds it difficult to meet external financial expectations (Kim and Garman, 2003). The subjective experience of financial stress is strongly associated with many health problems (Arber et al., 2014), and financial difficulties cause more stress than many other everyday

Financial well-being in basic income experiment 97

problems (Kahn and Pearlin, 2006). The outcomes of stress include problems in executive functioning and attention disorders, which can negatively affect financial decision-making and planning (O'Neill et al., 2005). Long-term stress can also increase reactivity to other stressors in life, magnifying the effects of, for example, divorce or relationship problems and lead to further negative financial outcomes (Kim and Garman, 2003). Long-term stress also affects the formation of memories, and – especially in older age groups – memory difficulties are common when the lifetime stress burden is high (Kahn and Pearlin, 2006).

Financial behaviour is regarded as comprising a group of behaviours that have a direct effect on a person's financial situation, and which can be evaluated using either objective or subjective measures. Examples of the relevant kinds of behaviours are paying bills, saving, investing, budget management, spending, and debt management. Financial management can be measured in terms of whether a respondent feels he or she has the possibility of engaging in positive financial behaviour (e.g. paying bills by the due date). After comparing the basic income recipients to the control group recipients, we noticed that the basic income recipients seemed more capable of paying their bills on time and more in control of their finances, but again the differences were small when the sometimes/always categories were combined (the basic income group 92 percent and 84 percent for control group. A majority (72 percent) of the basic income recipients felt that they were always in control of their finances compared with 59 percent of the control group, whereas 7 percent of the basic income recipients and 16 percent of the control group felt they lacked control of their finances.

Financial management is associated with financial capability and financial behaviour. Financial capability (Vosloo et al., 2014) refers to an individual's ability to manage daily finances and enhance financial security. SFWB may increase the experience of capability and vice versa. Certain financial behaviours (e.g. paying bills, saving, investing, and budget management) can be either positive and stabilising, or negative and risk inducing. Interventions that target financial well-being often aim to make a positive change in some form of financial behaviour. Behaviour is also tied to a context, and the same behaviour in different contexts has different meanings. Researchers have debated the importance of financial literacy and basic financial skills, and how these skills are transmitted through parental and formal education. It is no doubt important that certain basic skills are developed, even if it is unclear how much they affect financial behaviour (Willis, 2011).

Financial management concerns the experience of control and the potential to engage in positive financial behaviour (paying bills on time). When comparing the treatment group to the control group, we found that the basic income recipients were more often able to pay their bills on time and more frequently believed that their financial situation was under control.

Financial freedom refers to individual possibilities to make reasonably independent financial decisions that are not coerced or that cause an unreasonable amount of stress (Brüggen et al., 2017). We asked respondents about their ability to make financially rational decisions, and the responses showed the least differences between the study groups, with 21 percent of the basic income recipients indicating that felt they had that ability compared with 18 percent of the control group.

In line with other measures of SFWB, a greater number of the basic income recipients (27 percent) felt that they had a financial backup (i.e. a financial emergency fund) than those in the control group (21 percent). It is also worth noting that over 40 percent in both groups felt that they never had any financial backup.

These findings accord with reported Finnish trends concerning savings, which show a considerable decrease in the last ten years (for details, please see the statistics from the Bank of Finland, 2008–18). Financial backup requires the opportunity to save, so that acute and unexpected costs can be covered. The size of any backup was not determined as the question aimed to measure preparedness for the future in general.

Measures of SFWB in Regression Analysis

The basic income recipients' income might have been higher than that of the control group although the data are re-weighted. Therefore, previously observed differences in SFWB might have been due to such income differences. In addition, SFWB is related to the financial situation of the whole household and includes the income and expenses of all household members. The relationship of basic income and SFWB was analysed in a regression analysis in which possible differences in income were controlled for. The categorical alternatives of SFWB were recoded into a dummy variable. The alternative 'always' was coded as 1 and the other alternatives as 0. The survey data and register data were linked, and thus, we were able to utilise the receipt of social assistance in 2018 as an additional control variable. The receipt of social assistance was indicative of low household income and no savings. The coefficients for the receipt of basic income and its statistical significance in relation to SFWB are reported in Table 8.3.

The results are consistent with previous descriptive findings. The receipt of basic income was negatively related to having financial worries and positively related to financial management, financial freedom, and having an emergency fund. The coefficients in relation to having financial concerns, engaging in

Financial well-being in basic income experiment 99

financial management, and having an emergency fund were also statistically significant when the receipt of social assistance was controlled for.

Table 8.3   Regression analysis results on subjective financial well-being (SFWB)

	Coefficient	p-value	
	Basic income		
I have financial worries.	−0.066	0.014	*
My financial situation is under control and I can pay my bills on time.	0.108	0.000	***
I can make reasonable financial decisions.	0.032	0.174	
I have an emergency fund.	0.063	0.009	**

Note: Explanatory variables: treatment indicator (receiving basic income) and social assistance. Statistical significance: *p-value < 0.05, **p-value < 0.01, ***p-value < 0.001

CONCLUSIONS

This chapter adds to the ongoing discussion on basic income (e.g. Van Parijs and Vanderborght, 2017) in proposing that examining the labour implications and cost-effectiveness of basic income from a productivity standpoint paints an incomplete picture. Other elements involved in income distribution that have significant influencing potential need to be considered to improve the well-being of those involved and their capacity to take part in and function in society as valued members. In other words, a combined perspective is needed that links SFWB and objective financial well-being, psychology, and economics, to widen the perspective on what is required for an effective, health-promoting life. The results presented provide a multidisciplinary account of how basic income can affect SFWB that is likely to be of value when used in making policy recommendations.

The basic income experiment and survey study aimed to examine whether a basic income had a specifically determinable effect on recipients' SFWB. We found that in all aspects of SFWB, the basic income recipients reported a higher SFWB and a better financial situation than those in the control group, but that in terms of stress and financial management, the differences were more subtle. When the receipt of social assistance was controlled for, the basic income recipients reported being less often worried, having better financial management, and being more often in possession of financial backup. The amount received in relation to basic income and the unemployment benefit was the same; however, the basic income recipients may have had a slightly higher income. The register data showed that the basic income recipients were employed on average just a few days more than those in the control group (Hämäläinen et al., 2020) and that the survey respondents in the treatment group received less social assistance (previously in this chapter). It is important to note that the benefit level did not change for the basic income experiment participants; they did not receive less than they had previously. Ensuring equality in terms of the amount received allowed for an evaluation of the effects of income structure. It has long been established within socio-economic research that people are attached to the status quo, and that loss of income tends to render people more unhappy than loss of potential gain (Van Praag et al., 2003; Layard et al., 2006).

In all public policy interventions where a sample of a population is subjected to an intervention of some kind, an issue arises concerning expectations and adaptation, which is also highly relevant to basic income experiments. Adaptation to increasing income will happen gradually; therefore, expectations are also more likely to rise with a rise in income, leading to a 'hedonic treadmill' (Van Praag et al., 2003; Layard et al., 2006). When life changes and the change leads to adaptation, this new state of things becomes the norm and expectations rise accordingly, which would leave SFWB mostly unaffected. A variation of adaptation is described in set point theory where it is suggested that an individual's well-being adapts to life changes and returns to a certain set-point of well-being determined by individual temperament (Brickman and Campbell, 1971) or more recently argued as set-range of well-being (Boehm and Lyubomirsky, 2009). Some life events, such as unemployment, are less easy to adapt to, possibly because they are closely related to everyday income and survival (Lucas et al., 2004). It seems that the SFWB of the basic income participants did not show evidence of adaptation over two years, which may indicate that basic income may have the potential to alleviate the negative effects of unemployment.

In previous research, it has been suggested that individuals who are satisfied with their income levels evaluate their income levels as higher than those who are unsatisfied with their income, despite the objective income levels involved (Prati, 2017). In other words, it is possible that SFWB rose in the basic income group, even when the objective income levels remained the same. It is also possible that the basic income recipients compared their situation favourably with the control group receiving unemployment benefits. When an income is compared with a reference group, the satisfaction on individual income is greatly affected by the income of that group, although there are individual differences. The effect of relative comparisons tends to be larger when comparisons involve similar types of individuals of the same age in the respective groups (Layard et al., 2008), and the potential effect of such comparisons still needs to be acknowledged. Stressors are associated with individual perspectives and attitudes, so even if an income level stays the same, a change in income structure may cause positive reactions. The affective evaluation of one's participation in an experiment aimed at simplifying and facilitating benefit transfers could also have positively altered individual SFWB.

Previous research (Finke et al., 2017) has found that people are inclined to see the future in a more positive light than their present situation. Positive future evaluations and the extent to which one believes one can influence one's future can motivate one to act in a way that improves one's personal financial situation (Summerville and Roese, 2008). It is noteworthy, especially considering the current volatile financial situation, that a large group of people indicated that they did not have any financial backup to prepare them for financial setbacks. Any intervention that could facilitate saving to improve short-term preparedness would appear to worth pursuing.

We suggest that basic income as a regular and predictable income transfer may enhance SFWB through facilitating individual financial management and decreasing financial stress. Reducing financial stress may improve executive functioning and consequently improve financial decision-making. This, in turn, can enhance the experience of financial self-efficacy. Long-term stress (especially caused by financial difficulties) is associated with learned helplessness, hopelessness, and inactivity, and is also considered a risk factor for depression and anxiety disorders.

SFWB affects physical and psychological health, family relations, quality of life, and happiness (French and Vigne, 2019). At the same time, it is important to note that SFWB is a fluctuating experience. Positive expectations of future financial opportunities may ease the stress of present difficulties. On the other hand, bleak prospects can be profoundly distressing. Individual hopes and expectations change during life as do societal realities. The dynamic interplay between these factors should be considered when SFWB is measured.

REFERENCES

Arber, S., Fenn, K. and Meadows, R. (2014), 'Subjective financial well-being, income and health inequalities in mid and later life in Britain', *Social Science and Medicine*, 100, 12–20.

Baird, S., McIntosh, C. and Özler, B. (2011), 'Cash or condition? Evidence from a CashTransfer experiment', *The Quarterly Journal of Economics*, 126(4), 1709–53.

Blomgren, J., Maunula, N. and Hiilamo, H. (2017), 'Do debts lead to disability pension? Evidence from a 15-year follow-up of 54,000 Finnish men and women', *Journal of European Social Policy*, 27(2), 109–22.

Boehm, J. K. and Lyubomirsky, S. (2009), 'The promise of sustainable happiness', in Lopez, S. J. and Snyder, C. R. (eds), *Oxford Library of Psychology. Oxford Handbook of Positive Psychology*. Oxford: Oxford University Press.

Brickman, P. and Campbell, D. T. (1971), 'Hedonic relativism and planning the good society', in Appley M. H. (ed.), *Adaptation-level Theory*. New York: Academic Press.

Brown, D. W., Balluz, L. S., Ford, E. S., Giles, W. H., Strine, T. W., Moriarty, D. G., Croft, J. B. and Mokdad, A. H. (2003), 'Associations between short- and long-term unemployment and frequent mental distress among a national sample of men and women', *Journal of Occupational and Environmental Medicine*, 45 (11), 1159–66.

Brüggen, E. C., Hogreve, J., Holmlund, M., Kabadayi, S. and Löfgren, M. (2017), 'Financial well-being: A conceptualization and research agenda', *Journal of Business Research*, 79, 228–37.

Chou, E. Y., Parmar, B. L. and Galinsky, A. D. (2016), 'Economic insecurity increases physical pain', *Psychological Science*, 27(4), 443–54.

Cooke, P. J., Melchert, T. P. and Connor, K. (2016), 'Measuring well-being: A review of instruments', *The Counseling Psychologist*, 44(5), 730–57.

Diener, E. (1984), 'Subjective well-being', *Psychological Bulletin*, 95(3), 542–75.

Diener, E. (2000), 'Subjective well-being: The science of happiness and a proposal for a national index', *American Psychologist*, 55(1), 34–43.

Diener, E. and Biswas-Diener, R. (2002), 'Will money increase subjective well-being?', *Social Indicators Research*, 57(2), 119–69.

Dolan, P., Peasgood, T. and White, M. (2008), 'Do we really know what makes us happy? A review of the economic literature on the factors associated with subjective well-being', *Journal of Economic Psychology*, 29(1), 94–122.

Easterlin, R. A. (1995), 'Will raising the incomes of all increase the happiness of all?', *Journal of Economic Behavior and Organization*, 27(1), 35–47.

Erikson, R. (1993), 'Descriptions of inequality: The Swedish approach to welfare research', in Sen, A. and Nussbaum, M. C. (eds), *The Quality of Life*. Oxford: World Institute for Development Economics Research, Clarendon Press, pp. 67–84.

Ferrer-i-Carbonell, A. (2005), 'Income and well-being: An empirical analysis of the comparison income effect', *Journal of Public Economics*, 89(5–6), 997–1019.

Finke, M. S., Howe, J. S. and Huston, S. J. (2017), 'Old age and the decline in financial literacy', *Management Science*, 63(1), 213–30.

Forget, E. L. (2011), 'The town with no poverty: The health effects of a Canadian guaranteed annual income field experiment', *Canadian Public Policy*, 37(3), 283–305.

Forget, E. L. (2013), 'Paying people to be healthy', *International Journal of Health Policy and Management*, 1(4), 245–6.

French, D. and Vigne, S. (2019), 'The causes and consequences of household financial strain: A systematic review', *International Review of Financial Analysis*, 62, 150–6.

Gibson, M., Hearty, W. and Craig, P. (2020), 'The public health effects of interventions similar to basic income: A scoping review', *Lancet Public Health*, 5 (3), e165–e176.

Goul Andersen, J. (2002), 'Coping with long–term unemployment: Economic security, labour market integration and well–being. Results from a Danish panel study, 1994–1999', *International Journal of Social Welfare*, 11(3), 178–90.

Gutter, M. and Copur, Z. (2011), 'Financial behaviors and financial well-being of college students: Evidence from a national survey', *Journal of Family and Economic Issues*, 32(4), 699–714.

Haagh, L. (2019), *The Case for Universal Basic Income*. Cambridge: Polity Press.

Heidenreich, M. (2015), 'The end of the honeymoon: The increasing differentiation of (long-term) unemployment risks in Europe', *Journal of European Social Policy*, 25(4), 393–413.

Hojman, D. A., Miranda, Á and Ruiz-Tagle, J. (2016), 'Debt trajectories and mental health', *Social Science and Medicine*, 167(C), 54–62.

Hämäläinen, K., Kanninen, O., Simanainen, M. and Verho, J. (2020), *Perustulokokeilun arvioinnin loppuraportti: Rekisterianalyysi työmarkkinavaikutuksista* [*Final Report of the Finnish Basic Income Experiment: Register Data Analysis on Employment Effects*]. Helsinki: VATT Institute Economic Research, VATT Muistiot 59.

Jakab, Z. (2012), 'Promoting health and reducing health inequities in Europe', *Lancet*, 380(9846), 951–3.

Johansson, S. (1973), 'Review symposium on the 1968 level of living survey in Sweden: The level of living survey: A presentation', *Acta Sociologica*, 16(3), 211–24.

Joo, S. and Grable, J. E. (2004), 'An exploratory framework of the determinants of financial satisfaction', *Journal of Family and Economic Issues*, 25(1), 25–50.

Kahn, J. R. and Pearlin, L. I. (2006), 'Financial strain over the life course and health among older adults', *Journal of Health and Social Behavior*, 47(1), 17–31.

Kenrick, D. T., Griskevicius, V., Neuberg, S. L. and Schaller, M. (2010), 'Renovating the pyramid of needs: Contemporary extensions built upon ancient foundations', *Perspectives on Psychological Science: A Journal of the Association for Psychological Science*, 5(3), 292–314.

Keyes, C. L. M. (2006), 'Subjective well-being in mental health and human development research worldwide: An introduction', *Social Indicators Research*, 77(1), 1–10.

Kim, J. and Garman, E. T. (2003), 'Financial stress and absenteeism: An empirically derived model', *Journal of Financial Counseling and Planning*, 14(1), 31–42.

Knabe, A., Rätzel, S., Schöb, R. and Weimann, J. (2010), 'Dissatisfied with life but having a good day: Time-use and well-being of the unemployed', *The Economic Journal*, 120(547), 867–89.

Kunze, L. and Suppa, N. (2017), 'Bowling alone or bowling at all? The effect of unemployment on social participation', *Journal of Economic Behavior and Organization*, 133, 213–35.

Layard, R., Mayraz, G. and Nickell, S. (2008), 'The marginal utility of income', *Journal of Public Economics*, 92(8–9), 1846–57.

Lucas, R. E., Clark, A. E., Georgellis, Y. and Diener, E. (2004), 'Unemployment alters the set point for life satisfaction', *Psychological Science*, 15(1), 8–13.

Malone, K., Stewart, S. D., Wilson, J. and Korsching, P. F. (2010), 'Perceptions of financial well-being among American women in diverse families', *Journal of Family and Economic Issues*, 31(1), 63–81.

Marmot, M., Allen, J., Bell, R., Bloomer, E., Goldblatt, P. and Consortium for the European Review of Social Determinants of Health and the Health Divide (2012), 'WHO European review of social determinants of health and the health divide', *The Lancet*, 380(9846), 1011–29.

Maslow, A. H. (1943), 'A theory of human motivation', *Psychological Review*, 50(4), 370–96.

Mays, J. (2019), 'Social effects of basic income', in Torry, M. (ed.), *The Palgrave International Handbook for Basic Income: Exploring the Basic Income Guarantee*. Houndmills, Basingstoke: Palgrave Macmillan pp. 73–90.

Ngamaba, K. H., Panagioti, M. and Armitage, C. J. (2018), 'Income inequality and subjective well-being: A systematic review and meta-analysis', *Quality of Life Research: An International Journal of Quality of Life Aspects of Treatment, Care and Rehabilitation*, 27(3), 577–96.

Netemeyer, R. G., Warmath, D., Fernandes, D. and Lynch, J. G. (2018), 'How Am I Doing? Perceived financial well-being, its potential antecedents, and its relation to overall well-being', *Journal of Consumer Research*, 45(1), 68–89.

Norvilitis, J. M., Szablicki, P. B. and Wilson, S. D. (2003), 'Factors influencing levels of credit-card debt in college students', *Journal of Applied Social Psychology*, 33(5), 935–47.

O'Neill, B., Sorhaindo, B., Xiao, J. and Garman, E. (2005), 'Financially distressed consumers: Their financial practices, financial well-being, and health', *Journal of Financial Counseling and Planning*, 16(1), 73–87.

Owusu-Addo, E., Renzaho, A. M. N. and Smith, B. J. (2018), 'The impact of cash transfers on social determinants of health and health inequalities in sub-Saharan Africa: A systematic review', *Health Policy and Planning*, 33(5), 675–96.

Paul, K. I. and Moser, K. (2009), 'Unemployment impairs mental health: Meta-analyses', *Journal of Vocational Behavior*, 74(3), 264–82.

Prati, A. (2017), 'Hedonic recall bias. Why you should not ask people how much they earn', *Journal of Economic Behavior and Organization*, 143, 78–97.

Sen, A. (1993), 'Capability and well-being', in Sen, A. and Nussbaum, M. C. and World Institute for Development Economics Research (eds.), *The Quality of Life*. Oxford: Clarendon Press.

Senik, C. (2009), 'Income distribution and subjective happiness: A survey'. Social: OECD, Employment and Migration Working Papers, No. 96. Paris: OECD Publishing.

Shim, S., Xiao, J. J., Barber, B. L. and Lyons, A. C. (2009), 'Pathways to life success: A conceptual model of financial well-being for young adults', *Journal of Applied Developmental Psychology*, 30(6), 708–23.

Smith, S. (2015), *Ending Global Poverty: A Guide to What Works*. New York: St Martin's Press.

Ståhl, C. and MacEachen, E. (2020), 'Universal basic income as a policy response to COVID-19 and precarious employment: Potential impacts on rehabilitation and return-to-work', *Journal of Occupational Rehabilitation*, available at https://doi.org/10.1007/s10926-020-09923-w (accessed 9 December 2020).

Summerville, A. and Roese, N. J. (2008), 'Dare to compare: Fact-based versus simulation-based comparison in daily life', *Journal of Experimental Social Psychology*, 44(3), 664–71.

Swarbrick, M. and Yudof, J. (2015), *Wellness in the 8 Dimensions*, Collaborative Support Programs of New Jersey, Working Paper.

Van Parijs, P. and Vanderborght, Y. (2017), *Basic Income: A Radical Proposal for a Free Society and a Sane Economy*. Cambridge, MA: Harvard University Press.

Van Praag, B. M. S., Frijters, P. and Ferrer-i-Carbonell, A. (2003), 'The anatomy of subjective well-being', *Journal of Economic Behavior and Organization*, 51(1), 29–49.

Veenhoven, R. (2002), Why Social Policy Needs Subjective Indicators, *Social Indicators Research*, 58(1-3), 33–46.

Vosloo, W., Fouche, J. and Barnard, J. (2014), 'The relationship between financial efficacy, satisfaction with remuneration and personal financial well-being', *International Business and Economics Research Journal*, 13(6), 1455–70.

Willis, L. E. (2011), 'The financial education fallacy', *American Economic Review*, 101(3), 429–34.

Winkelmann, L. and Winkelmann, R. (1998), 'Why are the unemployed so unhappy? Evidence from panel data', *Economica*, 65(257), 1–15.

Winkelmann, R. (2009), 'Unemployment, social capital, and subjective well-being', *Journal of Happiness Studies*, 10(4), 421–30.

World Health Organization (WHO), (2008), *Closing the Gap in a Generation: Health Equity through Action on the Social Determinants of Health, Final Report of the Commission on Social Determinants of Health*. Geneva: WHO.

Xiao, J. and Noring, F. (1994), 'Perceived saving motives and hierarchical financial needs', *Journal of Financial Counseling and Planning*, 5(1), 25–44.

Zyphur, M. J., Li, W. D., Zhang, Z., Arvey, R. D. and Barsky, A. P. (2015), 'Income, personality, and subjective financial well-being: The role of gender in their genetic and environmental relationships', *Frontiers in Psychology*, 6, 1493.

9.   The bureaucracy of claiming benefits

Miska Simanainen

INTRODUCTION

Citizens of welfare states often support extensive social benefit programmes, but also consider them as bureaucratic and inefficient (Svallfors, 2010). Part of the criticism may arise from citizens' experiences as beneficiaries. Sudden interruptions in benefit eligibility, delays in benefit decisions, and recovery of payments might reinforce the critical perceptions of these individuals. The complexity of benefit rules and practices, such as how benefits are adjusted to earnings, might also intensify citizens' perceptions of bureaucracy.

Perceptions of bureaucracy are an important phenomenon to study because they indicate the complexities involved in the administrative processes of welfare policies and the associated burden and costs of potential welfare recipients (cf. Handler, 2004; Handler and Hasenfeld, 2006). Moreover, the costs involved in claiming benefits might result in the non-take-up of benefits or discouraging beneficiaries from taking on jobs, especially when faced with temporary or part-time job offers (Brodkin and Majmundar, 2010; Currie, 2004; Moynihan and Herd, 2010; Kleven and Kopczuk, 2011).

The core idea of a basic income is to provide individuals with a regular minimum income without complex conditions or the need to interact with benefit officials. For example, Standing (1999: 362–3) argues that an unconditional basic income 'would simplify the complex schemes, make them more transparent, and reduce the amount of intrusive enquiry'. As a regular and automatic payment, a basic income should also reduce financial insecurity and increase the foreseeability of future cash flows (for more on the potential sources of financial insecurity, see Chapter 8 by Lassander and Jauhiainen).

In the ideal case of a basic income, individuals would be confident that they would receive the guaranteed stipulated amount, and that all additional income from employment or entrepreneurship would increase their monthly disposable income. In principle, a basic income should at least reduce the need to interact with benefit officials and release the beneficiaries from struggling with adjustments to benefits arising from other earnings.

Accordingly, advocates of a basic income often assume that the administrative processes and costs of distributing an unconditional basic income would be less than for distributing conditional benefits. The general view in the literature seems to be that reducing bureaucratic effort in benefit payment processes automatically leads to reductions in the burden caused to beneficiaries when claiming benefits (for a more thorough elaboration on the assumption, see De Wispelaere and Stirton, 2011). However, there is a large gap in the research literature on the effects of a basic income on the practical experiences of benefit claimants, and on the potential costs they face when trying to adjust to the complexity of conditional benefit schemes.

De Wispelaere and Stirton (2011) argue that the extent of administrative simplification that might result from the introduction of a basic income depends on the different design features of such a policy that determine whether it can truly replace or supplement the existing benefit framework. In the Finnish basic income experiment (2017–18), basic income did not fully replace the existing benefit system. The basic income model that was tested left the beneficiaries with the opportunity to apply for the other existing social benefits according to their original rules. Moreover, the register analysis on the use of social benefits in the experiment showed that a considerable proportion of those who were eligible for other benefits also applied for them (Hämäläinen et al., 2019 and 2020). To receive these additional benefits, the basic income recipients had to fulfil the benefit eligibility conditions and interact with the benefit and employment officials just as before the experiment. This would imply actions such as registering as an unemployed jobseeker, filling out employment plans, participating in active employment services, sending benefit claims, and providing information on earnings.

However, in the Finnish experiment, at least two things changed for the beneficiaries that were independent of whether they eventually applied for other social benefits apart from the basic income. First, they received the basic income of €560 regularly at the beginning of each month, regardless of whether they chose to apply for other social benefits retroactively. Second, the beneficiaries were aware that whatever the decision on their potential benefit claims was – or whether they chose to apply for it – they received at least €560 every month.

These changes in the benefits system motivated us to study the beneficiaries' perceptions of the bureaucracy of the social benefits system in the Finnish basic income experiment, thus leading to the posing of the main research question in this chapter:

Did the basic income recipients consider the benefits system as less bureaucratic than those who did not participate in the experiment?

The structure of the chapter is as follows. First, I present the data and methods used in the subsequent analyses. Second, I discuss the incentives of different population groups to apply for social benefits in the Finnish experiment. This discussion is relevant to the positing of a working hypothesis on how a basic income affects the perceptions of the bureaucracy of receiving benefits for different population groups. Thereafter, the findings on the perceptions of the participants are reported. Finally, the findings are summarised and discussed, including the potential ability of a basic income to reduce the bureaucracy in receiving benefits experienced by beneficiaries.

MEASURING PERCEPTIONS OF BUREAUCRACY IN RECEIVING BENEFITS

In the following analysis on the perceptions of bureaucracy, I will utilise data from a telephone survey conducted during the Finnish basic income experiment. The survey was targeted both at the participants of the experiment and at a sample of those who belonged to the control group of the experiment. In the analysis, I will utilise remodelled survey weights to correct for the bias caused by the unit non-response (for more information on the survey, see Chapter 5).

In the telephone interview, the respondents' perceptions of the bureaucracy of claiming social benefits were measured with the following question:

> When you think about the past two years, do you feel that there is too much bureaucracy involved when claiming social security benefits (Yes, No, Not sure)?

While the meaning of the question seems to be straightforward, the concept of bureaucracy may contain some ambiguity. It may not be entirely evident which bureaucracy is being referred to in the questionnaire. In the Finnish public discussions, the social benefits system is often described as too complex, non-transparent, unforeseeable, and discouraging beneficiaries to accept gig-like, part-time, or temporary job offers. A benefit system with such disadvantages is often labelled as bureaucratic. In the survey questionnaire, the concept of bureaucracy was used accordingly to refer to potential deficits of the benefits system.

In the following section, I explore the association between participation in the experiment and perceptions of bureaucracy by comparing the distributions of responses of the treatment and control groups. I will first analyse the responses of the whole study group and then separately the sub-groups formed according to the social assistance take-up, family type, and labour market position of the respondents. The background factors that define the sub-groups are self-reported and they represent the respondents' situation at the time of the survey interview (for more information on the study and background variables, see Table 9A.1 in the appendix).

I will provide statistical tests for the observed differences between the groups. The tests were calculated for each subgroup separately. In addition, the sensitivity of the observed differences between the treated and control groups was tested with a regression analysis that considers other factors that potentially explain the variety of perceptions of bureaucracy.

HOW IS PARTIAL BASIC INCOME AFFECTING DIFFERENT POPULATION GROUPS?

To hypothesise about the association between participation in the experiment and the experience of bureaucracy in claiming benefits, it is important to realise that in the experiment, some individuals continued to have the need and incentive to apply for other social benefits – especially those who received social assistance or had dependent children.

Households that receive social assistance often receive other basic social benefits such as unemployment benefits. In the experiment, the basic income was roughly equal to the basic amount paid as unemployment benefits. Despite the basic income replaced the basic unemployment benefit, the need and eligibility to apply for social assistance continued. Similarly, those with dependent children were eligible for a higher unemployment benefit (the so-called child component), and thus continued to have an incentive and a need to apply for it. As a result, the basic income experiment did not remove all bureaucracy from the claiming of benefits. Consequently, we should expect relative differences between the perceptions of the treatment and control group towards this bureaucracy according to the social assistance take-up and type of family.

The telephone survey included 586 persons from the experiment's treatment group and 1,047 from the control group. Those receiving basic social assistance at the time of the interviews for the treatment and *control groups* were 19 percent and *28 percent*, respectively. Of the treatment group (*control group*), 37 percent (*32 percent*) had dependent children, as indicated in Table 9.1.

The respondent's position within the labour market should also be considered relevant in the analysis. For those not receiving any social benefits, the basic income provided a pure minimum income and an earnings supplement. Moreover, it did not require any form of interaction with the officials to receive it.

The unemployed and those receiving other social benefits were only freed from eligibility conditions, duties related to claiming benefits, and the need to interact with officials if they decided not to apply for unemployment benefits. For students, however, the experiment worked as a replacement for existing benefits because the basic income was higher than the student grant.

110　　　　　　　　*Experimenting with unconditional basic income*

Table 9.1　　　Demographic analysis of respondents (treatment and control group)

	Treatment group	Control group
Respondents	586	1047
Household receiving social assistance	19%	28%
Household with children	37%	32%
Labour market position		
Wage earner/entrepreneur/farmer	35%	28%
Student	8%	10%
Unemployed/not in employment	37%	39%
Other	20%	23%

Consequently, the students should not have had the need or incentive to apply for other benefits in addition to the basic income.

There were relatively more wage earners, entrepreneurs, and farmers in the treatment group (37 percent) than in the control group (32 percent). About a quarter of respondents classified themselves as unemployed. The share of students in both groups was about 10 percent. The proportion of those unemployed and students was only slightly smaller in the treatment group than in the control group (Table 9.1).

EXPERIENCES OF BUREAUCRACY

Table 9.2 shows the responses of the treatment and control groups to the survey questionnaire about the perception of bureaucracy in receiving benefits. In the treatment group, a smaller share of individuals (57 percent) reported that there was excessive bureaucracy involved when claiming social security benefits than in the control group (64 percent). Significantly, more than half of the participants in the experiment still considered the claiming of benefits as too bureaucratic.

Participants who received social assistance reported more often that claiming social security benefits involved excessive bureaucracy (67 percent) compared with those who received social assistance in the control group (62 percent). However, the difference is not statistically significant. This result is somewhat expected since the design of the basic income experiment did not ease the eligibility conditions or the application procedure of the means-tested social assistance if the individual also received other basic social benefits.

For those unemployed, the responses were similar to those receiving social assistance. Unemployed participants reported more often that claiming social

The bureaucracy of claiming benefits 111

benefits involved excessive bureaucracy compared with the unemployed in the control group, but the observed differences were not statistically significant. In the experiment, the amount of the basic income was equivalent to the basic portion of the employment benefit. Thus, we would have expected that the unemployed in the treatment group would have reported negative perceptions about the bureaucracy of the benefits system less often than the control group. However, based on the register analysis on the take-up of unemployment benefits (Hämäläinen et al., 2019, 2020), most of the unemployed in the treatment group continued applying and receiving unemployment benefits and interacting with the employment officials, as they would have done outside the experiment. Noting this, the survey results on the unemployed are not surprising. The bureaucracy remained as in the case of social assistance recipients.

Students receiving the basic income reported experiencing less bureaucracy in claiming their benefits than students in the control group (Table 9.2). This result confirms our expectations because the basic income amount was higher than student grants and, thus, the students did not have a similar need to supplement their income with other benefits, as was the case with other categories of beneficiaries.

Table 9.2   *Experiences of bureaucracy by selected background factors*

	Treatment group	Control group	*p*-value
There is too much bureaucracy involved when claiming social security benefits: Yes	57%	64%	0.011
Social assistance	67%	62%	0.321
With children	52%	63%	0.014
Unemployed	64%	62%	0.674
Student	49%	64%	0.078
Wage earner/entrepreneur/farmer	49%	62%	0.002

Wage-earners, entrepreneurs, and farmers in the treatment group also experienced the benefits system as less bureaucratic than their peers in the control group. Finding explanations for this would require more information on the potential replacement of in-work benefits received by this group (adjusted unemployment benefits). It is also noteworthy that in addition to students, the wage earners, entrepreneurs, and farmers were those whose financial situation most likely improved because they received their basic income on top of their other potential income (earnings).

Participants with children reported experiencing bureaucracy in claiming benefits less often (52 percent) than their peers in the control group (63

112   *Experimenting with unconditional basic income*

percent). This result is somewhat unexpected as families are usually entitled to higher other benefits than the amount of the basic income in the experiment. The number of dependent children results in larger unemployment benefits and social assistance, and thus higher incentives to remain within the existing benefit system. The interpretation of the findings regarding families would require a more detailed picture of the benefits that the families received during the experiment.

In the previous analysis, we saw that a smaller share of respondents in the treatment group considered the social benefits system too bureaucratic compared with the control group (see also Table 9A.2 in the appendix). However, the association between participation in the experiment and perceptions of decreased bureaucracy should be analysed more thoroughly. This includes constructing a sensitivity test to determine if the association is observed even when controlling for other potential factors affecting perceptions of bureaucracy.

Table 9.3 includes the results of regression analysis for two different model specifications. The first model (*participation*) only includes a treatment indicator as an explanatory factor. The estimation of the coefficient for the treatment indicator (*participation*) is analogous to comparing response distributions between the treatment and control groups without considering other potential explanatory factors associated with the perceptions of bureaucracy. The odds ratios in the table indicate that participation in the experiment reduced the probability that the respondents reported excessive bureaucracy in claiming benefits (odds ratio < 1.0). In sum, those who participated in the experiment felt that claiming benefits was less bureaucratic than those who remained within the existing benefit system.

The second model in the table (*participation + controls*) controls for the take-up of social assistance, family type, labour market position, gender, age, education, health status, part-time employment, and the respondent's attitude to a basic income. These results – the estimated coefficient of the treatment indicator – show that the association between participation and perceptions of bureaucracy retains its size and direction, even though other potential explanatory factors are considered. In sum, even when the differences in the background factors are considered, a difference in the perceptions of the bureaucracy among the study groups is observed.

DISCUSSION AND CONCLUSIONS

In this chapter, individuals' perceptions of bureaucracy in claiming benefits are analysed from the Finnish basic income experiment. The study was motivated by the core idea behind the concept of a basic income; by being a regular and unconditional payment, a basic income should simplify the process of claiming benefits, reduce individuals' needs to interact with benefit officials and, in general, ease individuals' daily management of financial issues.

Table 9.3   Regression analysis (binary logistic) on the association of participation in the experiment and experiences of bureaucracy

	Coefficient (participation)	p-value	Odds ratio
There is too much bureaucracy involved when claiming social security benefits: Yes			
Participation	–0.30	0.0109	0.74
Participation + Controls*	–0.32	0.0100	0.73

Note: * Controls include take-up of social assistance, family type, labour market position, gender, age, education, health status, an indicator of part-time employment, and the respondent's attitude to a basic income.

In the Finnish experiment, the monthly basic income of €560 covered the basic part of the unemployment benefits (or other daily allowances) and was complemented by the opportunity to receive other social benefits (larger daily allowances), housing allowance, and social assistance. Thus, by design, the experiment did not result in a significant reduction in the bureaucracy of claiming social benefits if individuals continued to apply for other social benefits. According to a register study, at the end of the first year of the experiment, the share of those in the control group who applied for unemployment benefits was about 63 percent, and those in the treatment group around 47 percent (Hämäläinen et al., 2019, 2020). Moreover, there was only a slight drop in participation in employment services (Hämäläinen et al., 2019, 2020).

In this study, the bureaucracy of the benefits system was measured with a self-evaluative survey questionnaire that was targeted at both the participants and the control group of the Finnish experiment. The analysis indicated that, on average, those who participated in the experiment experienced claiming benefits as less bureaucratic than their peers who continued living on the existing benefit system. The association between participation and perceptions of decreased bureaucracy remained even when other explanatory factors were controlled. However, it is worth noting that more than half of the participants in the experiment still considered the claiming of benefits as too bureaucratic.

Some beneficiaries – those unemployed or receiving social assistance – reported excessive bureaucracy in claiming benefits more often in the treatment group than in the control group. Moreover, the results for those with dependent children were somewhat surprising and contradictory. In the study, families in the treatment group reported experiencing less bureaucracy in claiming benefits than those in the control group, although they most likely needed to continue applying for other social benefits. However, the sub-group analysis suffers from a small number of observations and, thus, these results should be interpreted with caution.

The study points to further analysis of the mechanisms that connect the receiving of a basic income to individuals' perceptions of bureaucracy. A more in-depth analysis could be performed by utilising register data on the take-up of social benefits and labour market transitions during the experiment and combining this with self-reported survey measures. Further analysis of the interview data utilised by Blomberg et al. (2020) (see also Chapter 12) could also provide explanations for the differences in the perceptions of different population groups to bureaucracy.

In this study, I focused on the bureaucratic burden felt by beneficiaries that result from the combination of needed benefit systems that supplement basic income support. A basic income policy designed to operate in parallel with other selective and conditional benefit systems clearly cannot remove all the existing administrative processes. Even if the payments of a basic income were purely unconditional and automatic, bureaucratic activities would likely be required for other purposes, such as the assessment of earnings-related benefits, complementing income assistance for expenses (housing benefits and social assistance) and income taxes. Such activities cannot be displaced by introducing a non-means-tested basic income policy. Consequently, we have no grounds to expect a drastic drop in beneficiaries' perceptions of the bureaucracy of this system.

The results of this study remain politically relevant, since in any feasible basic income system, 'the entire apparatus of welfare benefits would still have to remain in place, although benefits would, of course, be reduced by the amount of the basic income' (Barry, 2001: 65). Moreover, as Van Parijs (2001: 8–9) states,

> if a government implemented an unconditional income that was too small to cover basic needs – which […] would almost certainly be the case at first – UBI [unconditional basic income] advocates would not want to eliminate the existing conditional minimum-income schemes, but only to readjust their levels.

In this context, we may expect a slight improvement in the bureaucratic burden faced by the beneficiaries, but more importantly, as De Wispelaere and Stirton (2011) point out, start to consider how much we genuinely care about administrative efficiency compared with other goals that the basic income policy could help to achieve.

REFERENCES

Barry, B. (2001), 'UBI and the Work Ethic', in Van Parijs, P., Cohen, J. and Rogers, J. (eds), *What's Wrong with a Free Lunch?* Boston, MA: Beacon, pp. 60–9.

Blomberg, H., Kroll, C. and Tarkiainen, H. (2020), 'Elämää perustulolla – Perustulokokeilun työllisyys-, osallisuus-ja autonomiavaikutukset kokeiluun osallistuneiden haastattelukertomuksissa' ['Life on Basic Income – Basic Income Experiment Participant's Interview Accounts on the Effects of the Experiment on Employment, Participation and Autonomy'], in Kangas, O., Jauhiainen, S., Simanainen, M. and Ylikännö, M. (eds), *Suomen perustulokokeilun arviointi* [*Evaluation of the Finnish Basic Income Experiment*], Helsinki: Ministry of Social Affairs and Health, Raportteja ja muistioita, 15.

Brodkin, E. Z. and Majmundar, M. (2010), 'Administrative exclusion: Organisations and the hidden costs of welfare claiming', *Journal of Public Administration Research and Theory*, 20(4), 827–48.

Currie, J. (2004), 'The Take Up of Social Benefits', NBER Working Paper, available at https://www.nber.org/papers/w10488 (accessed 9 April 2020).

De Wispelaere, J. and Stirton, L. (2011), 'The Administrative Efficiency of Basic Income', *Policy and Politics*, 39(1), 115–32.

Handler, J. F. (2004), *Social Citizenship and Workfare in the United States and Western Europe: The Paradox of Inclusion*, Cambridge: Cambridge University Press.

Handler, J. F. and Hasenfeld, Y. (2006), *Blame Welfare, Ignore Poverty and Inequality*, Cambridge: Cambridge University Press.

Hämäläinen, K., Kanninen, O., Simanainen, M. and Verho, J. (2019), *Perustulokokeilun ensimmäinen vuosi* [*The First Year of the Basic Income Experiment*], Helsinki: VATT Institute for Economic Research, VATT Muistiot 56.

Hämäläinen, K., Kanninen, O., Simanainen, M. and Verho, J. (2020), *Perustulokokeilun arvioinnin loppuraportti: Rekisterianalyysi työmarkkinavaikutuksista* [*The Final Report on the Evaluation of the Basic Income Experiment: Register Analysis on Labour Market Effects*], Helsinki: VATT Institute for Economic Research, VATT Muistiot 59.

Kleven, H. J. and Kopczuk, W. (2011), 'Transfer Program Complexity and the Take-Up of Social Benefits', *American Economic Journal: Economic Policy*, 3(1), 54–90.

Moynihan, D. and Herd, P. (2010), 'Red Tape and Democracy: How Rules Affect Citizenship Rights', *The American Review of Public Administration*, 40(6), 654–70.

Standing, G. (1999), *Global Labour Flexibility: Seeking Distributive Justice*, Basingstoke: Palgrave.

Svallfors, S. (2010), 'Public Attitudes', in Castles, F. G., Leibfried, S., Lewis, J., Obinger, H. and Pierson, C. (ed.), *The Oxford Handbook of the Welfare State*, Oxford: Oxford University Press, pp. 241–51.

Van Parijs, P. (2001), 'Reply', in Van Parijs, P., Cohen, J. and Rogers, J. (eds), *What's Wrong with a Free Lunch?* Boston, MA: Beacon, pp. 121–7.

APPENDIX

Table 9A.1   Survey questions and response categories for the study and background variables

Questions on study variables	Available response categories
When you think about the past two years, do you feel that there is too much bureaucracy involved when claiming social security benefits?	Yes, No, Not sure
Questions on background variables	Available response categories
What sources of income does your household have (respondent/spouse/other household members)?	Wage/Business income, Pension, Unemployment benefits, Basic income, Social assistance/Income support, Other social security, Other income, Not sure
Which of the below alternatives best describes your household?	Single-person household, Couple without children, Household comprising more than one adult (over age 18), Household with children, Prefer not to reply
Which of the above best describes your position in the labour market at present?	Self-employed/a farmer, A wage or salary earner, A stay-at-home parent, A student, Unemployed, Retired, I'm not in paid work, I only get basic income payments, Other (please specify)

Table 9A.2   Distribution of response on the experiences of bureaucracy

	Treatment group (%)	Control group (%)
There is too much bureaucracy involved when claiming social security benefits		
Yes	57	64
No	36	31
Not sure	7	5

10. Trust, capabilities, confidence and basic income

Olli Kangas, Minna Ylikännö and Mikko Niemelä

INTRODUCTION

Had John Lennon and Paul McCartney been sociologists, the title of their most famous and most referenced article might have been 'All You Need Is *Trust*'. Indeed, trust is something we need in everyday life. We could not interact with others in any positive or productive manner if we did not trust them; similarly, without trust, we could not properly interact with public institutions and authorities.

Mutual trust is a prerequisite for any sustainable social organization. Societies with low levels of generalised trust in fellow citizens and institutions inevitably struggle with political instability and corruption; hence, when reforming social institutions and experimenting with new social policy models, the emphasis should be placed on how to increase and maintain trust and, in a Putnamian sense, get people 'to bowl together' (Putnam, 2000).

The academic literature has typically separated trust into two distinct forms: trust in one's fellow citizens, also called generalised trust, and trust in institutions. Whether people trust institutions, or other people for that matter, has an effect on the functioning of society (Fukuyama, 1995, 2011; Stiglitz et al., 2018); thus, the importance of trust should not be ignored when assessing the functioning of existing national institutions or the pursuit of new policies.

According to the Cambridge Dictionary, 'trust' is the belief that the other person is good and honest and will not cause harm, or that something is safe and reliable, while 'confidence' refers to the quality of being certain of one's own abilities and plans for the future. For the purposes of our analysis, we define confidence as one's reliance on oneself and one's perceived ability to cope, meet future challenges, and be an influential actor in one's own life.

Even in the scientific literature, the concepts of trust and confidence are frequently used interchangeably. However, from a sociological perspective, it is useful to distinguish between the two. While they are interwoven and

118 *Experimenting with unconditional basic income*

connected in many ways, they are not precisely the same (for a more detailed discussion, see for example Cofta, 2007). Both trust and confidence are related to the possibility of self-actualisation. The most prominent advocates of basic income, Guy Standing (2020) and Philippe Van Parijs (1995 and Van Parijs and Vanderborght, 2017), highlight the emancipatory value of basic income, which they view as greatly exceeding its monetary value. They also see basic income as an institutional device to enhance human agency and fortify individual self-governance and self-respect. These arguments have ideational resemblances to the works of Amartya Sen (1992, 1999, 2010) and Martha Nussbaum (2011), who emphasise the essential role of people's capabilities in creating well-being.

In this chapter, we ask how basic income, as an unconditional social transfer scheme, could be related to trust, capabilities and self-confidence. We start by discussing the concepts of trust, capability and confidence, presenting theory-based hypotheses and posing research questions on how basic income might be linked to generalised trust, trust in social institutions, (self-)confidence, and the set of capabilities needed to enable confidence building. After describing the outcome variables and methods used, we present the empirical analyses. The chapter ends with a general discussion of the results and their policy relevance.

ALL YOU NEED IS TRUST

Without trust, it would be difficult for people to interact with each other: life would be characterised by constant fear and full of vulnerabilities. Trust in fellow citizens can be seen as the glue that keeps societies together or the oil that lubricates human and economic transactions. Accordingly, a low level of trust in fellow citizens is correlated with low trust in the government, a low level of political efficacy, low confidence in one's own influence, lower voter participation, and less happiness and satisfaction in life (Putnam, 2000).

Perhaps the most well-known prophet of trust is Francis Fukuyama (1995, 2011, 2014), who emphasises, in several best-selling books, its crucial role in creating prosperous and economically sustainable societies. According to Fukuyama, a lack of mutual trust between fellow citizens and institutions has direct consequences for a nation's social order and economic trajectory. He further argues that 'a nation's well-being, as well as its ability to compete, is conditioned by a single pervasive cultural characteristic: the level of trust inherent in the society' (Fukuyama, 1995: 7).

Although trust makes life easier, vulnerability and uncertainty are always present in even the most trusting relationships (Heimer, 2001: 43). Historically, societies have developed different ways to reduce uncertainty and create trust, including various social institutions and social policy programmes. In particular, universal social policy programmes are believed to enhance trust in society (for example, Rothstein, 2005; Svallfors, 2012; Larsen, 2016). Such universal social policies effectively represent the reciprocal nature of trust, that is, while being trusted, we are inclined to trust others (Ostrom, 1990). Social security systems that are built on the principle of trust – as, typically, all universal benefit schemes are – generate more trust than programmes based on continued screening and means-testing. In the former case, clients are treated equally, and, most importantly, they are trusted. In the latter case, clients are instead subject to extensive discretion and needs assessment, which at times can be arbitrary. While only predictable institutions can generate trust, the key question is how predictably welfare state institutions work (Sztompka, 1999; Tyler, 2001).

One of the crucial elements of universal social policies and their ability to generate trust is linked to the concept of recognition (Honneth, 1992; Honneth and Frazer, 2003) and the public acknowledgement of a person's status as a dignified member of society (see also Fukuyama, 2019). In the field of social policy, recognition means that the institution in question acknowledges clients as autonomous agents and takes their claims seriously. Accordingly, clients' perceptions of the treatment they receive from the authority will be generalised to other institutions, consequently either increasing or breaking trust in both social institutions and the public authorities implementing them. In *Trust in the Law*, Tyler and Huo (2002: 136) analyse the implications of procedural justice, stating,

> …people do generalize from their personal experiences. People's perception of their treatment during an experience can have three types of broader impact: it shapes their trust in legal institutions and authorities; it shapes their trust in others in their community; and it shapes their identification with their community.

In the Nordic welfare states, universalism is a strong underlying principle during the implementation of social policies. The emphasis on the equality of citizens, instead of endless means-testing and screening, has created highly trusting societies. Indeed, comparisons between welfare regimes show that both generalised trust and trust in institutions are persistently higher in Nordic countries than in other welfare regimes. Further, trust is considered to be one of the key elements in the functioning of Nordic 'bumblebees', which, against all odds, have flown and continue to fly (for example, Andreasson, 2017; Halvorsen et al., 2016; Svendsen and Svendsen, 2016).

Against this theoretical and empirical background, we ask:

- *How do the treatment group (receivers of the basic income) and the control group differ in their levels of trust in the social security system?*

120   *Experimenting with unconditional basic income*

- *How do the treatment and control groups differ in their levels of trust in other societal institutions, including politicians, the legal system, and the police?*
- *How do the treatment and control groups differ in their levels of generalised trust?*

SELF-CONFIDENCE AND AGENCY IN ONE'S OWN LIFE

A Google search on 'confidence' produces millions of hits, most of them manuals on how to build and boost self-confidence, including '3 Ways to be Confident', '10 Things You Can Do to Boost Self-confidence', 'Confidence-building Exercises', and 'Confidence Coaching', to name just a few. The apparent popularity of such manuals indicates that, in modern society, self-confidence is regarded as a valuable personal asset that helps people succeed in their lives.

However, the benefits of high levels of confidence go far beyond the mundane pecuniary benefits these cheapjack manuals promise. Bénabou and Tirole (2002) distinguish three intrinsic values of confidence. First, the *consumption value* describes how favourably we feel about ourselves: a positive self-image makes people happier, and happiness is, in turn, correlated with other good qualities of life (Layard, 2006). For example, multiple studies have shown its strong relationship with health (Atherton et al., 2016; Mann et al., 2004), although the direction of causality – if there is any – is difficult to prove.

Second, the *signalling value* states that by believing in ourselves, we signal to other people that we have valuable skills and abilities, which is helpful, for example, for securing employment. Third, the *motivational value* describes how self-confidence increases our willingness to be involved in new projects and increases our goal attainment aspirations, which, in Maslow's (1987) classical hierarchy of needs, represent self-actualisation (Bénabou and Tirole, 2002).

Based on these theories, we ask:

- How do the treatment and control groups differ in their levels of confidence in their future?
- How do they differ in their confidence in their own economic situation?
- How do they differ in their confidence in being able to cope with difficult life situations?

To actualise their aspirations, people need both confidence and sufficient capabilities upon which to base this confidence. Through John Rawls' ideas about 'primary goods' in *Political Liberalism* (1993) and Amartya Sen's

(1992, 1999, 2010) emphasis on the role of people's capabilities, we move on to Martha Nussbaum (2011), who advances the idea of capability-building in human development. According to Nussbaum (2011: 193), there are two different forms of capabilities: an individual's own capabilities (internal capabilities) and those that are either fortified or hindered by social institutions and political systems (combined capabilities). Her central argument is that through combined capabilities, governments should advance measures that aim to strengthen people's internal capabilities.

In relation to the capability approach and basic income debate, we seek to answer the following:

- *How do the treatment and control groups differ in their capabilities to undertake meaningful work?*
- *How do they differ in their capabilities to improve their material level of living?*
- *How do they differ in their perceptions of their capabilities to influence societal issues?*

DATA, VARIABLES AND ANALYSES

Both generalised trust (trust in other people) and institutionalised trust (trust in the social security system, the legal system, and politicians) were measured on a scale from 0 to 10, where the value 0 indicated total distrust and the value 10 indicated the highest possible level of generalised or institutionalised trust (see Table 10.1). The question on generalised trust was worded as follows: 'Please evaluate on a scale of 0 to 10 if most people can be trusted, or if you can't be too careful in dealing with people. Zero means you can't be too careful, and 10 means that most people can be trusted.'

Respectively, the wording of the question on institutional trust was as follows, with the institutions being the social security system, legal system, police, the EU, parliament, politicians, and political parties: 'Please evaluate on a scale of 0 to 10 how much you trust each of the following institutions. Zero means you do not trust an institution at all, and 10 means you have complete trust in it.'

The same measures were used in the European Social Survey (ESS, 2018), which allowed us to place our results for trust in a wider Finnish and European

122 *Experimenting with unconditional basic income*

context (see Table 10.1). Questions on confidence and capabilities were posed as follows:

> How do you feel the following things have developed in your life within the last two years?
> Confidence in a) your own future, b) your own economic situation, and c) your ability to cope with difficult life situations;
> Capability to a) have a meaningful job, b) improve your material level of living, and c) influence societal issues.

The time period of two years refers to the experimental period. The answer options for the above questions on confidence and capabilities were: (1) bad, (2) fairly bad, (3) neither bad nor good, (4) fairly good, (5) good, and (6) I do not know. In subsequent analyses, the last alternative was treated as a missing value (except in Table 10.2). Statistical significance (sig.) of differences in the average values (Table 10.1) and the relative shares (Table 10.2) between the treatment and control groups were based on the test of means (Table 10.1) and χ^2-test (Table 10.2).

After presenting the cross-tabulated distributions of trust, confidence, and the respondents' perceptions of their capabilities, we merged the eight trust, three confidence, and three capacity variables into three additive and continuous variables.[1] The trust variable ranged from 0 to a maximum value of 80. The two other additive variables varied from the lowest value of 3 to the highest value of 15. We then used these new variables in the summative structural equation models depicting the heuristic description of the multidimensional associations between the outcome variables (i.e. trust, confidence and capabilities) and several background variables.

Structural equation modelling (SEM) is a convenient heuristic tool for elaborating the descriptive associations between variables. Structural equation models allow us to theoretically model loops between variables and test whether there are associations; thus, we could make hypotheses, for example, on associations between respondents' levels of education and their health status, and then with their economic problems, allowing us to elaborate direct and indirect associations. We used SEM to produce path diagrams and evaluate the goodness of fit of the models. For the sake of simplicity, we only report the root mean square error of approximation (RMSEA), which is a commonly used indicator for goodness of fit that ranges from 0 to 1. The smaller the value, the better the fit: while values less than 0.05 indicate a good fit, values greater than 0.10 indicate a poorly fitting model (Byrne, 2010: 80; Stata, 2011).

In the heuristic descriptions, we included all the variables gaining significance in the SEM models as explanatory variables, that is, age in six categories (27–35; 36–40; 41–5; 46–50; 51–5, and 56–61 years of age), gender (1 = female; 2 = male), education (1 = basic; 2 = vocational; 3 = high school; 4 =

college; 5 = applied university; 6 = university degree), subjective evaluation of own health status (1 = very bad; 2 = bad; 3 = fair/cannot say; 4 = good and 5 = very good), household size (1 = 1 person; 2 = 2 persons... 5 = 5 or more persons), feeling of bureaucracy ('If you think about your life over the last two years, do you feel that there was too much bureaucracy involved in getting social benefits?'; 0 = no; 1 = do not know; 2 = yes), and household economic situation (1 = Living comfortably on current income; 2 = Coping on current income; 3 = Do not know; 4 = Difficult to live on current income; 5 = Very difficult to live on current income). In the visual presentations, only statistically significant variables were included in the graphs.

TRUST, CONFIDENCE AND CAPABILITIES

The means of generalised trust and trust in institutions are shown in Table 10.1. The first observation is that Finland is a high-trust society: the level of trust with regard to all items was much higher among the Finnish European Social Survey (ESS) respondents than among those in the EU as a whole. The second observation is that the levels of trust are significantly lower among the unemployed than among the whole population; nevertheless, the observation that the Finnish unemployed are more trusting than average Europeans underlines the fact that Finland is a high-trust society.

However, when comparing either the unemployed or the experimental groups to the employed in Finland, Table 10.1 shows that the levels of trust in other people and institutions were lower in the former groups. Lower levels of trust among the unemployed may be because they, perhaps justifiably, blame the institutions for their misfortune, and, simultaneously, their misfortune may lead to a loss of generalised trust (Honneth, 1992; Hudson, 2006). When comparing the level of generalized trust and trust in institutions between the treatment and control groups of the basic income experiment, the treatment group displayed significantly higher levels of trust in all items, suggesting that after receiving basic income for two years, people are more likely to trust their fellow citizens and societal institutions, including the social security system.

Not all institutions are trusted equally, but some institutions are trusted more than others. Institutions enjoying high levels of trust are those for which there are no alternatives, such as the legal system, the police, and the social security system. Political institutions, which people can influence more or less directly, are less trusted. In our survey, these institutions included the EU, parliament, political parties and politicians. This pattern was the same in both our survey and the ESS (2018).

Next, we focused on the three aspects of confidence. As shown in Table 10.2, all the differences in opinions between the treatment and control groups were significant. We observed the highest confidence in coping with and

124 *Experimenting with unconditional basic income*

managing difficult life situations: two-thirds of the treatment group and more than half of the control group claimed that in the last two years, they believed they had a good or fairly good likelihood of coping with difficult life events. The lowest confidence levels were observed in respondents' perceptions of managing their financial situations. While 44 percent of the treatment group considered their confidence in managing their financial situation was good or fairly good, the corresponding share in the control group was 33 percent.

Table 10.1   *Institutional and generalised trust in the EU, in Finland and in the treatment and control groups (means)*

	European Social Survey 2018*				Experiment		
	EU (excl. Finland)	All Finns	Finns (excl. the unemployed)	Finnish unemployed	Treatment group	Control group	sig.
Social security	n.d.	n.d.	n.d.	n.d.	6.65	6.36	0.024
Legal system	5.18	7.17	7.20	6.19	6.73	6.46	0.044
Police	6.28	8.12	8.15	7.44	7.86	7.71	0.231
The EU	4.43	5.40	5.42	4.76	4.86	4.55	0.038
Parliament	4.41	5.91	5.94	5.23	5.19	4.72	0.002
Politicians	3.54	4.90	4.93	4.19	4.45	3.81	0.006
Political parties	3.50	5.03	5.06	4.22	4.58	4.18	0.005
Other people	4.91	6.94	6.96	6.33	6.66	6.32	0.007

Scale: 0 = complete distrust and 10 = complete trust, sig. = significance of the differences in means between the treatment and control groups. *Authors' own calculations; the European Social Survey Round 9 (2018); n.d. = no data.

Respondents rated their capabilities – or in Nussbaum's (2011) term 'internal capability' – lowest in regard to the self-assessed possibility of having a say in societal issues. Only about 32 percent of the treatment group and 28 percent of the control group reported that they were confident they could influence societal issues over the last two years. 51 percent of the treatment group assessed their ability to perform meaningful work as good or fairly good, while this share was 43 percent in the control group. Respondents' perceptions of their capabilities to improve their material level of living were somewhat lower in both groups (41 percent and 30 percent, respectively).

Table 10.2　*Levels of confidence and perceptions of own capabilities in the treatment and control groups*

	Group	Bad (%)	Fairly bad (%)	Neither good nor bad (%)	Fairly good (%)	Good (%)	Do not know (%)	Sig. χ^2
CONFIDENCE								
in own future	Treatment	6.6	7.3	24.4	36.6	25.6	1.5	0.000
	Control	10.3	11.7	28.3	30.3	18.6	0.8	
in own economic situation	Treatment	12.8	10.9	31.6	26.2	17.8	0.7	0.000
	Control	19.6	15.3	31.2	20.4	12.1	1.4	
in coping with difficult life situations	Treatment	6.0	4.4	21.5	35.0	30.8	2.2	0.003
	Control	8.0	7.7	25.3	32.6	24.1	2.3	
CAPABILITY								
to have a meaningful job	Treatment	15.5	9.7	19.9	25.7	25.6	3.6	0.014
	Control	19.8	12.8	20.2	22.7	20.5	4.4	
to improve material level of living	Treatment	14.0	11.3	27.6	23.7	16.9	6.5	0.000
	Control	20.7	16.3	28.9	18.7	11.1	4.2	
to influence societal issues	Treatment	14.8	17.6	29.4	17.9	14.5	5.8	0.000
	Control	22.7	20.2	24.7	18.7	9.2	4.6	

BASIC INCOME, TRUST AND CONFIDENCE: A MULTIDIMENSIONAL RELATIONSHIP

In this section, we provide tentative elaborations on how basic income might enhance people's trust and confidence. To do this, we created a structural equation model that visualised the multi-layered interactions between the outcome and background variables (Figure 10.1). The model fit was not perfect, although it was satisfactory (RMSEA = 0.078).

As can be seen in Figure 10.1, there was no direct loop from treatment, that is, from receiving basic income to trust. However, indirect loops were revealed from treatment through economic problems and the experiences of bureaucracy to trust. The treatment group faced less bureaucracy when obtaining social benefits than the control group (see also Chapter 9), which is associated with lower levels of trust. Moreover, the treatment group reported fewer financial problems than the control group (see Chapter 8), which was positively related to the level of trust.[2]

Health affects people's ability to work and earn income (see Chapter 7), and, consequently, a strong and significant loop was seen in our model from subjective health to financial problems, which was, in turn, connected to trust. Furthermore, the smaller the household, the more severe financial problems it was likely to face. Educational attainment was positively connected to trust both directly and indirectly via health (higher education leads to better health) and economic problems (higher education leads to increased income).

One loop in our model ran from treatment to subjective health (significance = 0.010). On the basis of our survey, we cannot state the causality of the relationship between these two variables, although it receives some support from Forget's (2011, 2018) analyses of the Mincome experiment implemented in the 1970s in Canada (see also Costello et al., 2003). In our future research, we plan to merge register data on medical diagnoses with the use of prescribed medicines to corroborate whether receiving basic income actually caused better health in the Finnish basic income experiment or whether this was an artefact produced by the survey.

As we did for trust, we also conducted SEM for confidence (RMSEA = 0.079); visualisation not shown here). We were interested in both the relationship between treatment and confidence and the possible mediating role of capabilities when assessing the impact of treatment on confidence. Consequently, we used an additive variable measuring confidence as an outcome variable and an additive variable measuring respondents' capabilities as an independent background variable.

Figure 10.2 illustrates the loops from different background variables to confidence. The overall fit of the model was satisfactory (RMSEA = 0.073). Parallel to the model for trust, treatment had no direct connection to confidence; however, we observed an indirect loop from treatment to confidence through capabilities. Accordingly, we also observed an indirect loop from experiences of bureaucracy to confidence through capabilities, signifying that basic income and, more generally, a less bureaucratic social security system, play a role in capability building, which then positively impacts confidence-building.

Both direct and indirect loops were also seen through capabilities from financial problems, subjective health, and age to confidence, emphasising their importance in both capability- and confidence-building. Financial problems and age are negatively connected to capabilities; that is, more severe financial problems and a higher age predict lesser self-assessed capabilities; if one succeeds in capability-building, one should also gain more (self-)confidence.

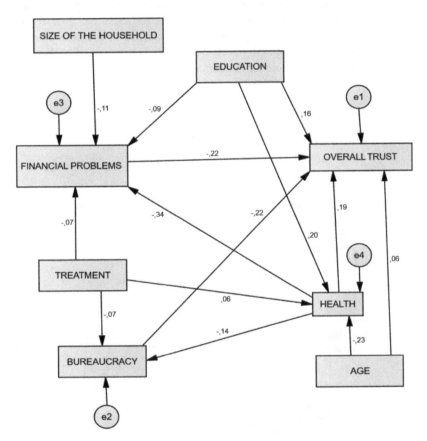

Figure 10.1   Heuristic model of associations between trust and receiving basic income and the background variables

Regarding the other variables, educational attainment had a direct association with confidence and an indirect association through financial problems and household size. Having a decent income is essential both for capability- and confidence-building; however, as our results show, the worse one's subjective health and the lower one's educational level, the more financial problems are likely and the more difficult it is to acquire and maintain capabilities and build confidence in oneself and one's future.

Outside of our main field of interest, we observed a direct negative loop from subjective health to experiences of bureaucracy, which indicates that either those with health issues confront the quite bureaucratic social administration more often than those with better health or that their rare acquaintances with the administration are more bureaucratic due to, for example, the more complex health issues to be solved when applying for social benefits. In sum, Figures 10.1 and 10.2 summarise the findings detailed in previous chapters and visualise the multi-dimensional connections between a set of background variables and trust, confidence and internal capabilities.

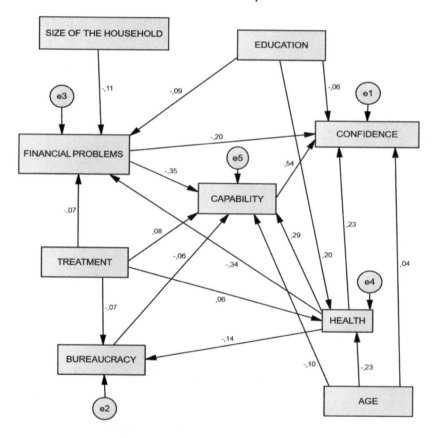

Figure 10.2   Heuristic model on associations between capability and receiving basic income and the background variables

CONCLUSIONS

In this chapter, we were interested in the relationships between basic income, trust, confidence and internal capabilities. We asked whether the level of trust in other people and societal institutions, confidence in oneself and in one's future, and the assessed set of capabilities differed between those who received basic income in the Finnish basic income experiment and a control group.

The overall conclusion we can draw from the results of our analysis is that receiving basic income increases trust and confidence, although indirectly. To enhance people's trust and confidence, a decent income and good health are prerequisites: the more severe financial problems a household faces, and the more health problems a person has, the more difficult it is to enhance trust and confidence, even if social benefits are paid unconditionally.

A mundane and bold explanation for the observed higher levels of trust among basic income receivers might be that there is an unobserved heterogeneity between the survey respondents in the treatment and control groups. The analyses presented herein are based on a survey that, unfortunately, had low response rates; thus, the representativeness of the data can be legitimately questioned. However, if our tentative findings are corroborated either by previous empirical findings or by relevant theories, or preferably by both, then we can be more confident in our results, and it might be more interesting to tell a story that is grounded in the ample theoretical literature on trust and how it can evolve.

Both financial and health problems are common in the target group of the Finnish experiment, which comprised unemployed job seekers who received flat-rate unemployment benefits from the Social Insurance Institution of Finland (instead of earnings-related benefits from the country's unemployment funds) at the beginning of the experiment. These unemployed job seekers have typically been unemployed for a long period, for example, due to health problems (see also OECD, 2020). Indeed, as shown in Table 10.1, trust was lower among both the treatment and control groups than among non-unemployed fellow citizens. However, both trust and confidence were significantly higher in the treatment group than in the control group, indicating that basic income may enhance both, even if only indirectly.

In this chapter, we were also interested in the role of capabilities in confidence-building. Obviously, we cannot state any causal relationships between these two variables or other variables used in the SEM; however, as a heuristic tool, SEM helped us elaborate descriptive associations between variables. In the latter structural equation model (Figure 10.2), we observed an indirect loop from treatment to confidence through capabilities, asserting that receiving basic income positively correlates with capabilities and capabilities positively impact confidence. This result is unsurprising considering the vast literature on the central role of capabilities in well-being and life in general.

Theoretically, the higher levels of trust and self-confidence observed among the recipients of basic income may be explained by ideas of recognition and dignity, as posited by Honneth and Frazer (2003: 9), who argue '…that neither redistribution alone nor recognition alone can suffice to overcome injustice today; thus, they need somehow to be reconciled and combined'. Only recognition and redistribution together can allow for the right kind of justice, namely the ideal of 'participatory parity', which guarantees that each subject is afforded equal participation in public life, as demanded by Sen (1999, 2010) and Nussbaum (2011).

On the one hand, Frazer's ideas can be applied when trying to understand why a basic income might enhance trust and confidence. A recognition of clients' needs is an important aspect of decent treatment, although, on the other hand, recognition can also be used as an argument *against* basic income: a universal, homogeneous and unconditional benefit such as a basic income does not recognise individual or group-based differences in the same way that more targeted benefits do. However, targeted benefits generally include a lot of screening and discretion, which may cause feelings of unjust processes when social benefits are applied. If the system is not able to recognise the individual's needs and, at worst, bypasses them completely, the likelihood of breaking trusting relationships between the social security system and citizens is high.

To conclude, we need trust, but it is not all we need: trustworthy institutions are also required. Following Heimer's (2001) line of argumentation, we propose that those institutions that treat clients with dignity and decency and protect them from various vulnerabilities and risks in life enhance trust, strengthen self-confidence, and fortify capacity-building. A quotation from Standing (2020: 3) brings these ideas closer to the debate on basic income: 'A basic income would also strengthen social solidarity, including human relations: it would be an expression that we all are part of a national community, sharing the benefits of the national public wealth created over our collective history'.

The main lesson from the Finnish basic income experiment could be understood as follows. Decent minimum income protection – be it basic income or the Finnish variant of residence-based basic security – is a necessary condition for the fulfilment of the grand goals the protagonists of the basic income advocate. However, this is not a sufficient condition for achieving these goals. In addition, we also need the amplitude of social, health care, educational, and employment services in order to support individuals to fully utilise their internal capabilities.

Finally, considering the empirical results from our own survey and the vast academic literature on trust, confidence, and capabilities, we can confidently argue that the questions of the relationships between basic income and trust, basic income and confidence, and basic income and capabilities are of the utmost relevance, and that enhancing trust and confidence, strengthening citizens' capabilities and ensuring decent social security should be the most important goals when reforming the current social security systems in Finland and elsewhere.

NOTES

1. Cronbach's alpha for the eight trust variables was 0.919, for the three confidence variables 0.821, and for the three variables measuring capabilities 0.709.
2. This result was also corroborated by analyses performed on the ESS 2018 data.

REFERENCES

Andreasson, U. (2017), *Trust – The Nordic Gold, Nordic Council of Ministers Analysis Report*. Copenhagen: Nordic Council of Ministers.

Atherton, S., Antley, A., Evans, N., Cernis, E., Lister, R., Dunn, G., Slater, M. and Freeman, D. (2016), 'Self-Confidence and Paranoia: An Experimental Study Using an Immersive Virtual Reality Social Situation', *Behavioural & Cognitive Psychotherapy*, 44(1), 56–64.

Bénabou, R. and Tirole, J. (2002), 'Self-Confidence and Personal Motivation', *The Quarterly Journal of Economics*, 117(3), 871–915.

Byrne, B. (2010), *Structural Equation Modelling with AMOS*, London: Routledge.

Cofta, P. (2007), *Trust, Complexity and Control: Confidence in a Convergent World*, Chichester: John Wiley & Sons.

Costello, E. J., Compton, S. N., Keeler, G. and Angold, A. (2003), 'Relationships between Poverty and Psychopathology: A Natural Experiment', *JAMA*, 290(15), 2023–9.

ESS (2018), Round, E. 9, European Social Survey Round 9 Data, Data File edition 3.0, Norway: NSD – Norwegian Centre for Research Data, Data Archive and Distributor of ESS Data for ESS ERIC, available at doi:10.21338/NSD-ESS9-2018 (accessed 11 December 2020).

Forget, E. L. (2011), 'The Town with No Poverty: The Health Effects of a Canadian Guaranteed Annual Income Field Experiment', *Canadian Public Policy*, 37(3), 283–305.

Forget, E. (2018), *Basic Income for Canadians. The Key to a Healthier, Happier, More Secure Life for All*, Toronto: James Lorimer and Co.

Fukuyama, F. (1995), *Trust. The Social Virtues and the Creation of Prosperity*, London: Pelican Books.

Fukuyama, F. (2011), *The Origins of Political Order. From Prehuman Times to French Revolution*, London: Profile Books.

Fukuyama, F. (2014), *Political Order and Political Decay. From the Industrial Revolution to the Globalisation of Democracy*, London: Profile Books.

Fukuyama, F. (2019), *Identity: Contemporary Identity Politics and the Struggle for Recognition*, London: Profile Books.

Halvorsen, R., Hvinden, B. and Schoyen, M. A. (2016), 'The Nordic Welfare Model in the Twenty-First Century: The Bumble-Bee Still Flies!', *Social Policy & Society*, 15(1), 57–73.

Heimer, C. (2001), 'Solving the Problem of Trust', in Cook, K. S. (ed.), *Trust in Society*, New York: Russell Sage Foundation, pp. 40–88.

Honneth, A. (1992), *The Struggle for Recognition: The Moral Grammar of Social Conflicts*, Cambridge: Polity Press.

Honneth, A. and Frazer N. (2003), *Redistribution or Recognition?: A Political-Philosophical Exchange*, London: Verso.

Hudson, J. (2006), 'Institutional Trust and Subjective Well-Being across the EU', *Kyklos*, 59(1), 43–62.

Larsen, C. A. (2016), *The Institutional Logic of Welfare Attitudes: How Welfare Regimes Influence Public Support*, London: Routledge.

Layard, R. (2006), *Happiness. Lessons from a New Science*, London: Penguin Books.

Mann, M., Hosman, C., Schaalma, H. and de Vrieset, N. (2004), 'Self-Esteem in a Broad-Spectrum Approach for Mental Health Promotion', *Health and Education Research, Health Education Research*, 19(4), 357–72.

Maslow, A. H. (1987), *Motivation and Personality*, Delhi: Pearson Education.

Nussbaum, M. C. (2011), *Creating Capabilities: The Human Development Approach*, Cambridge, London: The Belknap Press of Harvard University Press.

OECD (2020), *Faces of Joblessness. A People-centred Perspective on Employment Barriers and Policies*, Paris: OECD.

Ostrom, E. (1990), *Governing the Commons: The Evolution of Institutions for Collective Action*, Cambridge: Cambridge University Press.

Putnam, R. (2000), *Bowling Alone: The Collapse and Revival of American Community*, New York: Simon & Schuster.

Rawls, J. (1993), *Political Liberalism*, New York: Columbia University Press.

Rothstein, B. (2005), *Social Traps and the Problem of Trust*, Cambridge: Cambridge University Press.

Sen, A. (1992), *Inequality Re-Examined*, New York and Oxford: Clarendon Press, Oxford University Press.

Sen, A. (1999), *Development as Freedom*, New York: Oxford University Press.

Sen, A. (2010), *The Idea of Justice*, London: Penguin Books.

Stata (2011), *Structural Equation Modelling, Release 12*, TX: College Station: A Stata Press Corporation.

Stiglitz, J., Fitoussi, J. and Durand, M. (eds) (2018), *For Good Measure: Advancing Research on Well-Being Metrics Beyond GDP*, Paris: OECD.

Standing, G. (2020), *Battling Eight Giants: Basic Income Now*, London: Tauris.

Svallfors, S. (2012), 'Welfare States and Welfare Attitudes', in Svallfors S. (ed.), *Contested Welfare States. Welfare Attitudes in Europe and Beyond*, Stanford: Stanford University Press, pp. 1–24.

Svendsen, G. and Svendsen, G. (2016), *Trust, Social Capital and the Scandinavian Welfare State*, Cheltenham: Edward Elgar Publishing.

Sztompka, P. (1999), *Trust. A Sociological Theory*, Cambridge: Cambridge University Press.

Tyler, T. (2001), 'Why Do People Rely on Others? Social Identity and the Social Aspect of Trust', in Cook K. S. (ed.), *Trust in Society*, New York: Russell Sage Foundation, pp. 285–306.

Tyler, T. R. and Huo, Y. J. (2002), *Trust in the Law: Encouraging Public Cooperation with the Police and Courts*, New York: Russell Sage Foundation.

Van Parijs, P. (1995), *Real Freedom for All: What (If Anything) Can Justify Capitalism*, Oxford: Oxford University Press.

Van Parijs, P. and Vanderborght, Y. (2017), *Basic Income: A Radical Proposal for a Free Society and a Sane Economy*, Cambridge: Harvard University Press.

11. What explains the popular support for basic income?

Miska Simanainen and Olli Kangas

INTRODUCTION

There is growing interest in understanding the popular support for basic income in Finland and globally. On the one hand, researchers have tried to evaluate the level of support in different countries, and, on the other hand, to explain the variation of support within populations. In addition to scientific curiosity, there are practical reasons for surveying population support. These reasons are closely linked to politics and policymaking: for example, political parties aim to understand the opinions of the electorate to frame their political agenda in a way that resonates with opinions among their possible voters and maximises their political support in elections.

During the last two decades, support for basic income has been stable in Finland. Surveys carried out before the Finnish basic income experiment showed that about 60 to 70 percent of Finns were in favour of universal basic income (Airio et al., 2016; Andersson and Kangas, 2005). However, recent studies on popular support have provided highly divergent results. Differences in the results of separate surveys are likely related to differences in the definitions of basic income given in the questionnaires. Previous research has shown that there tends to be a substantial framing effect on the level of support for policy issues (Rasinski, 1989). Moreover, such general questions as 'Are you in favour of or against basic income?' and 'Is basic income good or bad?' tend to produce much higher support levels than more specific questions that aim to explain the content of the basic income model (Pulkka, 2018). One obvious feature of general survey questions on basic income is that they do not give any indication to the respondent about the possible costs of implementing basic income. In some Finnish surveys, the respondents were given more detailed information about the costs and tax levels needed to finance the benefit. Such more-detailed information decreased the support levels to lower than 30 percent (Airio et al., 2016).

As regard public support for basic income, Finland is ranked in a middle position internationally. The 2016 wave of the European Social Survey (ESS) included a question about basic income. The scheme was described as a universal transfer that everyone receives from the state, regardless of any other sources of income. In the ESS survey, basic income was described as covering essential living costs and replacing many other social benefits. Meanwhile, the strongest support for basic income was found in Russia (73 percent) and Israel (65 percent), and the weakest support was found in Sweden, Switzerland and Norway (37, 35 and 34 percent, respectively). In Finland, 65 percent of the population supported the basic income model as worded in the ESS (Fitzgerald, 2017).

In their comparative study, Roosma and van Oorschot (2020) found that, in Europe, basic income is supported in countries with low levels of social spending and high levels of material deprivation. Parolin and Sjöland (2020) showed that in countries with high union density, support for basic income is lower than in countries with lower unionisation rates. Given these findings, Finland appears to be an interesting case: its social spending is one of the highest in the world, material and social deprivation among the lowest, the welfare state is rather generous, and the unionisation rate is the highest in Europe. However, support for basic income in Finland seems to be much higher than in many other countries.

In this chapter, we are interested in the underlying reasons for the support for basic income, that is, why some people are more inclined to favour and others to oppose universal and unconditional income transfers. In previous studies on the support for basic income, socio-economic and demographic factors, such as gender, age, education and income, and political affiliation have been shown to be important explanatory variables (Andersson and Kangas, 2004, 2005; Pulkka, 2018; Roosma and van Oorschot, 2020; Simanainen and Kangas, 2020). In our subsequent inspections, we extend the analysis by studying other potential determinants of basic income support. These include (1) income inadequacy and insecure employment relations, and (2) perceptions of the causes of social problems and specific opinions about basic income. We explore the above-mentioned potential explanatory factors by utilising survey data from two opinion surveys conducted after the Finnish experiment.

The study sheds light on the role of material conditions (income and employment) and attitudinal aspects in explaining basic income support within the Finnish population.

The rest of the chapter proceeds as follows. First, we present the theoretical motivation for our research questions and the survey data used in the empirical analyses. The empirical sections focus on different potential explanations for popular support.

136 *Experimenting with unconditional basic income*

We analyse how income inadequacy and insecure employment relations are associated with the likelihood of supporting basic income. Then, we analyse how perceptions of 'deservingness' (whether individuals' social problems are the result of their own actions or rather of social structures) are linked to the popular support of basic income. Thereafter, we focus on the association between basic income support and specific opinions on the characteristics of basic income. In the final section, we summarise our findings and discuss their societal relevance.

THEORETHICAL FRAMEWORK, OBJECTIVES AND METHODS

Income Inadequacy and Insecure Employment

There are many doomsday prophesies that robots will take over human labour and that there will be massive disappearance of paid (human) work in the future (Frey and Osborne, 2017). The development of the digital mode of production has been seen to lead to mass unemployment. While the prophesies about the end of work may be too premature, the new digital economy will likely change the characteristics of employment in the future; for example, it has been calculated that one-third of the traditional jobs in Finland could disappear and be replaced by new types of employment (Pajarinen and Rouvinen, 2014). In other countries, this process may be even faster. Technological change may also lead to polarisation in labour markets: employment bifurcates into the expansion of low-paid and precarious employment on the one hand and high-skilled employment with secure positions on the other hand. Moreover, the share of middle-skilled routine jobs may diminish (for example, Frey and Osborne, 2017; Goos et al., 2010).

In his *Global Labour Flexibility*, Guy Standing (1999) analyses major trends in labour markets and concludes that flexibility means increasing insecurity that gradually threatens the sustainability of the entire production system. Standing (2011, 2016) further develops the idea of the 'precariat' as a danger-ous class whose problems must be solved. There are two aspects to the problem of the precariat: the first pertains to the unsecure position between employment and under-employment, and the second to inadequate income protection that the class faces. Due to these problems, people in the precariat are volatile, may create instability in the society, and may become frustrated and easy prey for populist and extreme social and political movements, argues Standing. Thus, in a Polanyian sense (Polanyi, 2001 [1944]), a new social policy system is functionally needed to fix the problems of capitalism and prevent the economic system from destroying itself. The advocates of basic income see basic income as the new social policy system answering the problems created by technological change (Standing, 2016; see also Bregman, 2017).

Attitudes and opinions in general and attitudes toward the welfare state in particular are sensitive to individuals' positions in the social stratification system (Larsen, 2006; Roosma and van Oorschot, 2020; Svallfors, 2012). In this study, we hypothesise that those in insecure labour market positions are more likely to support universal basic income than those coping better or having more secure labour contracts. In the following empirical section, we aim to shed light on the potential association between insecure employment and popular support for basic income. In particular, we analyse whether there are any systematic differences in the opinions of those who have permanent jobs versus fixed-term employment contracts, and of those who are working full-time or part-time, or who have only zero-hour contracts. Furthermore, we analyse how people's perceptions of income adequacy are associated with their opinions on basic income.

Values, Attitudes and Item-specific Opinions

Values define what is good and bad in our society (Rokeach, 1973). There is a correspondence between values and attitudes, and in the transition from value preferences to various issue attitudes (Jacoby, 2006). However, purely based on individuals' value structures, we cannot say much about individuals' attitudes and opinions on more specific social questions (Zaller, 1992). Individuals can share the same values (such as freedom and happiness) but their opinions on practical social and political issues and, hence, on wished-for policy options may be very different. Therefore, we have to narrow our scope and step down from values to focus on attitudes on social matters and to more specific issue opinions.

Attitudes and opinions are more volatile and less stable over time than values, and they may change when new information and experiences are received. Attitudes are states of mind representing individuals' propensity to respond in a certain way to a given stimulus (for example in opinion surveys), whereas issue opinions are more specific, bound to a specific and more detailed question.

In our analyses, we assume that attitudes pertain to a more generic way of thinking about the reasons for becoming a welfare recipient. Van Oorschot and Halman (2000) distinguish between two general explanations or popular perceptions of why some individuals have fallen into poverty, whereas others have not (see also van Oorschot, 2000; Andersson and Kangas, 2004, 2005; Niemelä, 2008; van Oorschot et al., 2017). According to the first brand of explanations, 'individual blame', people face problems because they lack will-power. Oftentimes, also the welfare state is blamed: it is seen to create

138 *Experimenting with unconditional basic income*

overly strong incentives for people not to take care of themselves, and as seducing people into idleness (for example, Murray, 1984).

The second category of explanations, 'social blame', pertains to a number of social injustices and social problems created by societal structures and changes. According to this line of thinking, the existing measures that the welfare state offers are not strong enough to help the poor out of poverty.

There is an abundance of more specific arguments presented in favour of and against basic income. The proponents of basic income regard it as a source of emancipation and real freedom (Van Parijs, 1995; Standing, 2017; Van Parijs and Vanderborght, 2017), solutions to various problems of precarious employment (Standing, 1999, 2011), and as a way to diminish bureaucracy and simplify the overly complicated and non-transparent 'jungle' of social benefits. Communitarians support basic income because they see that it would enhance voluntary work, facilitate activities in the third sector, and fortify their responsibilities toward fellow citizens (Etzioni and Platt, 2008). On the other side of the demarcation line, opponents are afraid of detrimental labour market effects – basic income would decrease labour supply (for a discussion, see Knotz, 2019). Moreover, there are arguments that the one-size-fits-all approach is not a good strategy: basic income does not take into consideration individual circumstances and therefore, on top of basic income, myriad other benefits and services would still be needed. Otherwise, those in the weakest positions would be left without adequate support. At the end of the day, basic income would not reduce bureaucracy; on the contrary, bureaucracy would increase (see, for example, De Wispelaere and Stirton, 2013).

Based on the aforementioned ways of reasoning about the characteristics of basic income, we develop a battery of item-specific questions to look into popular perceptions on the potential consequences of introducing a basic income (see Table 11A.1 in Appendix). In this study, we hypothesise that the two attitudinal dimensions, that is, individual and social blame, are systematically related to more detailed and item-specific opinions about basic income and, more importantly, to the popular support for introducing basic income in Finland.

Data and Methods

To find evidence on the research questions presented in the previous section, we utilise data from two survey studies. First, the subsection on income inadequacy and insecure employment draws on data from a population survey carried out via telephone from February–March 2020. The survey contains responses from 2500 respondents. The data sample is weighted by age, gender, and place of residence to represent the total Finnish population. Second, data on attitudes and item-specific opinions are from a thematic opinion survey conducted in the same period. The data include responses from a survey sample of 1002 respondents and represent the mainland Finnish population.

For descriptive analyses, we present cross-tabulations of the distribution of opinions for different survey questions. To study the associations between the variables, we utilise regression analysis. In the analyses, we control for the known demographic and socio-economic determinants of the variables and present the results only for our variables of focus. To squeeze the number of variables included in the analyses, we rely on factor analysis to determine whether it is meaningful to construct additive summative variables out of several survey questions. The validity of the additive summary variables is evaluated using Cronbach's alpha.

EXPLAINING THE SUPPORT FOR BASIC INCOME IN FINLAND: EMPIRICAL EXPLORATIONS

Income Inadequacy and Insecure Employment

A population survey conducted in early 2020 as part of the evaluation project of the Finnish basic income experiment explored the association between experienced income inadequacy and insecure employment relations and the support for basic income in Finland. According to the study, at the population level, the experience of inadequate household income was associated with support for basic income: the more difficult the respondent's perceived financial position was, the more likely he or she was to support the introduction of a basic income. About 43 percent of the respondents who indicated that they had no difficulties meeting their needs supported basic income. On the other hand, about 54 percent of those who had some difficulties in meeting their needs with household income, and about 74 percent of those who had major difficulties, reported supporting basic income (Simanainen and Kangas, 2020).

Among those who were employed, the type of employment contract was associated with attitudes toward basic income as well. Both part-time and fixed-term work contracts increased the probability of supporting basic income. About 44 percent of people with full-time and permanent work contracts supported the idea of introducing basic income in Finland. For those with a permanent but part-time contract, the share was 53 percent. Meanwhile, 58 percent of those with a fixed full-time contract supported basic income. Finally, the support rate for basic income was as high as 71 percent in the group with a fixed part-time contract (Simanainen and Kangas, 2020).

Table 11.1 presents a regression analysis of the association between income inadequacy and type of employment and the support for basic income with controls for gender, age, municipality group, labour market position, education, income and household type. We find statistically significant estimates

140   *Experimenting with unconditional basic income*

for the association between income inadequacy and type of employment (fixed-term and part-time contracts) and support for basic income. Moreover, having a fixed contract is a stronger determinant of support than working part-time. With additional control variables included, the explanatory power of the models is about 5 percent. The relatively low explanatory power of the model motivates us to explore other potential explanatory factors for the support of basic income in the population.

Table 11.1   *Regression analysis results on the determinants of support for basic income in Finland 2020: income inadequacy and insecure employment*

	Coefficient	p-value	adj. R^2	N
Type of employment (model 1)			0.04	1355
Full-time, permanent (reference)	–	–		
Full-time, fixed-term	0.23	0.07		
Part-time, permanent	0.09	0.54		
Part-time, fixed-term	0.50	0.01		
Zero-hour contract	0.34	0.27		
Inadequate income (model 2)	0.24	0.01	0.06	2360

Notes: In Model 1, explanatory variables include type of employment, income inadequacy, gender, age, municipality group, education, income and household size. Model 2 includes income inadequacy, gender, age, municipality group, labour market status, education, income and household size. The dependent variable is measured with the following survey question: 'What do you think about the following statement? A basic income should be introduced as a permanent part of the social security system in Finland: strongly agree (5), somewhat agree (4), neither agree nor disagree (3), somewhat disagree (2), strongly disagree (1) and cannot say (excluded from the analysis)'. Income inadequacy is measured with: 'Which of the following best describes your household income at present? We live comfortably on our current income or we are doing OK (0), we have difficulties or we are barely getting by (1), not sure (excluded)'.

Deservingness: Individual or Social Blame?

General opinions on the reasons why people have social and financial problems and need support from the welfare state are strongly related to more specific opinions on the welfare state, its characteristics, scope, size, and legitimacy. In Table 11.2, we present the six questions used in the opinion survey to measure respondents' views on the causes of unemployment: whether they are related to individual factors (own fault), or to various societal problems and structural changes in the society. Similarly, the respondents could express their opinions about why people are poor and if it is too easy to obtain social benefits.

Table 11.2   Perceived causes for unemployment and poverty among the Finns in 2020

	Causes of unemployment			Causes of poverty		
	1. Own fault (%)	2. Societal problems (%)	3. Structural change (%)	4. People do not try hard enough (%)	5. Inadequate basic security (%)	6. It is too easy to live on social benefits (%)
Fully disagree	45.7	6.2	5.0	33.0	12.4	16.2
Partially disagree	36.9	26.7	18.1	37.0	37.2	25.0
Partially agree	13.5	49.8	56.5	22.4	33.6	35.0
Fully agree	2.5	11.2	13.0	4.6	11.3	20.6
Do not know	1.4	6.1	7.0	3.0	5.5	3.2

A majority of the respondents considered unemployment and poverty to be caused by factors beyond individuals' own control, whereas about half of the respondents considered that social benefits in Finland are too lucrative and too easy to live on. To determine the extent to which responses to these questions possibly cluster into social blame and individual blame dimensions, we ran a factor analysis. The answers loaded on two distinct factors, and the loadings were strong and clear. On the one hand, questions 2, 3 and 5 formed their own 'social blame' component and questions 1, 4 and 6 clustered on the 'individual blame' attitudinal dimension. Based on these results, we formed two additive variables that were used in the regression models presented in Table 11.3. Cronbach's alpha was 0.628 for social blame and 0.679 for individual blame.

According to the analysis, gender is not significantly related to individual or social blame. Whereas age increases the propensity to emphasise social explanations, age is not significantly associated with individual blame. Although education and income are strongly correlated, the association between education and income vis-à-vis social blame and individual blame moves in different directions. While higher levels of education are positively associated with social blame and negatively associated with individual blame, the opposite is true for income. A closer analysis shows an interesting interaction: those with high educational attainments but low income tend to blame societal factors,

142   *Experimenting with unconditional basic income*

whereas high-income earners with low educational achievements are more prone to blame individuals.

Both dimensions are correlated with political affiliations. If we use the voters for the National Coalition Party (the Conservatives) as a reference point, voters for all other parties – with the exception of the Centre Party – are significantly more against blaming the individual when background variables are controlled for. As far as social blame is concerned, only voters for the Social Democrats, the Left Alliance, and the Greens significantly deviate from the voters for the National Coalition.

Attitudes on Deservingness, Item-specific Opinions, and Support for Basic Income

The respondents could respond separately to each item-specific question about the anticipated consequences of introducing basic income in Finland. The response scale ranged from 0 (totally disagree) to 10 (totally agree). The means for each question are presented in the appendix (Table 11A.1). In the positive attributes, the means varied from a low of 5.71 for 'Social spending would decrease' to a high of 6.84 for 'Social security for short-term employees and the self-employed would improve'. In the negative item-specific opinions, the lowest mean 5.04 was for 'Because of duplicate benefits paid, the social security system would become more complicated' (mean = 5.04) and the highest one for 'Responsibilities between individuals and the state would become blurred' (mean = 5.53). The means of the responses show that the positive aspects have a slightly stronger acceptance than the negative ones. The Finns seem to have at least a lukewarm positive perception to the specific outcomes of basic income.

As in the case of the attitudinal dimensions of deservingness, we ran factor analysis to reduce the number of variables. The item-specific questions were loaded into two factors. Based on these results, we formed two additive variables with high consistency. Cronbach's alpha for the positive dimension was as high as 0.899 and for the negative dimension it was 0.857. Thereafter, we ran regressions to study the connections between demographic background variables and political affiliations, and positive and negative item-specific opinions on basic income.

Regarding positive opinions, income had a negative and significant regression coefficient. Those in higher income groups were sceptical about the beneficial aspects of basic income. Gender, age, and education were not significant. In comparison with the voters for the Conservatives, voters for the Greens, the Left Alliance, and Social Democrats had significantly more positive views, whereas the Centre Party and the Finns Party

What explains the popular support for basic income? 143

Table 11.3   *Regression analysis results on the determinants of support for basic income in Finland 2020: deservingness and opinions on the characteristics of basic income, coefficients and p-values*

Model	M1	M2	M3	M4	M5
Social blame	0.07		0.05	0.06	0.06
	(<0.001)		(<0.001)	(<0.001)	(<0.001)
Individual blame	−0.10		−0.07	−0.07	−0.06
	(<0.001)		(<0.001)	(<0.001)	(<0.001)
Positive opinions		0.21	0.19	0.18	0.17
		(<0.001)	(<0.001)	(<0.001)	(<0.001)
Negative opinions		−0.04	−0.02	−0.04	−0.03
		(<0.001)	(0.216)	(0.007)	(0.047)
Party affiliation					
Conservatives (reference)					
Finns Party					0.18
					(0.083)
Centre					0.17
					(0.173)
Greens					0.41
					(<0.001)
SDP					0.15
					(0.172)
Left Alliance					0.32
					(0.019)
Adj. R^2	0.08	0.18	0.23	0.30	0.31

Notes: Model 1 considers only social blame and individual blame; Model 2 considers only positive and negative attributes of basic income; Model 3 = Model 1 + Model 2; Model 4 = Model 3 and age, gender, income and education controlled for; and Model 5 = Model 4 and political affiliation. The dependent variable is measured with the following survey question: 'What do you think about the following statement? A basic income should be introduced as a permanent part of the social security system in Finland: strongly agree (5), somewhat agree (4), neither agree nor disagree (3), somewhat disagree (2), strongly disagree (1) and cannot say (excluded from the analysis)'.

144 *Experimenting with unconditional basic income*

voters did not deviate from the Conservatives. With regard to negative attributes, age and gender were significantly associated with critical opinions. Criticism increased when moving from younger to older age groups and from women to men. Education significantly decreases negative opinions, such as voting for the Left Alliance, Social Democrats, Centre or the Greens.

Table 11.3 gives a numeric summation of the discussion presented above. Attitudinal dimensions have a highly significant association with support for basic income, and the association remains significant, even when the two variables pertaining to item-specific opinions (Model 3) and political affiliations are added to the model and demographic background variables are controlled for (Model 5). Positive item-specific opinions are highly significantly linked to support for basic income in all the models, whereas negative perceptions have weaker connections and their coefficients sometimes lose significance. Of the political affiliations depicted in Model 5, only voting for the Greens and the Left Alliance is a significant determinant of a positive basic income opinion.

The first, attitudinal model explains 8 percent of the variation (Adj. R^2) in the support for basic income. The second model, with specific characteristics of basic income as independent variables, performs better and increases the variance explained to 18 percent. If we combine both the attitudinal and item-specific variables, as in Model 3, the R^2-values increase further. However, introducing demographic controls (Model 4) or political affiliations of the respondents (Model 5) did not substantially increase the variance explained.

Based on this study, we cannot establish whether values, attitudes, and opinions come first followed by party affiliation, whether it is vice versa, or whether they are formed simultaneously. The cross-sectional and one-dimensional analysis carried out above cannot reveal all the multidimensional interactions between various demographic, socio-economic, and other background variables, attitudes, item-specific opinions of basic income, and political affiliations. In the concluding section, we attempt to provide a heuristic description of the possible multidimensional relationships of different factors behind the popular support for basic income.

CONCLUSIONS AND DISCUSSION

This chapter focused on different factors explaining the support for basic income in Finland. We used data from two opinion surveys to explore the potential determinants of popular support.

We first analysed how income inadequacy and insecure employment relations are associated with the likelihood of supporting or opposing basic income. Our analyses showed that fixed-term full- and part-timers are more likely to support basic income than are those who have full-time and permanent contracts or part-timers with permanent jobs. This result fits our expectations: own experience of insecurity in the labour market is likely to affect how people view the desirability of basic income. According to the results, inadequate income increases the probability of supporting basic income.

Opinions on policy issues are also based on individuals' value preferences, which, in turn, are related in a number of ways to how people perceive societal problems. Previous studies show that support for social policy is strongly linked to the so-called 'deservingness' principle, that is, who should get what and on what grounds (van Oorschot et al., 2017). In the second part of our study, we focus on this value-based attitudinal dimension. Individual blame, pertaining to the view that social problems and welfare needs are a result of individuals' own actions. Social blame, meanwhile, refers to the societal roots of individual problems. These two dimensions appear to have significant ramifications for the support for basic income. Those who emphasise individual reasons tend to be sceptical of unconditional transfers, whereas the opposite is true for those who emphasise social blame: they tend to support basic income. The two dimensions of deservingness are also strongly linked to an individual's political affiliation. Voters for left-wing parties and the Greens are more inclined to emphasise the social blame paradigm than are voters for other parties.

From the analyses of deservingness, we then moved to more specific questions on the possible outcomes of introducing a basic income scheme. Not surprisingly, proponents regard basic income as a solution to many problems of the present social security system and the world's societies, while opponents of basic income emphasise its possible detrimental behavioural effects. Similar to deservingness, these item-specific dimensions are important determinants of the support for basic income.

If we then compare the relative significance of various background factors, our tentative conclusion is that, on the one hand, socio-economic characteristics and labour market statuses of respondents are important explanatory factors for basic income, but on the other hand, attitudinal dimensions in general and deservingness criteria in particular are even more relevant.

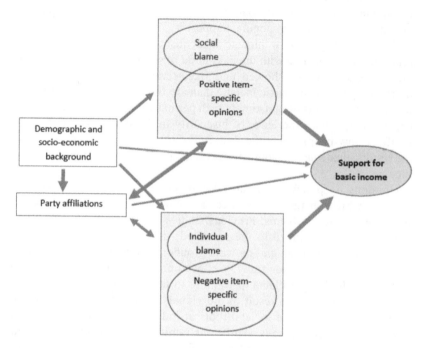

Figure 11.1 Summary of the relationships between demographic properties and labour market positions, political affiliations, views about deservingness, item-specific opinions concerning basic income, and support for basic income

Figure 11.1 summarises our previously presented analyses. The thickness of an arrow indicates the strength of the relationship between the study variables. Demographic factors and socio-economic status are linked to party preferences. Those with higher positions in the social hierarchy tend to vote for right-wing parties, adhere to individual blame explanations, and have negative views of the possible outcomes of basic income. Those on the lower ladder of the social hierarchy and uncertain labour market positions are more likely to emphasise societal reasons for individuals' problems and evaluate basic income in positive terms. As indicated by thicker arrows, the attitudinal dimensions are strongly associated with the likelihood of support for basic income. Double-headed thick arrows describe the dialectic interaction between values, attitudes, and item-specific opinions.

To more reliably study these linkages and even establish causality between the variables, we would need longitudinal data. Collecting such data is a task for future studies.

REFERENCES

Airio, I., Kangas, O., Koskenvuo, K., and Laatu, M. (2016), 'Tasaveroon pohjautuviin perustulomalleihin suhtaudutaan varauksellisesti' ['Scepticism against flat-rate tax based basic income models'], available at https://tutkimusblogi.kela.fi/arkisto/2942 (accessed 15 December 2020).

Andersson, J. O. and Kangas, O. (2004), 'Popular support for basic income in Sweden and Finland', in Standing, G. (ed.), *Promoting Income Security as a Right: Europe and North America*, London: Anathem Press, pp. 289–302.

Andersson, J. O. and Kangas, O. (2005), 'Universalism in the age of workfare: Attitudes to basic income in Sweden and Finland', in Kildal, N. and Kuhnle, S. (eds), *Normative Foundations of the Welfare State: The Nordic Experience*, London: Routledge, pp. 112–29.

Bregman, R. (2017), *Utopia for Realists and How We Can Get There*, London: Bloomsbury.

De Wispelaere, J. and Stirton, L. (2013), 'The politics of unconditional basic income: Bringing bureaucracy back in', *Political Studies*, 61(4), 915–32.

Etzioni, A. and Platt, A. (2008), *A Community-Based Guaranteed Income*, Oxford: The Foundation for Law, Justice and Society, University of Oxford.

Fitzgerald, R. (2017), 'Assessing support for universal basic income', available at https://www.europeansocialsurvey.org/findings/singleblog.html?a=/findings/blog/essblog0010.html (accessed 15 December 2020).

Frey, C. B. and Osborne, M. A. (2017), 'The future of employment: How susceptible are jobs to computerisation?', *Technological Forecasting & Social Change*, 114, 254–80.

Goos, M., Manning, A., and Salomons, A. (2010), *Explaining Job Polarization in Europe: The Roles of Technology, Globalization and Institutions*, London: London School of Economics, CEP Discussion Paper, No. 1026.

Jacoby, W. G. (2006), 'Value choices and American public opinion', *American Journal of Political Science*, 50(3), 706–23.

Knotz, C. (2019), 'Why countries "get tough on the work-shy": The role of adverse economic conditions', *Journal of Social Policy*, 48 (3), 615–34.

Larsen, C. A. (2006), *Institutional Logic of the Welfare Attitudes: How Welfare Regimes Influence Public Support?*, Chippenham: Ashgate.

Murray, C. (1984), *Losing Ground: American Social Policy 1950–1980*, New York: Basic Books.

Niemelä, M. (2008), 'Perceptions of the causes of poverty in Finland', *Acta Sociologica*, 51(1), 23–40.

Pajarinen, M. and Rouvinen, P. (2014), *Computerization Threatens One Third of Finnish Employment*, Helsinki: ETLA Brief 22.

Parolin, Z. and Sjöland, L. (2020), 'Support for a universal basic income: A demand–capacity paradox?', *Journal of European Social Policy*, 30(1), 5–19.

Polanyi, K. (2001 [1944]), *The Great Transformation: The Political and Economic Origins of Our Time*, 2nd edn, Boston: Beacon Press.

Pulkka, V.-V. (2018), 'Finland shares unconditional money, but the public view remains polarised', IPR Blog, available at http://blogs.bath.ac.uk/iprblog/2018/01/23/finland-shares-unconditional-money-but-the-public-view-remains-polarised/ (accessed 14 December 2020).

Rasinski, K. A. (1989), 'The effect of question wording on public support for government', *Public Opinion Quarterly*, 53(3), 388–94.

Rokeach, M. (1973), *The Nature of Human Values*, New York: Free Press.

Roosma, F. and Van Oorschot, W. (2020), 'Public opinion on basic income: Mapping European support for a radical alternative for welfare provision', *Journal of European Social Policy*, 30(2), 190–205.

Simanainen, M. and Kangas, O. (2020), 'Speaking to those who know it best: Does participation in an experiment explain citizens' attitudes to basic income?', *Journal of International & Comparative Social Policy*, 36(3), 1–15.

Standing, G. (1999), *Global Labour Flexibility,* Houndmills: Macmillan.

Standing, G. (2011), *The Precariat: The New Dangerous Class*, London: Bloomsbury.

Standing, G. (2016), *The Corruption of Capitalism. Why Rentiers Thrive and Work Does Not Pay*, London: Bite Back Publishing.

Standing, G. (2017), *Basic Income: And How We Can Make It Happen*, London: Pelican Books.

Svallfors, S. (ed.) (2012), *Contested Welfare States. Welfare Attitudes in Europe and Beyond*, Stanford: Stanford University Press.

Van Oorschot, W. (2000), 'Who should get what, and why? On deservingness criteria and the conditionality of solidarity among the public', *Policy & Politics*, 28(1), 33–48.

Van Oorschot, W. V. and Halman, L. (2000), 'Blame or fate, individual or social?', *European Societies*, 2(1), 1–28.

Van Oorschot, W., Roosma, F., Meuleman, B., and Reeskens, T. (eds) (2017), *The Social Legitimacy of Targeted Welfare: Attitudes to Welfare Deservingness*, Cheltenham: Edward Elgar Publishing.

Van Parijs, P. (1995), *Real Freedom for All: What (If Anything) Can Justify Capitalism?*, Oxford: Oxford University Press.

Van Parijs, P. and Vanderborght, Y. (2017), *Basic Income. A Radical Proposal for a Free Society and Sane Economy*, Cambridge MA and London: Harvard University Press.

Zaller, J. R. (1992), *The Nature and Origins of Mass Opinion*, Cambridge: Cambridge University Press.

APPENDIX

Table 11A.1   Means for item-specific question on the characteristics of basic income (0=fully disagree, 10=fully agree)

Item	Mean
If basic income was implemented:	
Bureaucracy in social security would decrease	6.52
Social spending would decrease	5.71
It would be easier to accept short-term and low-paid jobs	6.77
Social security for short-term employees and the self-employed would improve	6.84
Tax avoidance and fraud in social security would decrease	6.13
The unemployed would have better possibilities to participate in society	6.60
Individuals' freedoms to decide about their own business would increase	6.65
Those most in need would be left without adequate support	5.05
Low-paid 'slave' labour would increase	5.27
Idleness and laziness would increase	5.44
Responsibilities between the individual and society would be blurred	5.53
Because of duplicate benefits, the social security system would become more complicated	5.04
The ability of the social security system to respond to changes in the labour market would diminish	5.23

12. Life on basic income – Interview accounts by basic income experiment participants on the effects of the experiment

Helena Blomberg, Christian Kroll and Laura Tarkiainen

INTRODUCTION

The aims of the Finnish basic income experiment were strongly associated with the target population's employment status effects, since the main goals were to strengthen employment incentives and remove the conditionality of unemployment benefits. However, basic income proponents argue that the effects of basic income should be scrutinised in a broader sense than a narrow labour supply framework. For example, Van Parijs (2013) and Davala et al. (2015) claim that basic income is an emancipatory and participatory income promoting individuals' real freedom. In addition, as argued by Calnitsky (2016: 28), labour supply results tell little about how recipients experience basic income, and understand and interpret its effects. Thus, research on basic income experiments would benefit from considering various aspects of social and psychological consequences, as well as personal accounts by experiment participants on their effects.

In this chapter, we examine the effects of the Finnish basic income experiment by analysing qualitative interview accounts of 81 people who participated in the two-year experiment. In our theory-driven content analysis, we utilise Hannah Arendt's theory (Arendt, 1998 [1958]) on labour, work, and action modalities and Inger Jansson's interpretation of basic income's effects on these modalities (Jansson, 2019). By analysing interviewees' accounts in the light of Arendt's labour, work and action modalities, we aim to achieve a deeper understanding of the various effects of the basic income experiment.

We start by briefly introducing previous research on basic income and discussing our theoretical underpinnings. Then, we present our data and analysis

Life on basic income

process. Next, we examine the interviewees' accounts of the effects of utilising the framework of the labour, work and action modalities. In the concluding section, we reflect on our findings more broadly.

ON THE EFFECTS OF A BASIC INCOME

As pointed out elsewhere in this book, the concept of basic income has been discussed from a variety of theoretical and practical vantage points. For example, in Finland, basic income has been given multiple conflicting definitions, because it has been posited as a response to various issues, such as problems of welfare bureaucracy, fulfilment of social rights, incentives for paid work, and insecurity of 'precarious' employment (Perkiö, 2020a, 2020b). Thus, although basic income has often been presented as a simple and unified idea, concrete policy proposals have included varying goals and interpretations of it (De Wispelaere and Stirton, 2004). In the Finnish basic income experiment, the final design parameters can be regarded as the result of not only political, but also legal, institutional, and budgetary considerations and constraints (see De Wispelaere et al., 2018: 16).

Generally, existing research on basic income has largely focused on the normative discussions of its application, particularly with regard to work and employment (for reviews, see Kangas and Pulkka, 2016; Widerqvist, 2013). On the one hand, basic income is thought to incentivise paid work and provide a safety net and bargaining power to those who are subjected to insecure, poorly protected, and low-paid working conditions. Basic income is, for example, assumed to support those who perform sporadic and irregular entrepreneurial activities as well as project-based creative work (Jansson, 2019; Kangas and Pulkka, 2016). On the other hand, it is argued that basic income may present a risk of trapping precarious workers in insecure employment conditions (see Birnbaum and De Wispelaere, 2020).

Furthermore, it is claimed that basic income obscures the division between 'work' and 'non-work' (Pateman, 2004), when taking into account not just paid work in the labour market, but also the range of non-commodified forms of activities, such as domestic work, care work, community engagement, and voluntary work. In addition, basic income is thought to make it easier for an individual citizen to reduce working time, to take a break between jobs, to have the means to undertake further training, or to become self-employed (Van Parijs, 2001). Thus, it is argued that basic income challenges the centrality of paid work and decreases the shame and deleterious effects of unemployment (Sage, 2019). By various means, basic income may enhance individuals' freedom, autonomy, and emancipation (e.g. Standing, 2017; Van Parijs, 1995, 2013).

Because of its universality principle, basic income has been considered to eliminate explicit or implicit moral judgements and to reduce benefit stigma (Calnitsky, 2016; McKay, 2007). It has been perceived as providing a humane alternative to conditional traditional means-tested workfare programmes (Hamilton and Mulvale, 2019).

While empirical evidence on various issues regarding the effects of basic income often seem inconclusive to date, existing studies have often followed a quantitative methodological approach. In the relatively scarce body of qualitative work on basic income experiments, some studies have reported reduced stigma under an unconditional regime with a mixed group of recipients (Calnitsky, 2016), while others have reported that basic income has positive effects on recipients' self-dignity and experiences of trust (Bohmeyer and Cornelsen, 2019). In addition, basic income has outperformed traditional conditional welfare programmes with respect to long-term financial and future planning, improved nutrition, housing stability, physical and mental health, and social connections with friends and family (see Hamilton and Mulvale, 2019).

BASIC INCOME IN THE LABOUR, WORK AND ACTION MODALITY FRAMES

As pointed out above, a basic income can be assumed to affect people's employment and life trajectories in various ways, although it is far from clear how, since the assumptions presented include conflicting and contradictory ideas and conclusions. By approaching the Finnish basic income experiment from the perspective of participating individuals, we aim here to account for people's various social contexts in which 'everything affects everything'. Hence, our point of departure is that basic income should be assessed in relation to individuals' larger life situations and social contexts. We assume that people as actors pay attention to various aspects of life when making decisions related to paid employment and activities outside the labour market.

Arendt's (1998 [1958]) theory, known as vita activa, provides a theoretical framework that takes into account these various aspects. The main principle of the theory is that human activity is conditioned under three modalities: labour, work and action. These three modalities include everyday survival and consumption, utility and production; creating permanence and coexistence among humans; and human flourishing.

Arendt's thought has increasingly inspired researchers interested in welfare policy and occupational science, including some interested in basic income (Jansson, 2017, 2019; Sauer, 2015; Suuronen, 2018). For example, Jansson (2019) analysed Arendt's theory vis-à-vis people's occupational patterns and their experiences of occupational meaning. According to this view, the

Life on basic income 153

rationale underlying claims for basic income relies on different ideologies that can all be examined through the lens of labour, work and action modalities. Therefore, the effects of basic income should be assessed through not just one but all modalities, since people participate more or less in all of them. First, the 'labour' modality refers to the abolishment of bureaucratic payment transfer systems and work that secures everyday survival through paid work. Within the labour modality, basic income may help to liberate people from impossible demands of the labour market, but may also result in the risk of them becoming passive consumers, unable to fully participate in other modalities, that is, work and action. Jansson (2019: 132–4) seems to associate the Finnish basic income experiment's aims to alter the so-called bureaucratic and welfare 'traps' related to low-paid and sporadic jobs primarily with the labour modality.

Second, the 'work' modality refers to diminishing poverty and enhancing self-determined lives and work performed to create useful, permanent and sustainable production, beyond just survival. This could mean that with basic income, people may have better options to refuse jobs that are unethical or deleterious to both humans and the environment. This type of thinking emphasises the meaning of paid work and work communities as a means to guarantee individuals' autonomy and well-being. Finally, the 'action' modality refers to human activity performed in relation to other people in the public sphere, such as voluntary work. Within the action modality, basic income may enhance participation and shared political activity in forms other than paid work. Hence, basic income may enable actions that aim to deepen democracy and shared political and/or participatory activity among citizens (Jansson, 2019).

DATA

To obtain the type of qualitative data needed, the Social Insurance Institution of Finland delivered our research group's interview invitation and informed consent form to half (988 people) of the basic income experiment participants by mail. Those willing to participate in a face-to-face interview were asked to mail their consent forms directly to our research group, which was the only party with access to the interview data at any stage. This procedure was the result of the study being an independent part of the experiment's evaluation by a research group at the University of Helsinki. Therefore, the transfer of personal data was contingent on the explicit consent of the basic income experiment participants only. Taking into account this procedure, in which reminders were not allowed, our initial goal was to receive at least 50 signed consent forms. However, the expectations were exceeded, and a total of 106 informed consent forms were obtained during the period 3 February–16 March 2019.

We chose to conduct semi-structured interviews, which enabled us to freely discuss several themes relating to participants' experiences. The interviews

Table 12.1 Interviewees' background information (number of persons)

Gender	Female	42
	Male	38
	Non-binary	1
Age	25–34 years old	18
	35–44 years old	21
	45–61 years old	40
	No information	2
Residency	Uusimaa (including greater Helsinki area)	27
	Southern Finland	21
	Western Finland	24
	Northern and Eastern Finland	9

dealt with three core themes: (1) participants' general life situation and well-being; (2) unemployment, work, and bureaucratic encounters; and (3) interviewees' experiences as basic income experiment participants.

In our data collection, we kept conducting interviews until we reached a point at which we were assured that the accounts of basic income and the experiment started to resemble each other (e.g. Hennink et al., 2016). We ended up interviewing 81 people, notably more than our initial goal.

The interviews were conducted in quiet and easily accessible locations[1] that were suitable for the interviewees and caused them no extra expenses to travel to. Three people employed for the project conducted the interviews. The first pilot interview was conducted on 14 January 2019 and the remaining 80 interviews between 7 February 2019 and 4 June 2019; 74 interviews were conducted in Finnish, four in Swedish, and three in English.

The interviews lasted between 27 minutes and 2 hours 22 minutes. In total, we ended up with 88 hours and 1 minute of recorded interview material. The interviews were transcribed verbatim, resulting in 3893 pages of transcribed data. All data extracts used in this chapter were anonymised and translated into English.[2] We present information on the interviewees' backgrounds in Table 12.1.

Approximately two-thirds of our interviewees reported that they had gained paid employment during the experiment; 25 interviewees had been working in either longer fixed-term or permanent positions; and 14 had undertaken short-time and/or on-demand work. Five interviewees worked in creative fields and six were entrepreneurs. Five interviewees performed work supported by a pay subsidy. Around one-third of the interviewees did not gain any form of paid employment during the experiment. Of these interviewees, nine had studied full time, one had acted as (an unofficial) caregiver, six had

Life on basic income

been receiving activation services that promoted employment, and 12 were not involved in any of these activities.

ANALYSIS

For our analysis, we first read our data to make sense of it as a whole. Then, for closer analysis, we collected all data passages that dealt with interviewees' accounts of the experiments' effects. For the next stage of the analysis, we applied theory-driven content analysis on relevant data passages that were organised in correspondence with prior theoretical knowledge (Elo and Kyngäs, 2008).

We analysed our data with respect to the labour, work, and action modalities identified by Arendt (1998 [1958]), as well as the assumed effects of basic income on these activities (see Jansson, 2019). Nearly all of the interviewees touched upon these three modalities in one way or another while making sense of their experiences, for example, by making multiple justifications when describing factors that contribute to unemployed people's access to paid employment. By analysing these three modalities, we aimed to exemplify the diversity of interviewees' social contexts and manifold accounts of the experiment's effects. However, by focusing on the analysis of these modalities, we excluded several intriguing interview themes that were beyond the scope of our analysis.

The Labour Modality

We identified two different ways in which the interviewees described the effects of the basic income experiment related to labour modality activities: everyday survival and consumption. The first way concerns interviewees' descriptions that portray the basic income experiment as having been meaningful for meeting their basic human needs and allowing them to secure necessary consumption through paid employment. The second way is associated with accounts in which the interviewees described the minimal or non-existent effects the experiment had on their employment, living conditions, and/or consumption.

In interview accounts in which basic income was said to have strengthened the labour modality, the enhanced possibilities for accepting, in particular, short-time, part-time and gig jobs were highlighted. Some interviewees stated that favourable tax conditions that were a part of the experiment design had resulted in them taking jobs that had otherwise been too poorly paid and insecure. Others, in turn, had regarded their basic income as allowing them to decline job offers perceived as being too insecure or having very poor working conditions. For some interviewees, basic income had provided economic security, enhancing their life situation between different jobs, gigs, or contracts. In particular, this security was associated with part-time and zero-hour contracts in which earnings were varied and job contracts were characterised by breaks in between.

> During the basic income experiment, I was in a work trial that resulted in temporary contracts, and then an on-demand work contract. (--) When the experiment started, it immediately affected my mindset, that if I could get even small bits of work, I could have a chance to support myself. (--) Well, my salary was not amazingly high, so it [basic income] was a good supplement and I was able to get on very well with it during the experiment. And when I finished the temporary contract and got another, it was still really a good help for me. In particular, last summer, when I left that temporary contract and started this on-demand contract, it was an extra good supplement, as my earnings were really uncertain at the time. So it [basic income] brought loads of security to my life. (Interviewee 71)

The interviewees, however, talked about the labour modality in various ways, representing different ways of reasoning. For example, for some interviewees, the basic income experiment offered an opportunity to seek new options in the labour market, whereas others said that they had postponed their plans to study, for example, since it was worthwhile to work full-time and to have the untaxed basic income on top of their earnings. Hence, many interviewees stated that having a salary and basic income strengthened their ability to undertake long-term economic planning, for example, to consume, save money, and afford both basic necessities and small luxuries (see Hamilton and Mulvale, 2019: 588–90). However, some interviewees experienced economic difficulties and extra bureaucratic stress between jobs during the experiment, since unemployment insurance funds and trade unions had little knowledge of how the basic income affected earnings-related daily unemployment allowances.

Still, basic income combined with a salary was described as offering some of the interviewees a better living standard, instead of only covering everyday survival (cf. Jansson, 2019). During the experiment, some interviewees were able, for instance, to buy proper winter clothes or household appliances, to repair their car, to go to the cinema, to visit a restaurant, or to go to the hairdressers. Some interviewees had been able to invest in culture, travel, home decorating, visiting relatives, or children's recreational activities. Therefore, combining the basic income with a salary offered many interviewees a sense of security and continuity in their lives.

> I feel that I am economically a little bit stronger now. On my own, I happened to find a therapist whom I meet once a month. Just speaking about my issues has helped me to move forward with my life. [...] Basically, this basic income has paid for my therapy, which has helped me to cope in working life. (Interviewee 4)

Life on basic income 157

Basic income was described as being particularly motivating in situations in which it was combined with a salary paid from subsidised work. However, not all interviewees had internalised the benefits of the untaxed basic income until subsidised work started, that is, keeping the basic income untaxed on top of any earnings. On the one hand, basic income was portrayed as strengthening incentives for working in the intermediate labour market. On the other hand, the experiment caused disappointment to some interviewees, since despite their hopes and wishes, they did not gain access to 'proper jobs' within the open labour market owing to work ability limitations.

> When I got [from subsidised work with basic income] nearly the same sum as those who work as regular labourers, it motivated me insanely to work. To be honest, I was really upset when it [basic income] ended. I am a client of integrated services [Multi-sectoral Joint Service Promoting Employment], and the staff there told me many, many times that now it would be a profitable time to seek a job as one can get some extra money. [...] I have to say that it has bothered me that I didn't realise I could go somewhere earlier. Or, I don't know. [...] I had no work capacity then [...] I had long, long episodes in rehabilitative work and at the time, I had no strength to do proper jobs. I sort of have to admit it [not having working ability] to myself. Well, even these days, I sometimes have problems with my ability to cope, and my feelings are not always very good. (Interviewee 32)

Some interviewees described situations in which they had found it difficult to find employment, because they lacked work ability, or had only partial work capacity due to mental health issues, homelessness, or an otherwise difficult life situation. However, in these situations, some people gained paid employment at the end of the second year of the experiment. In these interview accounts, success in gaining employment is portrayed as a long-term project in which not just basic income but also support from officials and non-governmental organisations (NGOs) is described as meaningful. However, during the experiment, some participants were able to make longer-term plans for the future and to 'sort things out' after prolonged periods of unemployment.

> I must have been quite difficult to employ before I got into this basic income experiment. I had problems with my driving licence and it looked like a knot that would not open in any way. [...] When this basic income thingy started, I got some type of drive. I immediately thought that, God dammit, I have 2 years to get my shit together, to do as I want to. And so it went. I am very satisfied with all the things I achieved during these 2 years. And as a cherry on the top, during the last month, I found a place to work, which seems relatively long lasting. [...] I mean, this experiment gave me 2 years' timeframe to see the horizon. That really, now I have time to breathe. (Interviewee 74)

The other way to describe the effects of experiments on the labour modality deals with descriptions of minimal or non-existent effects. In these cases, the

158   *Experimenting with unconditional basic income*

interviewees had, for example, agreed to take on jobs prior to knowing about the experiment and/or jobs were easy to accept despite the experiment. Hence, the experiment was associated with little meaning vis-à-vis labour modality.

In other of these accounts, the interviewees made sense of the labour modality by presenting structural explanations for their situations. In these descriptions, the interviewees shared their aspirations with respect to the labour modality; however, heterogeneous reasons, such as their place of residence, age, disability, long-term illnesses, their educational background, and/or migrant status influenced their opportunities to gain employment (see also Calnitsky and Latner, 2017: 375, 390). Some interviewees also included descriptions in which the experiment was portrayed as 'unsuccessful' or 'wasted' in their cases, since their health or work ability did not allow them to strengthen the labour modality as a basic activity in their lives. Thus, in these cases, the experiment time was not described as differing significantly from the time of receiving traditional welfare.

> Well, all kinds of [services for promoting employment] have been tried. But I just can't [participate in them for health reasons]. [...] If I think about [basic income] financially, I was 100 percent sure when it came, as it came so steadily. But now [with traditional unemployment benefit] it comes in 4-week cycles, and it comes when it comes. [...] So it was a little easier [with basic income]. [...] Otherwise, I can't say, whether my [life situation] would have been any different. In the same way, the sun rises in the morning and sets in the evening. (Interviewee 2)

However, interviewees who had long-term illnesses and work ability limitations expressed that the basic income offered some kind of security owing to its regularity. The unconditionality of basic income was portrayed as meaningful for covering basic necessities, such as rent and medicine. However, the amount of the basic income in the experiment was described as too low to cover all necessities for everyday survival.

The Work Modality

The interview accounts for the effects of the experiment related to work modality activities deal with their descriptions of improved possibilities for making meaningful and sustainable decisions in the labour market. In particular, the experiment revealed that the work modality was strengthened in the case of interviewees who had either studied or worked as specialists, small business owners, or in creative fields.

Those interviewees who worked in creative fields stated that the basic income experiment had particularly positive effects in their situations in which freelance fees, hourly paid work and/or grants were combined. These interviewees stated that the basic income helped them to accept project-based and sporadic work, as it came with diminished bureaucratic load and lack of coercion and sanctions associated with traditional welfare. In addition, the basic income experiment was portrayed as having been helpful in terms of professional confidence and courage to pursue artistic aspirations, as well as strengthening general well-being, sense of control, and agency (see also Calnitsky and Latner, 2017: 392).

> Well, for sure, I can say that my well-being was better when I had basic income. It is about a feeling of freedom, and these psychological effects have been great. Whereas economically, the benefits have been nearly non-existent. But it is rather about not having that coercion in the background, so it increases creativity when you get the freedom. Then, creativity increases well-being. [...] So, it has provided me a feeling that I can focus on the matters that are relevant. [...] When the constant insecurity and regular hassle with benefits are gone, I mean the weariness of them, you can see that you are able to achieve miracles. When you don't always have to think whether I can accept this gig or not [without losing my benefits]. (Interviewee 6)

Interviewees who had worked in creative fields during the experiment said that the basic income was a relief for them owing to its economic predictability and stability. These aspects were portrayed as strengthening the interviewees' sense of security and helping them to free themselves from the stress related to income insecurity. However, these interview accounts on increased creativity were related to interviewees who had worked in creative fields prior to the experiment.

> Not much has changed, as I have reported my doings [to the Public Employment Services] in a similar way to before the experiment. I have had similar job gigs. The only positive thing I can say as an artist is that when you know that 560 euros will be deposited monthly into your account, I don't have to think about how much my monthly income will reduce my unemployment benefit. So, it has brought me some economic security. [...] And when you work in creative fields, it has a massive mental meaning. I mean what goes on in your head and what kinds of stress levels you have, so it has a significant meaning. [...] 560 euros is no astronomic sum at all. [...] Practically, it didn't increase my annual income at all, but it brought me some regularity. (Interviewee 13)

Some of the interviewees also stated that the experiment had freed them to educate themselves. In these accounts, descriptions of autonomy were emphasised, since during the experiment one could study without the Public Employment Services regulating the content, duration or means of those

160 *Experimenting with unconditional basic income*

studies. Thus, the basic income experiment freed some interviewees to channel their interests and motivated them to study instead of job seek.

> Well, if I am being totally honest, I have to say that it [basic income] has decreased [my job seeking] a bit. [...] But I have tried to perceive it in a way that I will now invest in my studies. First of all, I am a job seeker, so if I will get a job offer, I will prioritise it, and my studies will be secondary then. But I haven't been able to choose between these two. So, in that sense, my answer to your questions is that it [basic income] has made me a little bit passive. [...] However, it has rather enabled me to be myself. Because, if I use the word 'unemployed', the status of an unemployed person, I have never liked it at all. Because it has so much to do with the idea that society patronises me. [...] And work life for me [as a specialist] has been very independent and I have always been trusted. And all of a sudden, I am unemployed and all the trust is gone. So, in that sense, the basic income offered me the option to be trusted again. During these 2 years, I have been able to actualise myself, to participate in different events and study. (Interviewee 8)

The basic income experiment also helped some interviewees to upskill themselves in fields that would have been difficult or impossible to access with traditional conditional unemployment benefits. In these interview accounts, the possibility of advancing participants' studies was described as more meaningful than trying to achieve economic gains with basic income.

> I was studying in a field in which finding a job can be a little difficult. So [the basic income] was really a delightful thing for me [...] From time to time I thought, as I have that [anonymised] qualification, I could have gone to some [place of business] in Lapland for the summer, or some other place where there is a shortage of labour. But then again, it felt more meaningful to study. [...] I thought it was for my future. It was tempting to work, to get a basic income and salary, but then again, it felt more valuable and more important for me to find my own thing. (Interviewee 43)

Based on some of the interview accounts, the time during the basic income experiment was used to provide an option to find a balance in their general life situation, to practice 'self-seeking', to find one's 'own thing' or to reach for one's long-term hopes and dreams of finding meaningful work and activities.

> When I had basic income, I felt it was really good, as I didn't feel that my mental health was okay at that time. I had hoped that I could have received rehabilitation benefits for a little bit longer so I could have been a bit more relaxed at that point and taken care of myself better. But I had a slow pace with my mental health recovery and it would have required a little bit more time. But then I had this basic income option. [...] When I was pursuing my dreams [of studies], it helped me to work myself. My mental health is loads better now, I feel that I am really stable now. (Interviewee 40)

Life on basic income 161

In interview accounts related to aims to achieve one's long-term aspirations, some interviewees described how the basic income experiment had encouraged them to start their own small businesses, since they provided the option to experiment with self-employment without any major financial risk. However, some interviewees stated that basic income had no effect on these plans, since they were made prior to the experiment. Nevertheless, the ability to do meaningful things for a living is at the core of these experiences.

> In January, I realised that, hang on a second, I'm on basic income and I could afford to do this trick now. […] It was a lot easier and nicer to start a business, when I knew I had at least some income in the background. […] I thought that now I will try to do this, what I had been interested in doing. I thought that I have 2 years of time, and if everything gets fucked, at least I have tried it and I will not starve to death in between. Now, I have reached a point in which my business goes so well that there is no point of running it down, and get back on unemployment benefits. But then again, I have not got rich yet [so I have to do part-time work] […] The biggest change is that now I can do things that I have always wanted to. I had an opportunity to make my hobby as something that I could do for 12 hours per day in a way that someone is paying something for it. So, at the moment, it means a lot to me, that it is my life. […] But if the business needs to be shut down, I don't know. [My part-time job], for example, does not give me any of these feelings. It doesn't give any other feelings than that I wish this would be over for the day. (Interviewee 12)

The interviewees described how complex bureaucracy has prevented them from trying out self-employment prior to the experiment. However, these accounts also included statements that a two-year period was too short to establish a profitable business. In these interview accounts, the experiences were portrayed rather ambivalently, since they included descriptions of both self-actualisation and financial difficulties.

> I started my own business in autumn 2017, by invoicing the client through my own business. I don't know whether it would have been possible without this basic income, because I can't even imagine the hassle I would have had with the Social Insurance Institution of Finland. I would have needed to negotiate with them and send them all kinds of receipts for invoicing. That would have been intolerable. So basic income enabled that for me. I could start up my own business; however, in the end, it wasn't cost-effective. […] I had to close it down and think of other ways to invoice the clients then. […] So honestly, I can't brag that it was a great thing to start up a business, since it wasn't profitable. (Interviewee 9)

In addition, within the work modality, the basic income experiment also offered some of the interviewees meaningful employment options in their fields of specialisation, for example, by gaining more relevant work experience or having an option not to react the job offers of the Public Employment Services.

162   *Experimenting with unconditional basic income*

The Action Modality

The interview accounts also included content that can be related to action modality activities, that is, descriptions of the basic income experiment's effects on interviewees' societal and political participation as well as actions and interactions benefiting other human beings. These accounts included illustrations of how the basic income experiment had provided some interviewees with opportunities to participate in different political activities, voluntary work, and other non-paid activities, such as care work.

Overall, in their interview accounts, the interviewees conceptualised various activities performed outside paid employment as work. For example, some interviewees described how receiving basic income had given them freedom to participate actively in different NGOs or cooperative activities, without being accountable to the Public Employment Services.

> [During the basic income experiment] I focused on activities of that co-operative. I was a chairperson of its board and a responsible account holder. [...] I could have applied for unemployment benefits, but I didn't, as I thought that basic income was enough. [...] I don't perceive myself as an unemployed person as I work so much. Even though I don't get any money out of it yet. [...] I believe I got a bit more self-confidence and ambition out of the fact that I didn't need to worry about the money or to all the time have to demonstrate to the Social Insurance Institution of Finland or the Public Employment Services that I need money and I do things in an active manner. I believe that basic income had a positive effect on my confidence and strength. (Interviewee 50)

Some interviewees stated that receiving basic income encouraged them to perform voluntary work, since there was no risk of losing benefits. However, typically, these interviewees had done voluntary work prior to the experiment too.

> If I still would have that basic income, I could do some voluntary work. I have been working in a helpline service and as a support person. [...] I could do something actually meaningful, and reasonable things too. But, now I am sort of hanging here and waiting, waiting, and waiting. (Interviewee 3)

Some interviewees described how basic income had inspired them to undertake social and political activities, for example, to advocate for basic income or to deepen their knowledge of social policy in general. Some interviewees stated that as a result of the experiment, they had followed the news and daily politics in more detail, readjusted their political views, or participated in different events dealing with basic income. In addition, some interviewees shared their aspirations for participating in basic income studies as a means of being 'useful' for future research. Thus, some interviewees expressed their desire to

Life on basic income 163

help with and be part of knowledge production vis-à-vis basic income (see also Calnitsky, 2016: 30).

> For sure, I wanted to participate [in this study], and with great inspiration, I am involved. This is a hot and topical issue around the world. I am very satisfied that I got selected, and I really hoped to participate in this face-to-face interview. Surely, this is a slow and tough way to influence, but this is how it works. (Interviewee 70)

Some interviewees also described how they had the flexibility to help and assist people during the experiment by adjusting their time use. This help included, for example, shopping for groceries for relatives, taking their neighbours' dogs out for walks, or babysitting their grandchildren.

> I do gigs [at work] because my parent has early dementia and my husband is on a sickness benefit. [...] So also for my husband's sake I haven't been taking on permanent work, in case there will be situations that I couldn't have time off to help him. But now, when I do gigs, I can plan my schedule a little bit. [...] The guaranteed minimum income [basic income] provided me some alone time so I could regain some strength, too. [...] Also, during those 2 years, I was able to give a bit more time to my children and grandchildren, so I could make my working hours a little flexible. [...] So it [basic income] gave me own kinds of security and enough strength to cope with my family life. (Interviewee 47)

In the interview accounts, caring for relatives was portrayed as being easier in situations in which basic income was combined with self-employment and paid labour. These accounts overlapped all three modalities, since having the chance to focus on meaningful activities also freed energy to support close ones.

> I take care of my brother's everyday life so that he survives. [...] Even though I am not an official guardian, I take care of all kinds of stuff he needs. [...] I have to say that during last year, I felt I was alive again. As I was able to actualise myself [in my own business] and do and try new things. [...] I remembered who I am again. Because of my family issues, I had years, a couple of years when I didn't think about myself at all. I just worked for other people, took care of them and helped them, so I sort of forgot who I am. I was sort of living some other person's life in a way. So during last year, I was able to focus on my own thing, even though I helped others, but I was prioritising myself. (Interviewee 16)

In particular, some interviewees stated that basic income had enabled them to help their ageing relatives who needed daily assistance, for example in cases of acute illnesses. In the interviewee accounts, the care work of elderly

164   *Experimenting with unconditional basic income*

relatives was placed on a parallel with paid full-time work, compensated by basic income.

> In my family, both my parents got ill at the same time. They are rather aged, so I have been acting as a voluntary care worker for a couple of years now. It has been a life situation that has occupied me a lot and it took time, since I have a different place of residence than my parents. So, I have moved to their place and been there physically. So, I haven't thought about work issues; rather, I have been making sure that my parents' everyday life flows, all their medical issues are in order, they have been to the doctors. [...] So I kind of think that this voluntary care work, I perceive it as work, it has been work what I have done with my basic income salary. [...] I said to my mother that you don't have to give me any money. That I perceive that this basic income money is my salary that I will take care of you two. That you don't have to be in any elderly care institution or be assisted by strangers. (Interviewee 28)

In addition, interviewees who were out of the paid labour market during the experiment described the economic security of basic income as meaningful for their social relationships and ability to help others.

> I have been told that I was remarkably happier [during the experiment than now], maybe it was the peace I had with the money being always in my account. It brought so much security to my life. Now, when I don't have it, I am told that I am a similar bugbear as before. So in the autumn, I realised that God damn it, the time will come to its end. So, I had a little panic about what to do. [...] So now when this citizen's wage [basic income] ended, I didn't even have a chance to visit the swimming hall with my friend, as I needed to save money for the bus ticket. [...] I was too comfortable with my good situation. So, when it ended, it was quite a drop to anxiety. (Interviewee 10)

Thus, within the action modality, some interviewees stated that the basic income had an effect on their mental and general well-being, which influenced their ability to interact with other people on an everyday basis.

CONCLUSIONS

In this chapter, we analysed interview accounts by 81 participants in Finland's basic income experiment for the effects of the experiment vis-à-vis three modalities: labour, work and action (cf. Arendt, 1998 [1958]; Jansson, 2019).

The interview accounts of activities relating to the *labour modality* were varied. Some of the interviewees described the experiment as having had a substantial effect on their labour market behaviour, employment, and daily consumption. For example, the financial incentives of the experiment encouraged some of the interviewees to seek employment or hold on to their jobs, which were often low-paid and had relatively insecure working conditions. Some of the interviewees pointed out that the incentive to hold on to such jobs

Life on basic income 165

was connected to the additional income provided by the basic income, compensating for a low salary. According to the interview accounts, for some the basic income had instead given rise to the opportunity to change jobs, reduce hours worked, or decline jobs offers perceived as meaningless in essence or as exploiting workers' rights. Such power to say 'no' to undesirable jobs has been one of the central arguments for many proponents of a basic income (cf. Jansson, 2019; Van Parijs, 2013; Widerquist, 2013).

Some of the interviewees instead recounted that the experiment had little if any effects on their activities relating to the labour modality. In particular, interviewees who perceived themselves as having limited work capacity described the experiment as having had only minor effects on their lives. When having difficulties accessing paid employment, the basic income covered only the minimum necessities and daily consumption, if even those. Many of these interviewees also described difficulties in taking part in work and action modality-type activities, a situation which had, however, prevailed even before the basic income experiment. However, in such situations, basic income was still often described as enhancing the experience of financial security and continuity, as well as decreasing negative bureaucratic load and stress related to 'coercive' activation.

The interview accounts for the effects of the experiment also related to the *work modality*, which can be associated with self-determined life and sustainable as well as ethical production as a means to guarantee individuals' autonomy and well-being (cf. Arendt, 1998 [1958]; Jansson, 2019). In particular, the interviewees who had worked in creative fields described the basic income experiment as having strengthened their autonomy and ability to undertake meaningful work. In addition, the interview accounts related to self-employment and studying were associated with meaningfulness and ability to fulfil one's own long-term aspirations.

The interview accounts also included activities that can be associated with the *action modality*. Some interviewees described how receiving a basic income had provided them with the opportunity to undertake voluntary work and activities, such as care work, which had strengthened their experience of well-being. Thus, part of the benefits of the experiment had to do with the participants considering modes of social participation, such as performing non-paid voluntary or care work, to be more legitimate when obtaining basic income than when receiving unemployment benefits. In addition, some interviewees perceived such modes of participation as giving them the option of identifying themselves as working rather than belonging to the category of the unemployed (cf. the discussion on a basic income obscures the limits of 'work'). Thus, our results seem to lend some support to claims (e.g. Pateman, 2004) that basic income (experiments) may obscure perceptions of the division between 'work' and 'non-work', in our case, clearly affecting people's self-identity in positive ways.

The effects of the basic income experiment vis-à-vis the three modalities of labour, work and action were to some extent overlapping. Hence, the effects are varied and only partially fit the modality framework. Based on our analysis, people act by considering factors relating to all modalities in their activities. This means, for example, that an ability or will to accept a job is often tangled with more general reflections on work, family, economy, health and well-being. Often, these reflections seem connected to the variation regarding the premises of the interviewees, which are substantial even within the quite limited group studied (recipients of basic unemployment benefits from the Social Insurance Institution of Finland). Overall, the interview accounts on the effects of the experiment were often positive, but not all of them were. In particular, some interviewees who remained outside of paid employment described themselves as having 'failed' in the experiment, since they were not able to access the labour market. Thus, the interviews also reflect the explicit employment-related aims of the experiment.

However, the diversity in the accounts indicates that a basic income may respond to diverse social needs and various life situations in multiple ways (cf. Calnitsky and Latner, 2017: 390). Thus, our results can be interlinked with varied theoretical assumptions of basic income effects (for assumptions, see, for example, Jansson, 2019; Standing, 2002; Torry, 2019; Van Parijs, 2013; Widerqvist, 2013), although these often depart from the assumption that basic income is introduced to all members of society.

While our results point to some similarities with previous empirical qualitative interview study findings regarding positive aspects of basic income (Hamilton and Mulvale, 2019), making comparisons with such research and experiments is challenging, since they differ in design, objectives, and general socio-political contexts. The Finnish basic income experiment was strongly tied to employment policy goals, lasted for only two years, and had a relatively low monthly payment, albeit tax exempt. The target group comprised only recipients of basic, flat-rate unemployment benefits, and the experiment group was fairly small (2000 people). Such factors, as well as the broader framework of the welfare system as a whole, have to be considered when assessing our empirical results and conclusions.

In the 'Nordic welfare state'-type context, in which all residents are, as a rule, covered (at least) by some comparatively low, but statutory means-tested last-resort economic benefits, receiving (tax-exempted) unconditional basic income instead of flat-rate basic unemployment benefits, as in the case of the experiment participants, seems to have had varied consequences.

Most participants emphasised increased economic predictability and greater degrees of freedom of action as positive aspects of the income. However, for people engaged in (some) gainful employment, the basic income also presented the opportunity to increase living standards, and thus, to move from a life of plain 'survival' somewhat closer to 'normal' consumption levels.

For experiment participants who were not, for any multitude of possible reasons, active in the labour market, the experiment seems to have had limited effects on (material) living conditions and (the quite modest) consumption levels: often, the basic income amount paid during the experiment, even with other possible supplementary benefits (social assistance, housing allowances, etc.) received, was described as too low to cover all the necessities for every-day survival.

NOTES

1. The locations of the interviews were as follows: 34 interviews at public libraries, 16 in meeting rooms, four at coffee houses/petrol stations, 25 at interviewees' homes, and two at interviewees' work offices.
2. Some semantic differences exist between the original and translated data extracts.

REFERENCES

Arendt, H. (1998 [1958]), *The Human Condition*, 2nd edn, Chicago, IL: University of Chicago Press.

Birnbaum, S. and De Wispelaere, J. (2020), 'Exit strategy or exit trap? Basic income and the "power to say no" in the age of precarious employment', *Socio-Economic Review*, available at https://doi:10.1093/ser/mwaa002 (accessed 12 December 2020).

Bohmeyer, M. and Cornelsen, C. (2019), *Was würdest Du tun? Wie uns das Bedingungslose Grundeinkommen verändert – Antworten aus der Praxis*, [*What Would You Do? How the Unconditional Basic Income is Changing Us – Answers from Practice*], Berlin: Econ Verlag.

Calnitsky, D. (2016), 'More normal than welfare: The Mincome experiment, stigma, and community experience', *Canadian Review of Sociology (Revue Canadienne de Sociologie)*, 53(1), 26–71.

Calnitsky, D. and Latner, J. P. (2017), 'Basic income in a small town: Understanding the elusive effects on work', *Social Problems*, 64(3), 1–25.

Davala, S., Jhabvala, R., Standing, G., and Mehta, S. K. (2015), *Basic Income. A Transformative Policy for India*, London: Bloomsbury.

De Wispelaere, J., Halmetoja, A. and Pulkka, V. (2018), 'The rise (and fall) of the basic income experiment in Finland', *CESifo Forum*, 19(3), 15–19.

De Wispelaere, J. and Stirton, L. (2004), The many faces of universal basic income, *The Political Quarterly*, 75(3), 266–74.

Elo, S. and Kyngäs, H. (2008), 'The qualitative content analysis process', *Journal of Advanced Nursing*, 62(1), 107–15.

Forget, E. L. (2011), 'The town with no poverty: The health effects of a Canadian guaranteed annual income field experiment', *Canadian Public Policy*, 37(3), 283–305.

Hamilton, L. and Mulvale, J. P. (2019), '"Human again": The (unrealized) promise of basic income in Ontario', *Journal of Poverty*, 23(7), 576–99.

Hennink, M. M., Kaiser, B. N., and Marconi, V. C. (2016), 'Code saturation versus meaning saturation: How many interviews are enough?', *Qualitative Health Research*, 27(4), 591–608.

Jansson, I. (2017), 'Lönearbete och medborgarlön – reflektioner utifrån Hannah Arendts vita activa' ['Paid work and basic income – Reflections based on Hannah Arendt's vita activa'], *Socialmedicinsk tidskrift*, 94(5), 603–9.

Jansson, I. (2019), Occupation and basic income through the lens of Arendt's vita activa, *Journal of Occupational Science*, 27(1), 125–37.

Kangas, O. and Pulkka, V. (eds) (2016), *Ideasta kokeiluun? Esiselvitys perustulokokeilun toteuttamisvaihtoehdoista* [*From Idea to Experiment – Preliminary Report on a Universal Basic Income*], Helsinki: Valtioneuvoston selvitys- ja tutkimustoiminnan julkaisusarja 13/2016.

McKay, A. (2007), 'Why a citizens' basic income? A question of gender equality or gender bias', *Work, Employment and Society*, 21(2), 337–48.

Pateman, C. (2004), 'Democratizing citizenship: Some advantages of a basic income', *Politics & Society*, 32(1), 89–105.

Perkiö, J. (2020a), 'From rights to activation: The evolution of the idea of basic income in the Finnish political debate, 1980–2016', *Journal of Social Policy*, 49(1), 103–24.

Perkiö, J. (2020b), 'Legitimising a radical policy idea: Framing basic income as a boost to labour market activity', *Policy & Politics*, 48(2), 277–93.

Sage, D. (2019), 'Unemployment, wellbeing and the power of the work ethic: Implications for social policy', *Critical Social Policy*, 39(2), 205–28.

Sauer, L. (2015), 'Das bedingungslose Grundeinkommen im Lichte der politischen Philosophie Hannah Arendts – Eine etwas andere Kritik der politischen Ökonomie', ['Unconditional basic income in the light of the political philosophy of Hannah Arendt – A somewhat different critique of the political economy'] in Osterkamp, R. (ed.), *Auf dem Prüfstand: Ein bedingungsloses Grundeinkommen für Deutschland?* [*On the Test Bench: An Unconditional Basic Income for Germany?*] Nomos: Sonderbände Zeitschrift für Politik 7, pp. 143–56.

Standing, G. (2002), *Beyond the New Paternalism: Basic Security as Equality*, London: Verso.

Standing, G. (2017), *Basic Income and How We Can Make It Happen*, London: Pelican Books.

Suuronen, V. (2018), 'Resisting biopolitics: Hannah Arendt as a thinker of automation, social rights, and basic income', *Alternatives: Global, Local, Political*, 43(1), 35–53.

Torry, M. (2019), *The Palgrave International Handbook of Basic Income*, London: Palgrave Macmillan.

Van Parijs, P. (1995), *Real Freedom for All: What (if Anything) Can Justify Capitalism?* Oxford: Oxford University Press.

Van Parijs, P. (2001), 'A basic income for all', in Rogers, J. and Cohen, J. (eds), *What's Wrong with a Free Lunch?*, Boston: Beacon Press, pp. 3–26.

Van Parijs, P. (2013), 'The universal basic income: Why utopian thinking matters, and how sociologists can contribute to it', *Politics & Society*, 41(2), 171–82.

Widerqvist, K. (2013), 'The basic income grant as social safety net for Namibia: Experience and lessons from around the world', in *Social Safety Nets in Namibia: Assessing Current Programmes and Future Options*, The Annual Symposium 2013 of the Bank of Namibia, pp. 43–67, available at https://www.bon.com.na/CMSTemplates/Bon/Files/bon.com.na/0f/0fa7f5ba-5585-4471-9511-1a42811bd0d1.pdf (accessed 18 December 2020).

13. Media coverage of the Finnish basic income experiment

Katja Mäkkylä

INTRODUCTION

In 2017–2018 Finland conducted a basic income experiment. The randomly selected experiment group consisted of 2000 unemployed persons between 25 and 58 years. The group received a monthly payment of €560, unconditionally and without means testing. The main purpose of the experiment was to study the effects of the basic income on employment and well-being. The Finnish basic income experiment was exceptional in many ways and generated interest worldwide. Coverage of the Finnish experiment, in both the Finnish and international media, has been remarkable before, during and after the experiment.

Social experiments cannot be implemented in a laboratory, but rather take place within communities, and their participants are individuals living their everyday lives. Social experiments occur in public; therefore, publicity is one characteristic of such experiments, and it is important to shed light on it. One way to study publicity is to study the media coverage of the issue.

The news media, among other forms of mediated communication, has a significant role in the construction of reality (Couldry and Hepp, 2018). One way the news media can construct reality is by *framing* how an issue is approached. Frames can be described as 'organizing principles that are socially shared and persistent over time that work symbolically to meaningfully structure the social world' (Reese, 2001: 11).

In this chapter, I explore coverage of the Finnish basic income experiment in both the Finnish and international media. Specifically, I address the research question of how the Finnish and international media have framed the Finnish basic income experiment. To study media coverage, its characteristics, and prevailing perspectives, I used media framing analysis, concentrating on identification of *media frames* and *frame-building*.

In this chapter, I first present media framing theory, and the theoretical and conceptual approaches to media frames, and the media framing process. Thereafter, sections on data and methods used in this study are presented. In

170   *Experimenting with unconditional basic income*

the following sections, I present the findings of the analysis, concentrating first on the Finnish data, then the international data, and then compare the findings of both datasets. In the final section, I summarise the findings and discuss their importance.

MEDIA FRAMES AND MEDIA FRAMING

Framing has been studied across different disciplines, such as political science, sociology, and media studies. Consequently, there are different approaches, theoretical perspectives, and methods of framing (Hertog and McLeod, 2001). In this chapter, the focus is on approaches that have emerged in media and communication studies.

Communication research has always had a strong focus on the effects of media; however, since the turn of the 20th century, there have been various paradigm changes. In some stages, media effects have been regarded as strong, while in others, the effects have been viewed as more limited. The latest stage, which can be described as 'social constructivism', began in 1980. The social constructivist paradigm emphasises the strong effects of mass media in constructing social reality; however, these effects can be perceived as limited with regard to the interaction between mass media and its audience (McQuail, 2005; Scheufele, 1999). In political communication studies, framing can also be viewed from the perspective of the social construction of meaning (Gamson and Modigliani, 1989).

Agenda-setting and *framing* are among the most frequently discussed approaches in political communication studies that aim to examine political news content and how it relates to audience knowledge, attitudes, and behaviour (Koch-Baumgarten and Voltmer, 2010). Agenda-setting refers to the belief that mass media defines the issues about which the audience forms opinions, and framing is 'based on the assumption that how an issue is characterized in news reports can have an influence on how it is understood by audiences' (Scheufele and Tewksbury, 2007: 11).

Framing studies have their origins in both sociology and psychology (Pan and Kosicki, 1993). Scheufele (1999) refers to this distinction in defining framing as both a macro-level and a micro-level construct. The focus is on *media frames* in macro-level analysis, and on *individual frames* in micro-level analysis, which refer to the frames in individuals' minds that help them process and interpret information. In this study, the focus is on *media frames*.

Gamson and Modigliani (1987: 143) suggest that the *media frame* is 'a central organizing idea or story line that provides meaning to an unfolding strip of events.... The frame suggest what the controversy is about, the essence of the issue.' Media frames can also be described as devices that help journalists organise a flood of information (Gitlin, 1980).

Media coverage of the Finnish basic income experiment 171

A frequently cited definition of framing is that of Entman (1993), who suggests that media framing consists of selection and salience; framing a news story means to select an aspect to reality and make it salient. Entman suggests that framing accomplishes this by defining problems, diagnosing causes, making moral evaluations, and recommending remedies.

According to Entman (1993), frames can be found in four different locations within the communication process: the communicator, text, receiver, and culture. Based on this classification, framing can be perceived as a process (de Vreese and Lecheler, 2012). Scheufele (1999) presented a framing process model consisting of different stages: frame-building, frame-setting, and the individual effects of framing. Frame-building refers to the internal and external factors that influence the construction of media frames within the newsroom. Internal factors can be considered media routines, such as values or organisational-level questions (Shoemaker and Reese, 1996), or news media's ideological orientation, political or otherwise (Scheufele, 1999). External factors that influence frame-building are the interactions between journalists and elites, interest groups, (Hänggli, 2012) or social movements (Snow and Benford, 1992). When the issue at stake is new for the journalists, it is more likely that elites will succeed in framing the issue in their own way (Scheufele, 1999: 166).

The basic income experiment introduced the concept of social experiments to the wider public in Finland for the first time. Furthermore, the Finnish media had not reported widely on this kind of issue previously, making it difficult to find research on media framing of social experiments. Nevertheless, media framing of basic income was studied previously. Perkiö et al. (2019) conducted a comparative study on media framing of basic income in Canada, Finland and Spain. They compared the frames used in academic literature, activist circles, and country-based debates with the frames used in the media, and discovered that in all three countries, basic income was generally regarded positively in news stories, with the *automation of work frame* being the most prominent frame. The study also suggested that, in Finnish news articles, the most prominent frame was the *labour activation frame*, which they explained as being due to the main purpose of the Finnish basic income experiment, which was to test the effects of basic income on work incentives.

In this chapter, the focus of the study is to determine how this new issue – the social experiment – is framed in the media. Since the issue had not been covered previously, also of interest is examining the internal and external factors that influence the construction of media frames to identify why the issue is framed in a certain way.

DATA AND METHOD

This research used two datasets: one collected from Finnish online news media and the other from international online news media. I examined these two datasets separately, then together by making comparisons between them.

The Finnish dataset comprises 347 articles published between 25 October 2016 and 29 April 2019 from Finnish online newspapers and news sites.[1] The selected articles were published in national and regional media outlets, tabloids, and media outlets associated with political parties. Many are short news articles, especially those published at the beginning of the experiment in January 2017, although there are also more extensive reports, editorials, columns, and opinion pieces. However, as the majority are news articles, I will use the general term *news article* here.

The international dataset includes 46 news articles published between 26 August 2016 and 8 December 2019 in online newspapers and news sites from outside of Finland. The selected articles were published in internationally well-known media outlets. The data are limited due to language constraints; consequently, the selected online newspapers mainly cover publications in English. In South Korea, for instance, the Finnish basic income experiment has gained much attention and been covered by the Korean media; however, due to the language barrier, these articles were not included.

Media coverage of the experiment was not spread out equally over this period, but concentrated on certain moments when the experiment's implementation proceeded in a significant way and there were related press releases, such as the beginning of the experiment in January 2017. The midpoint at the beginning of 2018 and the completion of the experiment at the end of 2018 were also moments that received much media coverage. A significant news spike came in February 2019, with the publication of experiment's preliminary results on the effects of basic income on employment and well-being.

The communication and information specialists at Kela helped me compile the datasets by using a media monitoring company to collect online news articles covering the Finnish experiment. In the data selection process, I paid attention to the online news articles' content. The results found via media monitoring were not all about the Finnish basic income experiment, but included some articles on basic income in general, with the Finnish experiment only mentioned. Articles such as these were separated from the data and were not included in the abovementioned number of news articles. The news articles included in the datasets are entirely, or at least partly, about the Finnish experiment.

Both datasets were also limited by the unavailability of some articles due to issues such as changes in web addresses or paywalls. These articles were excluded from the data. Television and radio programmes were also not included in the data; therefore, actual media coverage of the experiment was more extensive than was possible to include in this study's data. Nevertheless, the data broadly cover public discussion on the Finnish basic income experiment.

Media Framing Analysis as a Method

There is a significant variety in methodological approaches to media framing (Matthes and Kohring, 2008). Framing analysis starts by defining the frame and determining the frame type: issue-specific or generic (Matthes, 2009). Semetko and Valkenburg (2000) categorised generic frames used in news articles as economic consequence, conflict, human interest, morality, and responsibility frames. Media framing analysis can be qualitative or quantitative, and the coding process can be conducted either manually or with computer assistance (Matthes, 2009).

Frames can be deductively or inductively determined. The deductive approach uses frames identified and defined in earlier studies. In this approach, it is necessary to clarify the kinds of frames likely to be in news stories, to prevent them from being overlooked during the identification process. In the inductive approach, news stories are analysed carefully and with an open point of view, with the aim of identifying possible frames (Semetko and Valkenburg, 2000).

In the linguistic approach to media framing, the frames are identified in the text by '[analysing] the selection, placement, and structure of specific words and sentences in a text' (Matthes and Kohring, 2008: 260). Pan and Kosicki (1993) developed a linguistic approach, in which they identified the different framing devices used in texts: syntactical structure, script structure, thematic structure, and rhetorical structure.

Syntactical structure refers to the general structure of news stories (headlines, lead, episodes, background and closing). It also refers to choices regarding which experts to interview or quotations to use. Script structure refers to the tendency of journalists to organise a news story by asking who, what, when, where, why and how. Thematic structure refers to a theme that is 'presented or implied, and evidence in the forms of journalists' observations of actions or quotations of a source is presented to support the hypothesis' (Pan and Kosicki, 1993: 60). Rhetorical structure refers to rhetorical choices made within news texts. Metaphors and catchphrases are typical rhetorical devices, but numbers or rates can also be interpreted as such (Pan and Kosicki, 1993).

This was a qualitative study, and coding was conducted manually with the help of the Atlas.ti program. The frames were determined using an abductive approach, which combined inductive and deductive approaches (Layder, 1998;

174   *Experimenting with unconditional basic income*

Timmermans and Tavory, 2012). Unlike in Pan and Kosicki (1993), the unit of analysis in this study was the article, not the paragraph.

After data collection and selection, I began the analysis process by reviewing the selected news articles to obtain an overview of the data. Next, I applied an inductive approach and analysed a sample of news stories with an open point of view. In this step, I applied Pan and Kosicki's model and searched for the framing devices that signify a frame. The next step was an attempt to identify possible frames. I recognised that it was possible to identify generic frames commonly used in news media, which is why the method used in this study is more abductive than purely inductive or deductive. The generic frames identified were the *economic frame, conflict frame*, and *human-interest frame*. These frames created the initial codebook, but the codebook was completed with issue-specific frames: *the social experiment frame*, identified in both the international and Finnish datasets, and the *international attention* frame, identified in only the Finnish dataset. This approach allowed me to identify not only the frames commonly used in news articles but also the issue-specific frames, thus creating a more complete description of the issue's framing.

Frames often overlap, making it possible to identify more than one frame in a single news article. The more extensive the news article, the more likely it is that more than one frame can be found. However, one frame usually prevails in an article; therefore, in my analysis, I attempted to identify each article's prevailing frame. This was the most challenging part of my analysis. The economic frame was present in many of the news articles, and in some cases, it was difficult to determine whether it actually was the prevailing frame. Similarly, with the conflict frame, when the article addressed the issue in terms of conflict or disagreement, the subject of the disagreement was usually basic income's economic consequences or measures that should be taken regarding employment.

THE FINNISH BASIC INCOME EXPERIMENT CAN BEEN FRAMED IN MANY WAYS

In my analysis, I identified five frames in the data, including the *economic, conflict*, and *human-interest frames*. In previous studies, these were identified as prevalent news frames, and therefore can be considered generic frames (Neuman et al., 1992; Semetko and Valkenburg, 2000). In addition to these frames which journalists use often, two issue-specific frames were identified in news articles on the Finnish experiment, which I called the *social experiment frame* and the *international attention frame*.

In the *economic frame*, news issues are addressed in terms of the bottom line, profit and loss, and the economic consequences of social and political issues, such as their costs and gains, are the focus. The economic frame is used in news stories because the economic consequences of chosen policy options are seen to have significance for the audience (Neuman et al., 1992).

The *conflict frame* approaches the reported issue from the perspective of disagreement and conflict. The conflict frame is commonly used in news because journalistic practice emphasises telling 'both sides of the story,' and because creating an interesting story with tension requires presenting the good and bad or the right and wrong (Neuman et al., 1992). The presence of conflict is repeatedly referred to as one important news criteria when selecting which events will be news stories (de Vreese and Holli, 2001).

The *human-interest frame* describes news issues based on how they affect the lives of individuals or groups and by giving the issue a 'human face'. By using stories on an issue's human impact, it is possible to include direct expressions of emotions and evaluative statements in news articles, when journalists tend to avoid making these statements themselves in the name of objectivity (Neuman et al., 1992). With this type of frame, social and political decisions are presented using human stories, cases, and exemplars, which are said to be more effective than statistics presented in news articles (de Vreese, 2014).

The *social experiment frame* is an issue-specific frame, and it approaches the basic income experiment from the perspective of science and research. With this frame, political decision-making should make use of the results of scientific research, and scientific research should be conducted in such a way that it can be utilised in political decision-making.

The *international attention frame* is also an issue-specific frame, and was identified only in the Finnish dataset. With this frame, the basic income experiment is treated in terms of international media attention. Journalists describe international reporting on the Finnish experiment and the observations and representations of Finland and the Finnish people in the international media.

Frames in the Finnish Media

The economic frame was the most prominent frame in the Finnish data. The economic frame could be identified in many news articles, even when it was not the prevailing frame. The Finnish basic income experiment is an issue that concerns citizens' livelihood and income distribution in society; therefore, it is frequently framed in economic terms. When the Finnish media places the basic income experiment within the economic frame, the focus is on employment and work incentives. Therefore, the *employment frame* could be considered a sub-frame of the economic frame. This framing is essentially influenced by the experiment's main purpose, which was to understand how receiving a basic income affects participants' financial and employment status. The experi-

176 *Experimenting with unconditional basic income*

ment's participants were randomly selected unemployed persons who received unemployment benefits from Kela in November 2016.

> The basic income experiment promises to provide knowledge on how to combine low and occasional income with unemployment benefits. The weakness of our current social security system is that it is seen as making citizens passive. Finding a job, even when it is small and low-paid, should always be incentivised. The aim of the experiment is to look for answers to the question: in what situations do the unemployed have incentives to find a job? (*Keskisuomalainen*, 9 January 2017)[2]

The news media's political or ideological orientation also influences framing. Thus, the economic frame is especially prominent in business- and finance-oriented news media.

The conflict frame was identified in Finnish news articles that covered the basic income experiment from the perspectives of different political parties. Thus, disagreements and confrontations are described mostly between different political parties and their opinions. Basic income is unconditional and without work requirements by definition; however, most Finnish political parties support models in which income is conditional and recipients are obligated to search for work or be active in other ways. This is why the basic income experiment has been seen as a controversial issue.

The conflict frame was prominent in news media closely associated with political parties, which have written a lot on basic income and the basic income experiment. In their reporting, the party newspapers mostly aligned with their political party on social security, basic income, and the basic income experiment. The National Coalition Party and Christian Democrats also discussed Universal Credit, an alternative model to basic income previously introduced in the United Kingdom, which these parties believed could be successful in Finland.

However, some political parties also had internal disagreements on which basic income model they wanted to support. Therefore, conflicts appear not only between but also within political parties. These conflicts were described in the media especially in 2018 and at the beginning of 2019, before the parliamentary election in which social security reform was a central topic.

The disagreement between conditionality and unconditionality was again raised in the Finnish media at the beginning of the experiment's second year. In January 2018, the 'activation model' for unemployed persons came into effect, which included an obligation that people either actively search for work or participate in employment services to receive unemployment benefits (Kyyrä et al., 2019). Since the basic income experiment ran simultaneously with the activation model, they were usually presented in contrast to each other.

It was also possible to identify critical voices other than those of political parties. Some high-profile civil servants also expressed their opinions on the basic income experiment in Finland.

> The government launched the basic income experiment in January, and it has been closely followed worldwide. Now, the Chief Secretary of the Ministry of Finance, Martti Hetemäki, in his latest column has practically rejected the basic income that has been tested in the experiment. (*Helsingin Sanomat*, 19 July 2017)

In the Finnish media, the *human-interest frame* was prominent, especially in the national tabloids, which are the most widely read newspapers in Finland (Kansallinen Mediatutkimus, 2019). The human-interest frame described the Finnish experiment mainly from the perspective of its participants. When using this type of framing, participants' stories were mainly positive, and they often expressed that they felt lucky to be chosen as part of the experiment.

> Mr. Heikkinen, who has been unemployed for more than four years, stated he feels he is lucky, because he was one of the 2000 unemployed people who were randomly selected to take part in the basic income experiment. During the two-year experiment, Mr. Heikkinen will receive 560 euros, tax-free, in his account each month. (*Iltalehti*, 28 September 2017)

In the interviews with participants, the main considerations were their employment and livelihood; however, the experiment's effects on well-being were also highlighted. Some participants reported that their stress decreased after they started to receive a basic income. However, there were participants who reported that receiving basic income had no impact on their lives, or that it made things more difficult for them.

The same focus on the effects of basic income on well-being was reflected in the news articles which reported the results of a survey study conducted as a part of the evaluation study. In the survey, individuals from both the treatment and control groups were asked about their health and well-being, as well as their trust in other people and in institutions in society and their confidence in their own future and in their ability to influence things. The survey results showed that, compared with the members of the control group, those in the treatment group (i.e. the experiment's participants) felt less stressed and more confident (see Chapters 7, 8 and 10 in this volume).

Stories on participants appeared, especially in tabloids and national media. However, only a small group of participants appeared in the media. Among the 2000 participants, 24 provided interviews to different media outlets. This number was determined based on the number of individuals who were named in the news articles of the database. In the evaluation study the effects of the basic income experiment were studied through a phone survey (see Chapter

178 *Experimenting with unconditional basic income*

5 in this volume). In the survey, the participants in the experiment group and in the control group were also asked if they have given interviews to media regarding the basic income. A similar number of participants in the experiment group stated they had granted interviews to the media (see Table 13A.1 in the appendix).

Those who responded to requests for interviews by media outlets may not necessarily be a 'representative sample' of the experimental group. Although only a small number of participants shared their experiences and opinions in the media, their stories were widely covered, and thus contributed to how the experiment was portrayed to the public.

The *social experiment frame* could also be identified in the Finnish data. In this frame, the experiment is significant because it not only generates knowledge on basic income but also on incentive traps and the well-being of the unemployed. Accordingly, political decision-makers can apply this knowledge when planning social security reform. However, this framing was typically used when social policy or economics experts evaluate or criticise the experiment's implementation. Many experts agreed that social experiments are necessary, but repeatedly highlighted flaws in the basic income experiment. Some experts also suggested different models for the experiment. With this frame, the consensus was about the necessity of experiments, with more experiments on different issues suggested.

> Let us hope that the experiment gives practical knowledge on the questions hanging in the air and measures will be taken based on this knowledge. The model is barely ready, and there may be need for more experiments. Now, we finally get started. (Kaleva, 6 January 2017)

This frame was influenced by the communication strategies of the Finnish Social Security Institution (Kela), which implemented the experiment, and the Ministry of Social Affairs and Health, as a representative of public administration. Both actively communicated details about the experiment in press releases and on their social media channels at different stages of the experiment. Their press releases sent to media outlets were well received, and the reporting on the experiment was based largely on these press releases, repeating their viewpoints and what they chose to emphasise. Thus, those who planned and implemented the experiment were also able to influence the content and direction of public discussion on the topic.

In addition to these frames, the *international attention frame* was identified in the Finnish dataset. Finnish tabloids in particular reported on the experiment in terms of the international attention it gained. These articles usually summarised international media coverage on the issue and pointed out that Finland and the Finnish people have been noticed worldwide.

> Among others, the BBC, the Italian Rai1, the Swiss Radio Télévision Suisse, and the Japanese media outlets Asahi Shimbun and The Nikkei have contacted *Iltalehti* [Finnish tabloid] in order to ask for the contact information of the participants of the experiment. (*Iltalehti*, 28 September 2017)

In Finland, attention from international media outlets is considered exceptional and desirable, probably because relatively little is known internationally about Finland and it is a small player in global politics. The Finnish Ministry of Foreign Affairs and its Unit for Country Image, which works to enhance Finland's positive image, also noticed that the Finnish experiment gained a lot of attention worldwide. Consequently, they used the experiment to promote the country by presenting it as a typical Finnish social innovation.[3]

Frames in the International Media

The *economic frame* was also the most prominent frame in the international dataset. As with in the Finnish media, this frame's prominence can be explained by the main purpose of the Finnish experiment being to understand how receiving a basic income affects participants' financial and employment status.

The international media often framed the Finnish experiment from a broader economic perspective. The background information provided in this framing typically focuses on economic challenges, such as the economic recession Finland has faced in recent years. In explaining the economic challenges, some articles mention the economic sanctions directed towards Russia – an important trading partner of Finland – due to the Ukrainian crisis. The collapse of Nokia's mobile phone business and its influence on unemployment in Finland was also noted. Thus, the recession and increased unemployment were suggested as the motivation behind the basic income experiment.

> The Finnish economy has struggled for the last decade due to a string of problems, including high labour costs, a decline of Nokia's former mobile phone business and recession in neighbouring Russia, a major trade partner. (Reuters, 18 January 2017)

The economic frame in the international media was often influenced by the orientation of the media outlets. Many of the news articles in the dataset were published in business and financial news outlets, such as *Financial Times*, *Forbes* and *Business Insider*.

The *human-interest frame* could also be identified in the international media. It focuses on the personal stories of the experiment's participants. With this framing, a voice was given to people who had experienced periods of unemployment and struggled with the bureaucracy of social security. Without exception, the interviewees had a positive attitude towards basic income and the experiment. They described how participation in the experiment changed their lives, as well as sharing their opinions on the social security system and its flaws and suggestions on how to improve it.

> Ideas flow out of Järvinen as easily as water from a tap, yet he could exercise none of his initiative for fear of arousing bureaucratic scrutiny. (*The Guardian*, 1 November 2017)

International media outlets also applied *conflict frames*. When reporting on the Finnish experiment, a juxtaposition was often created between supporters and opponents of both the concept of basic income and the experiment itself. Notably, the supporters of basic income did not always support the experiment, but rather adopted a critical approach to it. They usually criticised the purpose of the experiment, initiated by the centre-right government of Prime Minister Juha Sipilä, or pointed toward what they viewed to be inadequate implementation. Further, international media outlets often portrayed trade union representatives as the main critics of basic income and the experiment, as they usually had reserved or negative attitudes towards both.

> Finnish politics is intricate: the Centre party, Greens and a far-left party back the study. So does a libertarian wing of the conservatives, hoping to pare the welfare state. Sceptics include traditional conservatives, many Social Democrats and big unions. (*The Economist*, 24 June 2017)

The *social experiment frame* could also be identified in the international media dataset. This frame is an issue-specific frame with a focus on the future, and treats political decision-making from the point of view of how we can construct a better future and more functional society. The vision of the future is often one in which automation and robotisation have replaced human labour, and basic income is needed to secure citizens' livelihood. This framing sees the use of scientific research in political decision-making to be of primary importance. In this frame, government employees and researchers did not present opinions on whether basic income should be introduced, but merely stated that the main purpose of the experiment was to generate knowledge for social security reform.

> Finland's centre-right government started the trial under a new framework that allows it to try various social policies through randomised tests. Mr. Kanerva says the goal is to make Finland 'the most innovative and experiment-friendly country by 2020'. (*The Financial Times*, 28 January 2018)

Media coverage of the Finnish basic income experiment

The Finnish Social Security Institution (Kela) and the Ministry of Health and Social Affairs influenced the use of this frame. Along with the enormous international attention on the experiment, press releases from Kela and the Ministry of Social Affairs and Health were also published in English and, in February 2019, press releases were published in German, French, Russian and Italian. The journalists at international media outlets also interviewed the researchers and authorities involved in planning and implementing the experiment.

Differences between the Frames in the Finnish and International Media

When comparing the framing in the Finnish and international media, the different premises in the collected data must be taken into account. First, the international media dataset consists of publications from large media outlets, whereas the Finnish data also include smaller regional newspapers and political party newspapers. Second, in many countries, the media has strong political and ideological dependence, and this naturally had an effect on how the basic income and the Finnish experiment were approached and framed. Still, when comparing the reporting on the issue in the Finnish and international media, it is possible to perceive differences.

In the international media, the issue was covered in terms of economics, employment, and the social security system. Participants' personal stories were often highlighted. These characteristics also appeared in the Finnish media, with mostly the same interviewees, experts and participants.

The differences in framing between the Finnish and international media can be identified in the social experiment frame. The international media represented the experiment and its results as significant to the changes in working life and explored its consequences, whereas the Finnish media approached the issue from the perspective of social security reform. In the Finnish media, basic income is not seen as something that could replace salaries that have disappeared due to automation and robotisation of work, but rather as a potential model to consider when planning and implementing social security reform.

The conflict frame was more frequent in the Finnish media than in the international media. The basic income experiment and the concept of basic income itself lead to strong positions in Finnish political parties. Many Finnish political parties have suggested alternative models to basic income. In international media, conflicts and disagreements were not described in such detail, and alternative models were not presented.

DISCUSSION ON FRAMES AND CONCLUSIONS

The Finnish basic income experiment has been framed as an economic issue, as an issue that creates conflict and disagreement, as a human-interest issue, as

182

Experimenting with unconditional basic income

a social experiment, and as an issue that draws international attention. As suggested above, media frames contribute to the construction of reality. What kind of reality do these media frames construct? Why are these frames selected or, in other words, why does the media choose these perspectives when reporting on the Finnish experiment?

The Finnish and international media have most commonly framed the Finnish experiment in terms of the economy and employment. The focus is on the effects of basic income on employment, and, more specifically, on work incentives. The purpose of the Finnish basic income experiment was to explore whether basic income could incentivise participants to work or start a business, and this purpose seems to have influenced media framing as well. The prevalence of this framing in media coverage highlights the potential economic consequences of basic income and provides less attention to other possible effects basic income could have on recipients. This finding is in line with Perkiö et al. (2019), who compared the frames used in academic literature to those used in the media, and found that in the Finnish media, the labour activation frame was the most prominent.

In the conflict frame, the focus was on the comments and proposals of different political parties regarding the experiment and basic income. In Finland, basic income is seen as an alternative alongside other social security models, and the political parties who support basic income have offered definitions and plans on how to implement a functioning basic income model, or another similar model. With this framing, the proposals of different political parties and actors are usually tied to questions on employment and incentive traps. Only the Left Party and the Green League offer basic income as a solution to increase individuals' liberty, autonomy and well-being. Thus, the conflict frame not only constructs reality full of tension and juxtapositions but also, in 'telling both sides of the story', offers different solutions to questions on social policy.

When the Finnish experiment is placed in the human-interest frame, the focus is on individuals and their experiences and feelings. With this framing, the experiment's participants and unemployed individuals were able to provide an alternative voice to the specialists and authorities who were repeatedly interviewed in the articles. In this frame, basic income's effects on participants' well-being were strongly emphasised. The same focus on how basic income affects well-being was reflected in the reporting of the survey data in which the experiment's participants were asked about their health and well-being as well as their trust in people and in institutions and confidence in their own future (Chapters 7, 8 and 10).

The social experiment frame emphasises the role of scientific research in policymaking. With this framing, the basic income experiment was described as a research project to produce knowledge on basic income and its effects. In

Media coverage of the Finnish basic income experiment

this frame, specialists and authorities did not take a stand for or against basic income. This presents the experiment as a value-free project or a tool for generating knowledge to influence policymaking.

The international attention frame sheds light on the significant international attention the Finnish experiment gained. This framing presented the Finnish experiment as an issue that draws mainly positive attention to Finland. The experiment was seen as unique, and Finland was viewed as a country that was leading the way in implementing social experiments. Mainly positive international attention towards the Finnish experiment in general contributed to the construction of a positive image of the country.

Focusing on frame-building can also help to improve understanding of the motivations behind news frames and the framing process. As suggested earlier in this chapter, frame-building is influenced by both internal and external factors (Scheufele, 1999).

Internal factors, such as news values or editorial processes, are especially reflected in the use of generic frames. Journalists apply the economic frame because the economic consequences of the issue – in this case, the basic income experiment in Finland – could have significance for members of the public. The employment issues strongly connected to the Finnish experiment are also important issues to the public. Use of the conflict frame reflects the journalistic tradition of telling both sides of the story. In the case of the Finnish experiment, political parties and authorities who did not support the idea of basic income or the tested basic income model usually told the 'other side of the story'. Journalists also applied the human-interest frame that enabled them to explain the abstract experiment in more concrete terms for a larger public. The human-interest frame makes a news story more appealing by highlighting individuals' experiences to evoke both emotions and opinions. Internal factors can also include the orientation of a particular news outlet, such as a political orientation, which was reflected in the issue's framing in Finnish news media associated with political parties. In addition, in both the Finnish and international datasets, the economic frame was prominent when the issue was presented in business- and finance-oriented news media.

The most influential external factor in the frame-building of the Finnish experiment has been the Social Security Institution (Kela) and the Ministry of Social Affairs and Health. Their press releases and social media updates were widely noticed, and influenced the way many media outlets framed the issue. Kela and the Ministry have framed the basic income experiment from the perspective of scientific research. With this framing, the basic income experiment and its results are primarily presented as tools for gathering knowledge for social security reform. Other external factors influencing frame-building are political parties, single politicians, public servants, or basic-income activists, who have offered their own framing to media outlets. With a relatively new

184 *Experimenting with unconditional basic income*

issue, it is highly likely that political parties and other elites will influence how it is framed. The basic income experiment introduced the concept of social experiments for the first time to the wider public in Finland. Therefore, the media's reporting on the Finnish experiment mainly followed the framing suggested by Kela and the Ministry.

The limitations that apply to this study are regarding the comparison between two different datasets. The Finnish dataset is larger and it covers smaller regional news media and media outlets associated with political parties, while the international dataset consists of internationally well-known media outlets. Smaller international media outlets, which were not included in the dataset, may have reported on the Finnish experiment in different ways.

This study focused on media frames and the factors that influence media-framing. Further studies could be conducted on the effects of media frames on the audience (i.e. how individuals in the audience interpret media frames). Thus, it would be possible to observe how media coverage of the Finnish basic income experiment has shaped the idea of basic income or the idea of social experiments among audience members. Finally, as public opinion is based on the audience's ideas and perspectives, public opinion may be the determining factor in the future of basic income and social experiments.

NOTES

1. A list of the online newspapers and news sites included in this study can be requested from the author.
2. The original language of the quotations of the Finnish news articles is Finnish. The author of this article has translated the quotations into English.
3. The Finnish Basic Income-Experiment 2017–2018. Retrieved from: https://toolbox.finland.fi/life-society/finlands-basic-income-experiment-2017-2018/

REFERENCES

Couldry, N., and Hepp, A. (2018), *The Mediated Construction of Reality*, Cambridge: Polity Press.

De Vreese, C. H. (2014), 'Mediatization of news: the role of journalistic framing', in Esser, F. and Strömbäck, J. (eds), *Mediatization of Politics: Understanding the Transformation of Western Democracies*, London: Palgrave Macmillan, pp. 137–55.

De Vreese, C. H., and Lecheler, S. (2012), 'News framing research: an overview and new developments', in Semetko, H. and Scammel, M. (eds), *The SAGE Handbook of Political Communication*, London: Sage, pp. 292–306.

De Vreese, J. P., and Holli, A. C. H. (2001), 'Framing politics at the launch of the euro: A cross-national comparative study of frames in the news', *Political Communication*, 18(2), 107–22.

Entman, R. M. (1993), 'Framing: Toward clarification of a fractured paradigm', *Journal of Communication*, 43(4), 51–8.

Finland's Basic Income Experiment 2017–2018, website, available at https://toolbox.finland.fi/life-society/finlands-basic-income-experiment-2017-2018/ (accessed 16 December 2020).

Gamson, W., and Modigliani, A. (1987), 'The changing culture of affirmative action', in Braungart, R. G. and Braungart, M. M. (eds), *Research in Political Sociology Vol. 3*, Greenwich: CT: JAI Press, pp. 137–77.

Gamson, W. A., and Modigliani, A. (1989), 'Media discourse and public opinion on nuclear power: A constructionist approach', *American Journal of Sociology*, 95(1), 1–37.

Gitlin, T. (1980), *The Whole World is Watching: Mass Media in the Making & Unmaking of the New Left*, Berkeley: University of California Press.

Hertog, J. K., and McLeod, D. M. (2001), 'A multiperspectival approach to framing analysis: a field guide', in Reese, S. D., Gandy, O. H., and Grant, A. E. (eds), *Framing Public Life: Perspectives of Media and Our Understanding of the Social World*, Mahwah NJ: Erlbaum, pp. 139–61.

Hänggli, R. (2012), 'Key factors in frame building: How strategic political actors shape news media coverage', *The American Behavioral Scientist*, 56(3), 300–17.

Kansallinen Mediatutkimus (2019), 'Lukijamäärät ja kokonaistavoittavuudet' [The National Media Research 2019, The Number of Readers and the Total Coverage], available at https://mediaauditfinland.fi/wp-content/uploads/2020/03/Lukijamaarat2019.pdf (accessed 16 December 2020).

Koch-Baumgarten, S., and Voltmer, K. (2010), 'Public policy and the mass media: the interplay of mass communication and political decision making', in Koch-Baumgarten, S. and Voltmer, K. (eds), *Public Policy and the Mass Media* (Vol. 66), London: Routledge/ECPR.

Kyyrä, T., Naumanen, P., Pesola, H., Uusitalo, R., and Ylikännö, M. (2019), *Aktiivimallin vaikutukset työttömiin ja TE-toimistojen toimintaan* [*The Impact of the Activation Model on the Unemployed and the Operations of TE Offices*], Helsinki: VATT Institute for Economic Research, VATT Tutkimukset 189.

Layder, D. (1998), *Sociological Practice: Linking Theory and Social Research*, London: SAGE Publications.

Matthes, J. (2009), 'What's in a frame? A content analysis of media framing studies in the world's leading communication journals, 1990–2005', *Journalism & Mass Communication Quarterly*, 86(2), 349–67.

Matthes, J., and Kohring, M. (2008), 'The content analysis of media frames: toward improving reliability and validity', *Journal of Communication*, 58(2), 258–79.

McQuail, D. (2005), *Mass Communication Theory* (5th ed.), London: Sage.

Neuman, W. R., Crigler, A. N., and Just, M. R. (1992), *Common Knowledge: News and the Construction of Political Meaning*, Chicago: University of Chicago Press.

Pan, Z., and Kosicki, G. M. (1993), 'Framing analysis: an approach to news discourse', *Political Communication*, 10(1), 55–75.

Perkiö, J., Rincon, L. and Van Draanen, J. (2019), 'Framing basic income: comparing media framing of basic income in Canada, Finland, and Spain', in Torry, M. (ed.), *The Palgrave International Handbook of Basic Income. Exploring the Basic Income Guarantee*, Cham: Palgrave Macmillan, pp. 233–51.

Reese, S. (2001), 'Prologue – framing public life: a bridging model for media research', in Reese, S., Gandy, O., and Grant, A. (eds), *Framing Public Life*, Mahwah, NJ: Erlbaum, pp. 7–31.

Scheufele, D. A. (1999), 'Framing as a theory of media effects', *Journal of Communication*, 49(1), 103–22.

Scheufele, D. A., and Tewksbury, D. (2007), 'Framing, agenda setting, and priming: the evolution of three media effects models', *Journal of Communication*, 57(1), 9–20.

Semetko, H. A., and Valkenburg, P. M. (2000), 'Framing European politics: a content analysis of press and television news', *Journal of Communication*, 50(2), 93–109.

Shoemaker, P., and Reese, S. (1996), *Mediating the Message: Theories of Influences on Mass Media Content* (2nd ed.), White Plains: Longman.

Snow, D. A., and Benford, R. D. (1992), 'Master frames and cycles of protest', in Morris, A. D. and Mueller, C. M. (eds), *Frontiers in Social Movement Theory*, New Haven, CT: Yale University Press, pp. 133–55.

Timmermans, S. and Tavory, I. (2012), 'Theory construction in qualitative research: from grounded theory to abductive analysis', *Sociological Theory*, 30(3), 167–86.

APPENDIX

Table 13A.1   *The number and percentages of persons interviewed in the media regarding the basic income experiment, according to a phone survey*

The number of times the person was interviewed	Experiment group		Control group		All	
	n	%	*n*	%	*n*	%
None	430	94.5	814	98.5	1244	97.1
1–5 times	17	3.7	11	1.3	28	2.2
5–10 times	3	0.7	1	0.1	4	0.3
More than 10 times	3	0.7	0	0.0	3	0.2
Unsure	2	0.4	0	0.0	2	0.2
In total	455	100.0	826	100.0	1281	100.0

14. The feasibility of universal basic income

Olli Kangas

INTRODUCTION

The Finnish government's experiment with universal basic income attracted exceptionally broad public interest both within Finland and around the world. Although universal basic income had been widely discussed in academic, popular, and policy circles for decades, Finland was the first country to give universal basic income a nationwide, controlled, randomised trial. Much of the feedback surrounding this pilot project has been positive (Chapter 13) and has lauded the Finnish government for bravely attempting to develop a new model of social security. However, reactions have not all been positive, and opponents of universal basic income have used the shortcomings of the Finnish experiment to argue against the efficacy of the basic income or related policies. Thus, proponents of universal basic income fear that the Finnish experiment weakened the political appeal of the scheme and diminished perceptions of its political feasibility. These fears are exacerbated by the fact that the results of the experiment are often taken out of context, simplified and misrepresented by policymakers and mass media seeking sensational news (Widerquist, 2018: 3).

The Finnish experiment merged universal basic income with the existing system of social security benefits in Finland. In order to properly define the functional division of labour between universal basic income and existing income transfer schemes – and because of the obligatory nature of the experiment – Finland devised special legislation pertaining to the experiment (Chapters 3 and 4). For instance, because Finland is a member state of the European Union (EU), it must adhere to the subsidiary principles of the EU. Although these principles hold that social policies are, in principle, the responsibility of national governments, in practice, the implementation of universal basic income in an EU member state brings national policy into conversation with EU-level agreements on the free movement of labour, labour legislation, and other aspects of coordination between member states. Indeed, the relationship between national universal basic income policy and EU-level legislation was considered when the research group began to plan the basic income experiment and to write the first report (Kangas and Pulkka, 2016; Chapter 3; see also Kalliomaa-Puha et al., 2017).

Thus, the Finnish experiment brings up questions regarding the possibility of implementing basic income in a single EU member state and the various EU-level constraints which would affect the implementation of such a policy (see Van Parijs and Vanderborght, 2017). Given that the Finnish experiment is central to many discussions regarding the feasibility of universal basic income, and the experiment's status as the only nationwide attempt to institute the income on a trial basis, this chapter discusses whether the experiment increased the feasibility of universal basic income in Finland. To assess the feasibility, we employ the often-used typology of the political feasibility of universal basic income provided by De Wispelaere and Noguera (2012; see also Torry, 2016). This typology suggests that the feasibility of the unconditional income transfer scheme depends on four factors – namely, strategic, institutional, psychological and behavioural factors. With help from this typology and evaluations of the Finnish experiment presented both in this volume and in earlier publications (for example, Kangas et al., 2019, 2020), we examine whether the experiment makes universal basic income seem like a viable option for future social policy in Finland.

This chapter proceeds in the following way. First, we briefly introduce the concept of political feasibility. Then, we introduce the four factors of political feasibility outlined above and discuss them in relation to the planning (Kangas and Pulkka, 2016) and evaluation (Kangas et al., 2019, 2020; Hämäläinen et al., 2020) of the Finnish experiment with universal basic income. Finally, we summarise our discussion and argue that the experiment's findings make it highly unlikely that universal basic income will be implemented in Finland in the near future.

POLITICAL FEASIBILITY

A policy is politically feasible 'when the background conditions are such that there is a reasonable probability of the policy becoming actualised in the foreseeable future' (De Wispelaere and Noguera, 2012). In other words, policies are politically feasible when reform is preferred to the status quo. Furthermore, scholars have asserted that 'political feasibility refers to constraints arising from human will, opposed to natural, physical, and technological impediments' (De Wispelaere and Noguera, 2012). Thus, it depends on the actions and interactions of human beings.

Politics implies agency and power relations. Both need to be taken into account when assessing the political feasibility of a given policy. Following

De Wispelaere, and Noguera (2012: 19), we distinguish between discrete and diffuse agency in this paper. Discrete agency belongs to readily identifiable actors that have specific, defined and distinctive interests, and the capacity to carry out reforms. Discrete agents are usually the most visible political agents (politicians, social elites, bureaucrats, and organisational actors such as trade unions). Diffuse agency is comprised of many kinds of actors and movements with little or no clear, strong, leadership or internal coherence (the general public, families with children, recipients of social assistance, etc.).

The distinction we make here is similar to Olson's (1965) distinction between privileged groups (usually small groups) with a concentrated interest and large groups with diffuse interests. Needless to say, both types of agents and agencies coexist and interact in different ways. We suggest that discrete and diffuse agents confront a different pair of the four factors affecting feasibility outlined above. Whereas discrete agents confront the strategic and institutional feasibility of universal basic income, diffuse agents confront its psychological and behavioural feasibility. Each of these four factors has important ramifications for our analysis, so we cover them all individually.

STRATEGIC FEASIBILITY

Strategic feasibility is linked to Weber's (1989 [1904–5]) and Geertz's (1973: 314) statement that policy ideas require strong and committed carriers to be feasible, even if they have a high level of public support. Before explaining further, it is useful to distinguish between cheap and expensive political support (De Wispelaere, 2015: 72–3). Whereas cheap support often vanishes in actual political struggles or when the presenter of an idea gains political power, expensive support demands strong commitment and participation from pressure groups to push an idea through to the realisation of a policy. In other words, cheap support is support which lacks 'either the commitment or the capacity to engage in the necessary political action to build a sustainable coalition around the policy' (De Wispelaere and Noguera, 2012: 22). We can see that universal basic income in Finland has cheap support insofar as studies have found that 60–70 percent of the Finnish public supports it in theory (for example, Andersson and Kangas, 2005; Airio et al., 2015; Chapter 11 in this volume) but only around 30 percent of the public supports universal basic income when confronted by the increases in tax rates that would accompany its implementation (Airio et al., 2016; Chrisp et al., 2020).

In Weber's (1989 [1904–5]: 90) famous analysis of the relationship between capitalism and Protestantism, he emphasised that ideas that have been effective in history have been supported by dominant or powerful social groups. Likewise, Geertz (1973: 314) wrote that ideas must be carried by powerful social groups in order to have powerful social effects. In other words, ideas must be institutionalised in order to be reified and actualised – they may not take hold or have an effect if they are not sufficiently revered, celebrated, defended, and imposed by a sufficiently powerful group of elites (discrete agents).

While there is a loose group of Finnish universal basic income enthusiasts representing diffuse interests, two small to medium-sized political parties in Finland, the Greens and the Left Alliance, provide discrete support for it. However, neither party can be classified as a powerful group because they do not possess the political power necessary to implement universal basic income. Finland's three largest political parties – the Social Democratic Party, the Finns Party, and the conservative National Coalition – are all against universal basic income. In a multi-party political system like Finland's, politicians must build coalitions between parties in order to successfully pass legislation and implement policy. One or two of those three bigger parties will be included in the subsequent coalition governments, which decreases the political feasibility of basic income.

Furthermore, social partners play crucial roles in the adoption and implementation of Finnish social policies. For instance, the Confederation of Finnish Industries and Finland's Central Trade Union Organisation have traditionally agreed upon a wide array of social policy questions relating to family leave, sick leave and pensions, during the course of centralised income policy negotiations (Alestalo et al., 1985). Both social partners (Chapter 2) and semi-private pension companies (Kangas, 2007) have demonstrated the value of social partners in Finnish policy by working together on pension policy. Due to their involvement in the political process, social partners 'own' these kinds of policy schemes and form an institutional barrier against political interference in those domains. Thus, for universal basic income or any other major social policy reform to pass, it must be supported by a robust coalition of political parties and social partners.

INSTITUTIONAL FEASIBILITY

Institutional feasibility is closely related to strategic feasibility. It refers to the administrative challenges posed by the implementation of a policy. These challenges pertain to updated citizen registers, implementing new payment tools, and monitoring payment of benefits (De Wispelaere and Noguera, 2012: 24–7). Given the accuracy and coverage of the population, social security, income and all other registers, there are no major problems in carrying out big social policy reforms in Finland.

Institutionalists emphasise that agents do not act in a vacuum; instead, they are constrained by previous policy actions, established institutions, and stable, conventional ways of acting and thinking in a given political arena.

Political power and agendas of yesterday remain impactful today, frozen in present-day institutions and cognitive paradigms. This situation both facilitates breakthroughs in some policy areas and rules out policy options or ideas in others (Mahoney and Thelen, 2010; Béland and Cox, 2011; Schmidt, 2010). For example, Finland's income-related unemployment protection system is fund-based, and its funds are mainly administrated by trade unions. Therefore, this formal institution might hinder the implementation of universal basic income (see Chapter 2). The same goes for Finland's employment-related pension scheme.

Current legislation can also constrain actors' choices and perception of viable policy options. As we described in Chapter 3, current legislation can pose a major hurdle to the successful implementation of universal basic income, largely because of the administrative and legislative challenges inherent in integrating the legislation with existing national and EU-level social security legislation and norms (see for example, Kangas and Pulkka, 2016, Kalliomaa-Puha et al., 2016; Tuovinen, 2017). Lawmakers confronted two distinct challenges at the national level. First, they had to ensure that universal basic income laws met constitutional and other legislative stipulations (Chapters 3 and 4; see also Scharpf, 2000; Van Parijs, 2000). Second, they had to define how other, existing social security benefits should be related to or integrated with universal basic income – i.e. which benefits should be replaced or reduced if the income were introduced, and if so, by what or by how much. In contrast, the EU-level challenges facing lawmakers revolved around whether universal basic income could fall under EU regulations regarding the coordination of social security systems (883/2004). In short, lawmakers pondered whether it was possible to implement a universal basic income scheme in only one EU member state considering the depth of EU-level coordination vis-à-vis national legislation (The European Parliament and the Council, 2004).

In addition, there is one element of institutional feasibility that is specific to Finland: the political role of municipalities. Finland contains over 300 municipalities, and each has its own political duties and purviews. These include the duty to organise social and health services and the right to collect taxes to finance the fulfilment of this duty. While planning the experiment, representatives of the municipalities expressed concern about universal basic income's possible impact on municipalities' tasks and budgets. In short, the municipalities were sceptical of the basic income at the time of the experiment (Vogt et al., 2017).

PSYCHOLOGICAL FEASIBILITY

Psychological feasibility refers to the general public's acceptance of a policy (in this case, universal basic income). General opinion surveys showed that

Finns' support for universal basic income ranged between 20 percent and 80 percent, depending on the formulation of survey questions (Pulkka, 2018). General framing, such as, 'Is universal basic income a good idea?' garnered high and robust support for it. In 2015, as much as 69 percent of the Finns said that it is a good or very good idea (Airio et al., 2015). The 2020 survey (see Chapter 11) that used the same question displayed significantly lower support levels (60 percent).

Furthermore, when survey respondents are told that taxes would be increased to pay for universal basic income, support for it drops to around 30 percent (Chapter 11; Airio et al., 2016; Chrisp et al., 2020). When survey questions are too general, they might paint too optimistic a picture of the possibilities of and popular support for universal basic income. The inverse is true for survey questions which are too specific. Even though research shows that it is unlikely that a universal basic income programme could be financed with increases in income tax alone (Van Parijs and Vanderborght, 2017; Andrade et al., 2019; Standing, 2020), the focus on tax revenue as the primary means to fund such programmes has undoubtedly skewed the psychological feasibility of the income and made the public's genuine support for it difficult to measure.

Because votes for politicians in democratic societies depend on constituencies' support, public opinion matters when these politicians set their policy and reform agendas. However, the simple 'bottom-up' view that constituents' opinions are directly and genuinely mirrored in political decisions is too simple and naïve. Democracy entails negotiations and is deliberative (Elster, 1998). Political elites negotiate and deliberate using techniques and devices which can effectively reframe, reformulate and manipulate public opinion. Thus, we can understand idea or policy framing as tools that elites use to legitimise their policy choices to the public (Campbell, 2002).

As we saw in Chapter 3, framing is an essential part of the political struggle of interpretation in which linguistic concepts and symbols give conceptual meaning to an issue and steer political debate. Ideas and policies are strategically framed so as to create a basis for political decisions and help political actors legitimise their decisions to their constituents. Via framing, political actors may, for instance, socially construct the sense of a need for policy reform (Kangas et al., 2014). Of course, politicians are neither the only nor the most powerful actors in framing political realities or future ambitions. As we saw in Chapter 13, national and international media alike framed public perception of the Finnish experiment and the basic income more generally, and as shown by Widerquist (2018) media oftentimes tend to be sensational rather than objective and spin the results to favour this or that interpretation.

BEHAVIOURAL FEASIBILITY

In order to be behaviourally feasible, a policy must neither fail to produce its desired outcomes nor produce counterproductive effects (De Wispelaere and Noguera, 2012: 29–32). Because the Finnish government undertook its experiment to determine whether basic income can effectively fortify incentives to seek paid work and combat disincentives, we should measure the behavioural feasibility of the experiment with reference to its effects on Finns' employment and incentive to work (Kangas et al., 2019, 2020). Evaluation of the experiment shows that universal basic income recipients did not work significantly more or less than the control population (Hämäläinen et al., 2020 and Chapter 6 in this volume). Thus, the experiment did not produce the desired outcome insofar as it did not increase or decrease Finns' employment.

This result opened the experiment itself up to vicious critiques, because its ability to enhance Finns' employment became the defining criteria of evaluation for many observers. However, evaluations of the experiment have demonstrated that it had many other effects. For instance, reception of universal basic income was positively and significantly associated with improvements in Finns' mental and social well-being (Chapter 7). Universal basic income recipients reported less financial and mental stress than their control counterparts (Chapter 8), and reported that they felt more confident, felt that they had more control over their lives, and felt that they were more trusting of other people and societal institutions (Chapter 10). Thus, when assessing the behavioural feasibility of universal basic income, researchers should attempt to weigh its recipients' quality of life alongside the large-scale economic effects of it.

CONCLUSION

This chapter asked whether Finland's pilot project with universal basic income increased the political feasibility of implementing universal basic income in Finland in the future by assessing its strategic, institutional, psychological, and behavioural feasibility. We will address each of these in turn, here, and then make more general comments regarding the pilot project's effects on the perceived feasibility of universal basic income in the future.

Regarding strategic feasibility, we found that universal basic income advocates do not form a discrete group powerful enough to impose their idea onto their peers. Instead, they form a diffuse group and lack the political power and organisation to translate their advocacy into powerful social action. Regarding institutional feasibility, we identified several rigid constraints which limit the implementation of universal basic income in Finland: the Finnish social security system (in which social partners have a strong influence on the admin-

194   *Experimenting with unconditional basic income*

istration of the main social insurance programmes), the ways in which political power and will are frozen in formal institutions, and the difficulty of coordinating national and EU-level policy with regard to universal basic income.

Here, we suggest that although modest basic income benefits could be carried out at the national level, true universal basic income would be difficult to enact in the EU – unless residents in a country which enacted universal basic income are willing to finance benefits that can be exported from the country to some other EU country or outside the EU. Regarding the psychological feasibility of the basic income, we found that popular support for it depends in part on how we measure it and that the relatively cheap popular support that it enjoys is not strong enough to make significant changes to the prevailing discourse surrounding social policy. Finally, regarding its behavioural feasibility, we found that the experiment did not necessarily have its intended effect on Finns' employment – or at least not significantly enough. However, we also suggested, in line with other studies (for example, Van Parijs, 1995; Standing, 2020; Bregman, 2017; Van Parijs and Vanderborght, 2017), that universal basic income may improve recipients' feelings of freedom, dignity and self-determination. This suggests both that basic income bears a huge burden of proof regarding its behavioural feasibility and that some analysts misplace this burden by emphasising only its potential employment, rather than any of its possible human, impacts.

Thus, there are serious obstacles in the political feasibility of basic income in Finland. Usually, exceptional times open up new possibilities. However, the COVID-19 pandemic has not increased or intensified political discussions on the implementation of basic income in Finland as it has done in many other countries. The main reason is that the welfare state's stress test caused by the pandemic has shown that the existing welfare state has worked very well under exceptional circumstances and it has cushioned the effects of the pandemic rather well. Only a very few temporary measures have been introduced to protect vulnerable groups (for example, Kangas & Kalliomaa-Puha, 2021). Institutional continuity rather than significant changes in the policy paradigm prevails. To sum up our analysis on the feasibility of basic income in Finland, we can conclude that for the time being universal basic income is not a realistic policy option. However, never say never.

REFERENCES

Act on The Basic Income Experiment (1528/2016; available in Finnish at https://finlex
.fi/fi/laki/alkup/2016/20161528) (accessed 14 December 2020).
Airio, I., Kangas, O., Koskenvuo, K. and Laatu, M. (2015) 'Kansa kannattaa perustu-
loa' ['People support basic income'], available at http://tutkimusblogi.kela.fi/
arkisto/2759 (accessed 19 December 2020).

Airio, I., Kangas, O., Koskenvuo, K. and Laatu, M. (2016), 'Tasaveroon pohjautuvaan perustuloon suhtaudutaan varauksellisesti' ['Scepticism about basic income that is based on flat-rate taxes'], available at http://tutkimusblogi.kela.fi/arkisto/2942 (accessed 19 December 2020).

Alestalo, M., Flora, P. and Uusitalo, H. (1985), 'Structure and politics in the making of the welfare state: Finland in comparative perspective', in Alapuro, R., Alestalo, M., Haavio-Mannila, E. and Väyrynen, R. (eds), *Small States in Comparative Perspective*, Oslo: Norwegian University Press, pp. 188–210.

Andersson, J. O. and Kangas, O. (2005), 'Universalism in the age of workfare: Attitudes to basic income in Sweden and Finland', in Kildal, N. and Kuhnle, S. (eds), *Normative Foundations of the Welfare State: The Nordic Experience*, London: Routledge, pp. 112–29.

Andrade, J., Crocker, G. and Lansley, S. (2019), 'Alternative funding methods', in Torry, M. (ed.), *The Palgrave International Handbook of Basic Income*, Cham: Palgrave Macmillan, pp. 175–90.

Béland, D. and Cox. R. H. (eds) (2011), *Ideas and Politics in Social Science Research*, New York: Oxford University Press.

Bregman, R. (2017), *Utopia for Realists and How We Can Get There*, London: Bloomsbury.

Campbell, J. L. (2002), 'Ideas, politics, and public policy', *Annual Review of Sociology*, 28, 21–38.

Chrisp, J., Pulkka, V-V. and Rincón García, L. (2020), 'Snowballing or wilting? What affects public support for varying models of basic income?', *Journal of International and Comparative Social Policy*, 36(3), 223–36.

De Wispelaere, J. (2015), *An Income of One's Own? The Political Analysis of Universal Basic Income*, Tampere: Tampere University Press.

De Wispelaere, J. and Noguera J.A. (2012), 'On the political feasibility of universal basic income: an analytical framework', in Caputo, R. (ed.), *Basic Income Guarantee and Politics*, New York: Palgrave Macmillan, pp. 17–38.

Elster, J. (ed.) (1998), *Deliberative Democracy*, Cambridge: Cambridge University Press.

Geertz, C. (1973), *The Interpretation of Cultures*, New York: Basic Books.

Hämäläinen, K., Kanninen, O., Simanainen, M. and Verho, J. (2020), *Perustulokokeilun arvioinnin loppuraportti: Rekisterianalyysi työmarkkinavaikutuksista* [*The Final Evaluation Report on the Basic Income Experiment: Register-based Analysis on Labour Market Effects*], Helsinki: VATT Institute for Economic Research, VATT muistiot 59.

Kalliomaa-Puha, L., Tuovinen, A-K. and Kangas, O. (2016), 'The basic income experiment in Finland', *Journal of Social Security Law*, 23(2), 75–88.

Kangas, O. (2007), 'Finland: labour markets against politics', in Immergut, E. M., Anderson, K. M. and Schoulze, I. (eds), *The Handbook of Western European Pension Politics*, Oxford: Oxford University Press, pp. 248–96.

Kangas, O., Jauhiainen, S., Simanainen, M. and Ylikännö, M. (eds) (2019), *Perustulokokeilun työllisyys- ja hyvinvointivaikutukset: Alustavia tuloksia Suomen perustulokokeilusta 2017–2018* [*The Basic Income Experiment 2017–2018 in Finland: Preliminary Results*], Sosiaali- ja terveysministeriö, Raportteja ja muistioita 2019:19].

Kangas, O., Jauhiainen, S., Simanainen, M. and Ylikännö, M. (eds.) (2020), *Suomen perustulokokeilun arviointi* [*Evaluation of the Finnish Basic Income Experiment*], Sosiaali- ja terveysministeriö, Raportteja ja muistioita 2020:15.

Kangas, O. and Kalliomaa-Puha, L. (2021), 'ESPN Thematic Report: COVID-19 impact on social protection and social inclusion policies: Finland', Brussels: European Commission.

Kangas, O., Niemelä, M. and Varjonen, S. (2014), 'When and why do ideas matter? The influence of framing on opinion formation and policy change', *European Political Science Review*, 6(1), 73–92.

Kangas, O. and Pulkka, V-V. (eds) (2016), *Ideasta kokeiluun? Esiselvitys perustulokokeilun toteuttamisvaihtoehdoista [From an Idea to an Experiment – Preliminary Report on Alternatives for Basic Income Experiment]*, Helsinki: Valtioneuvosto, Valtioneuvoston selvitys ja tutkimustoiminnan julkaisusarja 13/2016.

Mahoney, J. and Thelen, K. (eds.) (2010), *Explaining Institutional Change: Ambiguity, Agency, and Power*, New York: Cambridge University Press.

Olson, M. (1965), *The Logic of Collective Action: Public Goods and the Theory of Groups*, Harvard: Harvard University Press.

Pulkka, V.-V. (2018), 'Finland shares unconditional money, but the public view remains polarized', available at http://blogs.bath.ac.uk/iprblog/2018/01/23/finland -shares-unconditional-money-but-the-public-view-remains-polarised (accessed 20 December 2020).

Scharpf, F. (2000), 'Basic income and social Europe', in Van der Veen, R. and Groot, L. (eds), *Basic Income on the Agenda*, Amsterdam: Amsterdam University Press, pp. 155–60.

Schmidt. V. A. (2010), 'Taking ideas and discourse seriously: explaining change through discursive institutionalism as the fourth new institutionalism', *European Political Science Review*, 2(1), 1–25.

Standing, G. (2020), *Battling Eight Giants. Basic Income Now*, London: Tauris.

The European Parliament and the Council (2004), *Regulation (EC) No 883/2004 on the Coordination of Social Security Systems*, Brussels: The European Parliament and the Council.

Torry, M. (2016), *The Feasibility of Citizen's Income*, New York: Palgrave Macmillan.

Tuovinen, A.-K. (2017), *Perustuslainmukainen perustulokokeilu [Evaluation of the Basic Income Experiment in the Light of the Finnish Constitution]*, Helsinki: Kela, Working Papers 114.

Van Parijs, P. (1995), *Real Freedom for All: What (If Anything) Can Justify Capitalism?* Oxford: Oxford University Press.

Van Parijs, P. (2000), 'Basic income at the heart of social Europe: Reply to Fritz Scharpf', in Van der Veen, R. and Groot, L. (eds), *Basic Income on the Agenda*, Amsterdam: Amsterdam University Press, pp. 161–9.

Van Parijs, P. and Vanderborght, Y. (2017), *Basic Income. A Radical Proposal for a Free Society and a Sane Economy*, Cambridge, MA, and London: Harvard University Press.

Vogt, E., Porko, M., Hakola, J., Uotinen, S., Tyni, T., Lehtonen, S., Punakallio, M. and Lindberg, E. (2017), *Kunnat ja perustulo [Municipalities and Basic Income]*, Helsinki: Kuntaliitto.

Weber, M. (1989 [1904–5]), *The Protestant Ethic and the Spirit of Capitalism*, London: Allen & Unwin.

Widerquist, K. (2018), *A Critical Analysis of Basic Income Experiments for Researchers, Policymakers, and Citizens*, Cham: Palgrave Macmillan.

Index

ability to work 3, 56, 59–62, 64, 65, 66–7, 157, 158, 165
action modality 153, 165–6
    content analysis 162–4
activation model 52–3
    for unemployed persons 176
age 141, 142, 144
agenda-setting 170
Arber, S. 92
Arendt's theory of labour, work and action 5, 150, 152–3, 155–64
Atkinson, A. 21
attitudes 137–9, 144, 146
    on deservingness 142, 146
attrition 51
autonomy 153, 159, 165

basic allowance 11, 12
basic income 20, 21, 23, 31–2, 48, 50, 52–3, 64, 72, 89, 106–7, 109, 112–13, 138
    to achieve long-term aspirations 161
    and action modality 162–6
    for better mental health 160
    bureaucracy and 108, 110–12, 114
    Canada 58
    caring for relatives/ageing relatives 163–4
    (un)conditional 176
    and confidence in re-employment 65–7
    Dutch 58–9
    economic gains with 160
    economic security of 156, 164
    effects 151–2, 162, 166
        on employment 182
        on subjective well-being 95, 99
        on well-being 177, 182
    and employment 46, 47, 60–62, 68
    and EU legislation 25–7
    experimentation model 27–32

feasibility of 5
Finnish media 181
full 20, 22–3
    to invest in studies 160
    and labour modality 155–8, 164–5
    labour, work and action in 152–3, 155–64
    media framing of 171
    as money of trust 4
    Netherlands 58
    for NGO activities 162
    partial 20, 23–5
    policy 114
    for profitable business 161
    with salary 156–7
    for social and political activities 162
    for students 111
    trust and confidence 125–31
    universal *see* universal basic income
    for voluntary work 162
    for well-being 159
    and work modality 158–61, 165
basic income experiment 1–2, 6, 7, 13, 15, 18, 19, 32–3, 37, 44–5, 56, 72, 73, 75, 82, 84–6, 90, 107, 109, 113, 150–53, 155, 156, 159–62, 164, 166, 171
    activation model 52–3
    clarity of regulation 41
    data sources 46–50
    employment effects of 57–60
    equality 39–40
    evaluation of 3, 45–6, 50–53
    measuring SFWB in 94–8
    media coverage of 50
    media frames 174–5, 183
        Finnish 175–9, 181, 182
        international 179–82
    population surveys 50
    proportionality 40–41
    qualitative data 153–5
    regulation by law 41

for social security benefit 41–2
and unemployment 179, 183
Basic Income Experiment Act 31–2, 41, 42
basic income experiment bill 30–31
basic income recipients 99–100
and control groups 96–8
financial situation 93–4, 99
financial stress 96
basic social assistance 12
basic unemployment benefit 27, 29, 31, 33, 52–3, 109, 111
behavioural feasibility 193, 194
Bénabou, R. 120
benefit claiming 106–14
benefits for children and families 9–10
Blomberg, H. 5, 114
Brüggen, E. C. 92
budget 19, 29
bureaucracy 4, 138
and basic income 108, 110–12, 114
in benefit claiming 106–14
of benefits system 113
experiences of 109–12, 126, 128
perceptions of 106, 108–14
regression analysis 112, 113
traps 15
treatment group 126

Calnitsky, D. 58, 150
Canada, basic income 58
Canadian Guaranteed Annual Income 58
capabilities 4, 120–22, 124, 126–31
perceptions of 124, 125
cash transfer programmes (CCT) 71, 82, 85
CD see Christian Democratic Party (CD)
Centre Party 2
cheap support 189, 194
child allowance 9–10, 12
children benefits 9–10
Chou, E. Y. 92
Christian Democratic Party (CD) 31
cognitive bandwidth scarcity 81–2, 85
cognitive capabilities 73, 74, 78, 82–3, 85, 86
communication research 170
community effects 52
conditional unemployment benefits 52
Confederation of Finnish Industries 190

confidence 3, 4, 117–18, 120, 122–4, 126–31
levels of 124, 125
trust and 129
conflict frame 174–7, 180–83
conservative National Coalition 190
Constitutional Law Committee of the Parliament 38–42
constitutional preconditions 37–42
Constitution of Finland 37–8, 40
consumption value 120
content analysis 155
action modality 162–4
labour modality 155–8
work modality 158–61
control groups 39, 44, 51, 52–3, 60, 61, 64, 75–6, 78, 82, 84–6, 91, 94, 109, 110, 112, 113, 123–4, 129, 177
basic income recipients and 96–8
mental distress 85
responses of 110
see also treatment groups
COVID-19 pandemic 194
Cronbach's alpha 141, 142

data sources 46–50
Davala, S. 150
day care 9
democracy 192
depression 74, 95
deservingness 145
attitudes on 142, 146
individual/social blame 140–42
De Wispelaere, J. 18, 107, 114, 188, 189
diffuse agency 189
disability 75
discrete agency 189
Dutch, basic income 58–9

economic frame 174–5, 179, 183
economic recession 179
education 62, 141–2, 144
educational attainment 126, 127
employment 182, 193, 194
barriers 3, 64, 65, 67, 68
basic income and 46, 47, 60–62
health as a barrier to 64, 68
precondition for 64

probability of 62–4
rates 2, 13, 50
work ability and 66–7
employment effects 3, 27, 30, 33, 45–8,
   52–3, 55, 68, 82
   of basic income experiments 57–60
employment frame 175–6
employment relations 139, 145
employment services 62
employment status 75, 86
   health and 84–5
Entman, R. M. 171
equality 38–40
equilibrium effects 52
ESS *see* European Social Survey (ESS)
EU legislation 21, 25–7, 34, 191
European Social Survey (ESS) 94, 121,
   123, 135
evaluation 3, 45–6, 50–53
expensive support 189
experiences of bureaucracy 109–12, 126,
   128
   regression analysis 112, 113
experimentation legislation 38–9
experiments 50–52

face-to-face interviews 49
family benefits 10
feasibility of basic income 5
   universal *see* universal basic income
financial backup 98, 99
financial behaviour 97
financial capability 97
financial distress 96–7
financial freedom 98
financial management 97, 99
financial problems 126–9
financial situation of basic income
   recipients 93–4, 99
financial stress 3, 4, 68, 90, 92, 94, 96–9,
   101, 193
financial well-being 90–91
   subjective 91–3
Finland's Central Trade Union
   Organisation 190
Finnish media frames 175–9, 182
   versus international media frames
   181
Finnish Ministry of Foreign Affairs 179
Finnish Tax Administration 28–9

Finns Party 2, 190
fixed-term work contracts 139, 140, 145
flat-rate tax 20, 24, 25
Forget, E. L. 71, 85, 126
frame-building, internal and external
   factors in 171, 183
frames 173
   in Finnish media 175–9
   in international media 179–81
framing 170, 171
Frazer, N. 130
Fukuyama, F. 118
full basic income 20, 22–3
full-time work 61
   contracts 139, 145
fundamental rights 37–8, 40
   regulation 41

Gamson, W. 170
Geertz, C. 189
gender 141, 142, 144
generalised trust 117, 119, 121, 123–4
   see also institutionalised trust
Gibson, M. 72
Green League 2, 182, 190

Halman, L. 137
Hawthorne effect 51–2
health 3, 4, 6, 48, 51, 57, 64, 65, 68,
   71–6, 82, 85, 89, 90, 93, 95, 120,
   126–9, 158, 160, 177, 182
   defined 72
   and employment status 84–5
   inequities 89
   outcomes 85, 86, 92
   problems 59, 64, 65, 68, 96, 126,
   129
   subjective state of 76
health services 74–6, 85, 86, 95
health status 75, 84, 85, 92, 122, 123
Heimer, C. 130
Hetemäki, M. 177
home care allowances 10
Honneth, A. 130
household income 139
housing allowance 10, 12
human-interest frame 174–80, 182, 183
Hum, D. 58
Huo, Y. J. 119

ID *see* individual identity (ID)
incentive traps 15–16, 178, 182
income inadequacy 136–40, 145
income-related benefits 11, 12
income transfer 8–9, 32, 68
income traps 13–15
individual blame 137, 141–2, 145, 146
  see also social blame
individual frames 170
individual identity (ID) 46
insecure employment 136–40, 145
institutional feasibility 190–91, 193–4
institutionalised trust 117, 119, 121,
  123–4
internal capability 124
international attention frame 174, 175,
  178–9, 183
international media frames 179–82
  Finnish media frames *versus* 181
item-specific opinions 138–40, 142, 144,
  146

Jansson, I. 150, 152, 153
Jauhiainen, S. 4

Kangas, O. 2–5
Kela *see* Social Insurance Institution of
  Finland
Kosicki, G. M. 173, 174
Kroll, C. 5

labour activation frame 171
labour market services 55
labour market subsidy 11, 12, 27, 31, 60
labour modality 153, 164–5
  content analysis 155–8
labour, work and action 5, 152–3, 164–6
  content analysis 155–64
Lappalainen, K. 86
Lassander, M. 4
last-resort social assistance 58
Left Alliance 2, 190
Left Party 182
legislation 21, 25–7, 29–30, 191
  enabling the experiment 37–8
Lennon, J. 117
life satisfaction 73, 74, 76
long-term stress 97, 101
long-term unemployment 93

Mäkkylä, K. 1
marginal tax rates 13, 14
Marin, S. 55
Maslow's hierarchy of needs 90, 120
McCartney, P. 117
means-tested benefit schemes 82
media 169
media coverage 169, 172, 173, 179, 182,
  184
media frames 170, 182
  Finnish 175–9, 182
  international 179–82
media framing 171
media framing analysis 173–4
mental disorder 75
mental distress 73, 74, 76, 78, 85, 86
  regression results 84
  unemployment and 82, 84, 85
Mental Health Index (MHI-5) 74–6
mental well-being 82, 85, 86
MHI-5 *see* Mental Health Index (MHI-5)
Ministry of Social Affairs and Health 19,
  20, 31, 46, 178, 181, 183, 184
Modigliani, A. 170
motivational value 120
Mullainathan, S. 81
multidisciplinary evaluation 3, 19, 64,
  69, 99
municipalities, political role of 191
mutual trust 117, 118

national benefit schemes 26
National Coalition Party 2, 142, 176
negative income tax 20–22
Netemeyer, R. G. 92
Netherlands, basic income 58
news articles 172, 174
Niemelä, M. 4
Noguera J.A. 188, 189
non-discrimination principle 39, 40
Nussbaum, M. 4, 118, 121, 130
  internal capability 124

objective financial well-being 90, 92, 99
obligatory nation-wide field experiment
  27, 29, 33
obligatory participation 50
Olson, M. 189
online news articles 172

Index

Ontario Disability Support Program 58
opinions 4–5, 137–42, 144–6, 191–2

paid work/employment 151, 153–5, 157, 162, 166
Pan, Z. 173, 174
Parolin, Z. 135
partial basic income 20, 23–5
    effect on population groups 109–10
participation income 21–2
participation tax rates 13, 23–5, 32
part-time work 61–2
    contracts 139, 140, 145
Pega, F. 85
Pelzer, B. 82
perceptions of bureaucracy 106, 108–14
Perkiö, J. 171, 182
permanent work contracts 139, 145
PES *see* public employment services (PES)
planning the experiment 19–20
Polanyi, K. 136
policy framing 192
policy ideas 189
political affiliations 144, 145
political decision-making 180
political feasibility 188–9, 193
    behavioural 187–8, 194
    institutional 190–91, 193–4
    psychological 191–2, 194
    strategic 189–90, 193
political parties 2, 30–31, 176, 177, 181–4, 190
political power 191, 193, 194
population groups 109–10
population survey 138, 139
poverty 23, 141
powerful groups 189–90, 193
precariat 136
Prescott, D. 58
preventive social assistance 12
progressive income tax 13
proportionality 39–41
psychological distress 95
psychological feasibility 191–2, 194
Public Employment Services (PES) 62, 159, 162
public opinion 4–5
Putnam, R. 117

qualitative interview 153–5
    basic income effects on 150
        action modality 162–4
        labour modality 155–8
        work modality 158–61

randomised controlled trials 44, 45
    basic income experiment
        activation model 52–3
        data sources 46–50
        evaluation of 45–6, 50–53
randomised field experiment 33, 72
Rawls, J. 4, 120
    primary goods 120
realistic tax model 24
recognition 119, 130
re-employment 56, 60, 64–7, 69
register data 45–7, 51, 52, 60
regression analysis 61, 64, 74, 84
    experiment and experiences of bureaucracy 112–13
    measures of SFWB in 98–9
    support for basic income 139–41, 143–4
response distributions of survey questions 76–81, 83–4
rhetorical structure 173
right to social security 37
right to unemployment benefits 38
Rinne, A. 55
RMSEA *see* root mean square error of approximation (RMSEA)
Roosma, F. 135
root mean square error of approximation (RMSEA) 122

Scharpf, F. 27
Scheufele, D. A. 170, 171
scientific research 175, 180, 182–3
script structure 173
self-confidence 3, 4, 120, 127
    trust and 130
SEM *see* structural equation modelling (SEM)
Semetko, H. A. 173
Sen, A. 4, 130
    capabilities 90, 118, 120–21
SFWB *see* subjective financial well-being (SFWB)

Shafir, E. 81
signalling value 120
Simanainen, M. 3–5
Simpson, W. 58
Sipilä government 2
Sipilä, J. 16, 19, 31, 55, 180
Sjöland, L. 135
Social Affairs and Health Committee
    41, 42
social assistance 12–13, 94, 110, 112,
    113
    for households 109
    receipt of 98–9
social benefits 110–11, 113, 126
    claiming of 109–14
social benefits system 107, 108, 112, 114
social blame 138, 141–2, 145
    see also individual blame
social constructivism 170
Social Democratic Party 190
social experiment frame 174, 175, 178,
    180–83
social experiments 169
Social Insurance Institution of Finland
    (Kela) 2, 8–13, 28, 29, 31, 32, 45,
    46, 68, 129, 153, 161, 162, 176,
    178, 181, 183, 184
social isolation 76, 78
social policies 119, 190, 194
social security benefits 191
social security system 6–7, 10, 142, 145
Standing, G. 106, 118, 130, 136
Stirton, L. 107
strategic feasibility 189–90, 193
structural equation modelling (SEM)
    122–3, 125–6, 129
subjective financial well-being (SFWB)
    90, 91, 99–101
    defining 91–3
    measure
        in basic income experiment
        94–8
        in regression analysis 98–9
    response proportions of 96
    unemployment and 93
    see also health
subjective health 73–4, 76, 126–8
subjective well-being 45, 48, 82, 84
supplementary social assistance 12

support for basic income 134–5, 139–46,
    192
    attitudes on deservingness 142, 144,
        146
    income inadequacy 139–40
    individual blame 141–2
    insecure employment 139–40
    opinions 142, 144
    regression analysis 139–41, 143–4
    social blame 141–2
survey data 46, 48–9, 52, 60
    response rate 51
Swarbrick, M. 90, 94
syntactical structure 173

tabloids 177, 178
Tarkiainen, L. 5
tax revenue 192
thematic structure 173
Tirole, J. 120
treatment groups 39–41, 44, 45, 50, 51,
    53, 60–62, 64, 75–6, 78, 82, 84–6,
    91, 94, 109, 110, 112, 113, 123–4,
    129, 177
    bureaucracy 126
    mental distress 85
    mental well-being of 85
    responses of 110
    unemployed in 111
trust 4, 117–19, 122, 128–31
    basic income and 126
    and confidence 48, 117, 118,
        125–31
    generalised 117, 119, 121, 123–4
    institutionalised 117, 119, 121,
        123–4
    levels of 123
    and self-confidence 130
    see also confidence
Trust in the Law (Tyler and Huo) 119
Tuovinen, A. -K. 2
Tuulio-Henriksson, A. 3
Tyler, T. R. 119

UCT see unconditional cash transfers
    (UCT)
unconditional cash transfers (UCT) 71–2,
    78, 82, 85–6
unconditional social benefit 58, 59, 64

Index

unemployment 3, 71, 141, 179, 183
  activation model and 52–3, 55
  and mental distress 82, 84, 85
  and subjective financial well-being
    (SFWB) 93
unemployment benefits 27, 29, 31, 33,
    52–3, 55, 60, 68, 109, 111–13,
    129, 176
  right to 38
unemployment protection system 10–12,
    191
universal basic income 187–8
  behavioural feasibility of 187–8, 194
  institutional feasibility of 190–91,
    193–4
  political parties and 190
  psychological feasibility of 191–2,
    194
  strategic feasibility of 189–90, 193
Universal Credit 176
unrealistic tax model 24, 25

Valkenburg, P. M. 173
values 137, 144, 146
Van der Noordt, M. 82
Van Oorschot, W. V. 135, 137
Van Parijs, P. 27, 114, 118, 150
vita activa 152

Wahrendorf, M. 82

Weber, M. 189
welfare regimes 119
well-being 1, 3, 4, 6, 46, 53, 56, 57, 59,
    65, 68, 71, 72, 74, 76, 78, 82, 84,
    118, 130, 159, 165, 166, 169, 172,
    178
  basic income effects on 177, 182
  indicators 48–9, 51
  mental 82, 85, 86
  multidimensionality of 72–4
  subjective 45, 48, 82, 84
  subjective financial *see* subjective
    financial well-being (SFWB)
WHO *see* World Health Organization
    (WHO)
Widerquist, K. 33, 192
work ability 3, 56, 59–62, 64, 65, 66–7,
    157, 158, 165
work disincentives 13
work incentives 24
work modality 153, 165
  content analysis 158–61
World Health Organization (WHO) 72–3

Ylikännö, M. 3, 4
Yudof, J. 90

Zuelke, A. E. 72
Zyphur, M. J. 92